Hinkle & Co.

365 West Front Street, Cincinnati, Ohio.

NEW BOOK ON BUILDING.

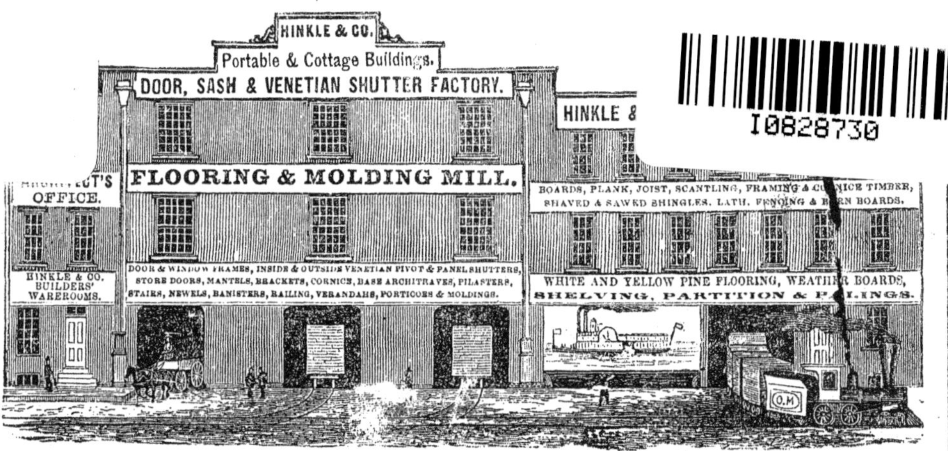

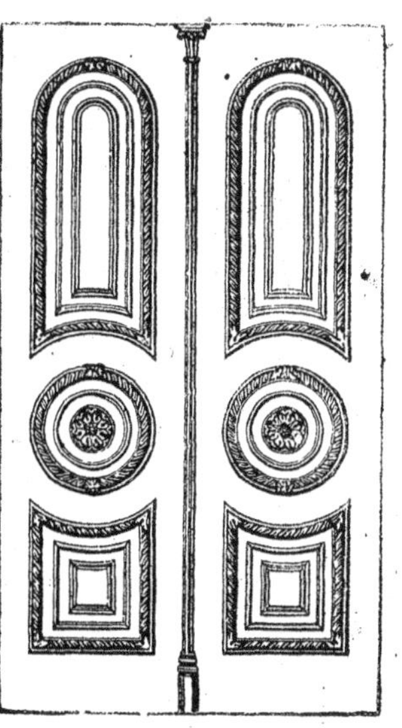

1869.

Elm Street Printing Company, Cincinnati

PHILIP HINKLE

Having purchased the entire interest of JOSEPH GUILD, the business hereafter will be carried on in the name of HINKLE & CO.

The proprietors have been engaged in the Building business in Cincinnati for thirty-seven years, and the last twenty-four years in manufacturing building materials for the South and West, where they have shipped the materials for several hundred houses annually. From their long experience and extensive trade in the South and West, they can refer to persons in almost any locality as to their responsibility, the quality of their work, and promptness in filling orders.

Our factory is in full operation, and with a heavy stock of manufactured carpenter work and seasoned lumber on hand, we are prepared to fill orders for either on short notice.

Persons intending to erect buildings, or wanting building materials, will find it to their interest to write or send their orders direct to us. We will then give them an estimate, mode of payment, and, if required, will give a reference to some person in their neighborhood as to our responsibility, the quality of our work, and our promptness in filling orders. The purchaser can then rest assured that he will get OUR manufactured materials, and will secure himself from imposition in having inferior work sent to him as OURS.

We frequently receive orders from strangers at a distance for our materials, wanted "immediately." We advise all such to send part of the money, near what they think it will cost, with the order, and any balance can be collected on delivery. This will insure the prompt filling of the order at our lowest cash prices.

Remember that our packages are marked

HINKLE & CO.

Sash and V Shutter Manufacturers,

CINCINNATI, OHIO.

Your attention is particularly invited to Preface, Description of Business, and the Plans of Buildings contained in this Book, varying in cost from one hundred and fifteen to three hundred and fifty thousand dollars.

Remember the first thing when about to build or alter is to obtain a good plan, bill of items, and specifications. *(See page 7.)*

CONTENTS.

OPINIONS OF THE PRESS ON

Hinkle & Co's New Book on Building.

New Book on Building.—Messrs. Hinkle & Co., formerly Hinkle, Guild & Co., have just issued such a book as every man needs who intends to build, or to remodel and repair, a house. It is an illustrated volume of over 100 8vo. pages, in which all the variety of wood work made by them (and they make all the varieties used in building,) is shown in profile, with the cost. Here are pictured moldings, architraves, bases, brackets, stairs, newels, balusters, rails, cornice, mantels, window frames, sash, doors, columns, etc., enough for any one to choose from. Here, also, are plans and elevations of 111 residences. Most of them are buildings planned by the best Cincinnati architects, and actually built, or being built, by some of our wealthiest and most tasteful citizens, and in the city and its beautiful suburbs They are not fancy plans got up to adorn the book, but those that have been adopted by practical men, on the recommendation of experienced architects The publishers of this volume have been extensively engaged in the manufacture of all kinds of wood work for building, for thirty-seven years. Their experience, and the high reputation they have acquired for promptness and integrity, give their patrons the best assurance that their orders will be satisfactorily filled. Any one wishing the book can obtain it by sending $1.00 to Hinkle & Co., 355 West Front Street, Cincinnati, O.—*Herald and Presbyter.*

An Important and Valuable Book.—The enterprising and well-known manufacturing house, Hinkle & Co., have published a book, which must prove of great value to architects, as well as to all who contemplate building. It is, in short, a practical and illustrative work, in which all the endless variety of wood work, made by them, used in building, from the tiny bead to the massive molding and elaborate stair case, are shown, with the cost; and not only this, but the plans and elevations of one hundred and eleven residences, most of them of buildings which have been erected, or are in course of erection, in the vicinity of this city, many of them located in those lovely suburbs of the city—Clifton and East Walnut Hills—which have become so famous all over the country. No one who contemplates erecting dwellings, who has not felt at a loss for plans of buildings to select from, and Messrs Hinkle & Co have, in this book, not only supplied this want, but have furnished data from which to estimate the cost. The value of this book is greatly increased by the vast experience of the publishers, who have been engaged in the manufacture of sash, doors, blinds, portable houses, and all wood work needed in building, for thirty-seven years. The price of the book is $1.00, and any person needing it can obtain a copy by remitting the price, and addressing Hinkle & Co.—*Cincinnati Price Current.*

A New Book on Building.—Messrs. Hinkle & Co., of this city, have published a book on building, which we doubt not will be found of great practical advantage to all those who contemplate the erection of dwellings. The suggestions and directions are all valuable, but the most important feature of it is, the great number of plans in it for all classes of houses. Most of them too, have the merit of having been practically tested near home, and the inquirer can have the satisfaction of seeing what would be the result of almost any plan he might adopt. We notice in it the plans of several of the most elegant houses in the vicinity of the city of Cincinnati. The cost of the work is $1.00.—*Cincinnati Chronicle.*

A Practical Publication.—The spirit of the age is opposed to theorizing. Practical ideas and practical men are leading the world, and the dreamers and fine elaborators are left far behind. Even a book, to be generally sought after, must be practical, terse, and direct to the subject. It must be the result of experience, or it were better that it had never been printed—especially if it assumes to teach the people of these times. These considerations induce us to again allude to the new book on building just issued by Messrs Hinkle & Co. The plans and elevations it contains are those of more than a hundred fine buildings already erected, from designs by the best architects, and, therefore, the results of the best experience. We are informed that by the aid of a carpenter we can erect a fine building, on any of the plans it illustrates, without help from an architect; and, as the price is but $1.00, this consideration alone will induce thousands to buy. —*Review.*

New Book on Building.—We have examined a new illustrated volume just published by Messrs. Hinkle & Co., of this city. It contains the plans and elevations of one hundred and eleven residences, already built, and known to be well approved. It is a practical work for popular use, consults every variety of taste, and gives plans for residences to cost from $115 to $35,000. Such a work meets a popular want that no one has heretofore been fortunate enough to supply. Price $1 00.—*Journal and Messenger.*

A Timely Book.—Messrs. Hinkle & Co., of this city, have just published "A new Book on Building" that every man who contemplates building or remodeling a residence should possess. It gives the plans and elevations of one hundred and eleven residences, etc., already built, from the designs of celebrated architects, embracing all the modern ideas and latest improvements, and a range of cost from $115 to $35,000, and contains, also, a great mass of information and suggestions of practical value to all who are in any measure interested in its subject. Such a work is timely, for it meets a general want that no one has heretofore attempted to supply. It costs but $1.00.—*Cincinnati Daily Enquirer.*

Hinkle & Co. have published a new book on building, which should be in the hands of every person proposing to build a residence. Besides a large amount of information in regard to materials and their cost, it contains seven hundred and twenty-six illustrations, including sixty-six plans of dwellings, with size and description of rooms. Many people build, but comparatively few plan properly; consequently, a large proportion of the buildings erected are neither handsome nor convenient. Here is a book that furnishes a variety of plans for houses, costing from $500 up to $300,000, drawn by first-class architects, which, if widely circulated, will lead to a marked improvement in the style of building in this country. Price $1.00.—*Cincinnati Daily Gazette.*

Messrs. Hinkle & Co., of this city, have fairly met a long-felt want by publishing "A New Book on Building." Nothing like it was ever before attempted, for it gives the plans and elevations of more than one hundred dwellings already built from designs of the best architects, and comprising all styles and prices, from the humble cottage at a cost of $115, to the princely mansion that is cheap at $350,000. Those who contemplate building, extending or remodeling any residence, church, school-house or similar structure, can save time and money by consulting this work and taking advice from its many illustrations and suggestions.—*Cin. Daily Times.*

HINKLE & CO.'S NEW BOOK —Lord Kames, in his Elements of Criticism, says, "The books we have upon architecture abound in practical instruction necessary for a mechanic, but in vain should we rummage them for rational principles to improve our taste." A man must be a mechanic before he can understand them, and then the ideas they convey are simply mechanical. They do not come home to the familiar comprehension of people at large, and such is not their design. A New Book on Building has just been published in this city, by Messrs. Hinkle & Co., however, that will not only improve the popular taste, but will give every body that examines it a succinct and comprehensive view of the rational principles that are at the foundation of the whole subject. It is eminently practical, illustrating the plans and elevations of one hundred and eleven houses already built, from the designs of the best architects, and authoritatively approved. They comprise a wide range of cost, from $115 to $350,000, and every variety of taste, as well as financial capacity, is consulted. Those who contemplate building, improving, or remodeling, should possess this volume, as its plans and suggestions are founded on the best practical experience, and are therefore invaluable to all who are not thoroughly posted. The price of this desirable brochure, which contains 726 illustrations, is only $1.00.—*Merchants' and Manufacturers' Bulletin, Cincinnati.*

NEW BOOK —Hinkle & Co., of this city, No. 365 West Front Street, have issued a new book on building that is highly interesting. The feature that will attract most attention is the costs and plans of private residences in and about the city. Nearly all the new houses are presented in this way.—*Cincinnati Commercial.*

We have received from Hinkle & Co., of Cincinnati, a book containing a great deal of valuable information to builders—such as plans for dwelling-houses, churches, colleges, etc., and engravings of architraves, moldings, counters, church pews, stair steps, etc. It will be sent free of postage on receipt of $1.00.—*Brandon, Miss., Republican.*

We acknowledge the receipt of a good sized book from Hinkle & Co., No. 365 W. Front Street, Cincinnati, O., containing a large number of plans of buildings, moldings, architraves, bases, brackets, stairs, newels, balusters, rails, cornice, mantles, window frames, sash, doors, columns, and almost every imaginable article used in house building. In addition, it contains much interesting information for persons about building. Messrs Hinkle & Co. have been engaged in the building business in Cincinnati for thirty-seven years, and now own one of the largest establishments in the United States.—*Dixie Farmer, Columbia, Tenn.*

We have received a book of plans of buildings, molding, etc., from Hinkle & Co., of Cincinnati, which has much to commend it to the careful attention of those about to erect either public or private buildings. Among its contents are, "Valuable Information on Building," "Portable Dwellings," "Stores," etc, description of business, bill of prices, and directions for sending orders, etc., which greatly aid one in deciding what he needs, as well as price of building. This firm is about to issue, July 1, 1869, "A New Book on Building," containing, in addition to this book, perspective views and plans of first and second floors of over 50 dwelling-houses in and around Cincinnati and elsewhere, with size of rooms, etc. In this book, plans can be found to suit every person contemplating building. Sent free of postage on receipt of $1.00 Address Hinkle & Co., Sash and Venetian Shutter Manufacturers, Cincinnati, Ohio.—*Ashtabula (Ohio) Telegraph.*

PRACTICAL BUILDING.—The works heretofore published with the design of assisting those about to build, have all been too cumbersome and impracticable. Messrs. Hinkle & Co., of this city, have just issued a new illustrated volume that, although unpretentious, will unquestionably meet the popular demand, and fill the great want on this important subject. It contains the plans of one hundred and eleven residences, already built and in process of erection, from the designs of the best architects, and addresses itself to every variety of taste. Its practicability will recommend it to every man that contemplates building, while its cheapness (only $1.00) brings within the reach of all.—*Christian World, Cincinnati.*

From Merchants' and Manufacturers' Bulletin.

CINCINNATI MANUFACTURES.

HINKLE & CO.'S BUILDERS' WAREROOMS.

As good wine needs no bush, so a great house, like that of Messrs. Hinkle & Co., at No. 365 West Front Street—said to be the largest of the kind on the continent—requires no word of commendation to extend its fame and usefulness. We propose, therefore, in describing it, to deal only with solid facts—the most prominent at that—and permit the reader to draw the inferences they suggest.

This house manufactures every description of wood work for buildings, and is a builders' warehouse, for the furnishing of everything appertaining to the business, and where the materials can be found ready-made for the finish of one hundred buildings Its lumber yard, in the Seventeenth Ward, covers five acres, and many millions of feet of lumber are there received and disposed of annually. Its smaller yard at the factory is also of goodly dimensions, sufficient to contain at least 4,000,000 feet of lumber, and is kept well supplied. Its warehouse and factory on Front Street occupy a front of 122½ feet, extending back 530 feet to the Ohio River. The factory proper is 60 by 150 feet, the warehouses 100 by 122½ feet, all four stories in hight, and substantially built of brick. Each story connects with a warehouse.

The basement is occupied by the steam-engine, a reciprocating saw-mill for resawing lumber and a packing-box factory. In the next story, which is on a level with the street, are the large flooring mills. The second story proper is filled with a great variety of machinery for the manufacture of sash, doors, blinds, etc. The third floor is principally used for putting work together.

On all the floors there are rail tracks for lumber cars, making the aggregate length of track 1,800 feet. These tracks extend from the street through all the warehouses to the rear of the manufactory, and through the basement out into the lumber yard. There are also transverse tracks that lead to an immense steam hoister, upon which the loaded cars are run and raised, or lowered to another floor, to suit the needs of the work in hand.

In the second story is an architect's office, where plans and drawings are made and valuable information furnished for every description of building. No sensible man builds a house without a plan well matured and approved by good authority, and practicable plans are best made where all the details of the work are understood.

It is inexpedient, in a notice of this kind, to go into all the details of the machinery and its economical management to produce the results attained by this establishment; and it is practically unimportant to everybody except the mechanic, so long as it is known that the results are attained legitimately and satisfactorily. Under this head it is probably enough to say that Messrs. Hinkle & Co. have furnished the wood-work for many of the finer residences in the vicinity of Cincinnati, and for many of the best in the West and South. Among those to which they especially refer, and illustrate in their new book on building, we find that some are in Louisiana, Mississippi, Arkansas, Tennessee, Kentucky, Missouri and Indiana, and are among the finest in those States; while those in this city and suburbs are among the most admired residences of our capitalists and leading business men. The portable houses and cottages they have furnished for new settlements in the territories are numbered by hundreds, and have always given satisfaction.

They take no contracts for building houses, but their specialty, to which we desire to call particular attention, is furnishing all the wood-work, of every name, style and description, that is wanted for any kind of building, ready dressed and fitted; and they do this at so near the original cost of the rough lumber that, after witnessing their whole modus operandi, the mystery still is how they can afford it. The labor-saving implements that are revolutionizing all our industries, leveling forests, cultivating corn and cotton, and advancing civilization through these means as well as through building houses by steam, furnish the solution of course; and, as they cheapen houses in the same proportion that they simplify toil, induce the rich to build better houses, and the poor to approximate nearer that earthly beautitude which is found in the estate of the freeholder, however humble.

Every man who designs building or improving a residence or other structure, in any part of the country, will exercise good judgment by consulting the catalogues and examining the work of this house before deciding on his plans, and, what is of some consequence in these times, he will save money by the precaution. The unanimous testimony of Messrs. Hinkle & Co.'s customers favors this view, and verifies all we have written of their facilities.

STAIRS.

HINKLE & CO.'S

Stair Department.

We call the attention of the public to our facilities for furnishing Stairs, from the plainest straight to the most elaborate circular or elliptic.

We furnish the Stairs all complete, ready to set up. Steps and risers glued and blocked, and housed into wall strings; Newel posts fitted into carriages; balusters turned, cleaned off and dovetailed; rails fitted up with screws, bored for balusters and cleaned off, with written directions for putting up, which can be done by any carpenter.

We also furnish, separately, newels of cherry, walnut, rosewood and mahogany, turned, veneered, octagon, fluted and carved. See page 30.

Balusters of cherry, oak, walnut and mahogany, turned octagon, fluted and carved. See page 30.

Rails, cherry, walnut and mahogany. See pages 27, 28 and 31.

Brackets. See page 30.

Persons ordering Stairs should give particular attention to the following: Give the width of hall, hight of story from top to top of floor, width of joists on landing on second floor. Send a drawing of Stair, or select one from page 29; kind of rail, selecting size and shape on pages 27, 28 and 31; give the length of step, the size of baluster and newel; give drawing of base in hall, that the molding of stairs may be the same pattern; say if circular corners are wanted, as dotted on figs. 2, 3 and 9, page 29.

There is no part of the inside finish of any building more ornamental than properly constructed Stairs, therefore, too much care can not be had in making a selection. We can please every taste, with Stairs of the best material and workmanship.

HINKLE & CO.'S
NEW
BOOK ON BUILDING;

MOLDINGS, ARCHITRAVES, BASE, BRACKETS,
STAIRS, NEWELS, BALUSTERS, RAILS,

CORNICE, MANTELS, WINDOW FRAMES,
SASH, DOORS, COLUMNS;

FORTY-FIVE

PLANS OF BUILDINGS;

CHURCH PEWS, STORE COUNTERS, PORTICOES, &c.;

SIXTY-SIX PLANS OF DWELLINGS,
WITH SIZE AND DESCRIPTION OF ROOMS ATTACHED;

FOR THE USE OF CARPENTERS AND BUILDERS.

ADAPTED TO THE STYLE OF BUILDING IN THE UNITED STATES.

CONTAINING VALUABLE INFORMATION ON BUILDING.

WITH SEVEN HUNDRED AND TWENTY-SIX ILLUSTRATIONS.

CINCINNATI:
PUBLISHED BY HINKLE & COMPANY.
1869.

ELECTROTYPED AT THE FRANKLIN TYPE FOUNDRY, CINCINNATI.

PREFACE.

Office of HINKLE & CO.,
Cincinnati, Ohio, 1869.

In presenting our new book on building, molding, etc, to the public, we call attention to the following Circular, and the accompanying plans of a few of the public buildings and private residences which we have furnished to different localities in different sections of our country. These plans will be found on pages 43 to 54, and will enable our readers to form a pretty good idea of the appearance and character of the buildings we are accustomed to furnish, and show that our manufactured work is used in public edifices and private residences of the first class.

Also, sixty-six plans of dwellings around Cincinnati and elsewhere, with size of rooms and description attached, costing from one hundred and fifteen to three hundred and fifty thousand dollars.

We have been for the last thirty-seven years, extensively engaged in the business of building houses, and manufacturing all kinds of carpenter work for the inside and outside finish of brick, frame, and stone buildings of every description. We constantly keep on hand a large and full assortment of all materials of this kind; we also keep on hand, for sale, a large amount of lumber for building purposes.

Our factory is the largest of its kind in the United States, and its location is convenient for shipping our goods. It is situated on the bank of the Ohio River, just east of the Gas Works. It is near the depot of the Ohio and Mississippi, Indianapolis and Cincinnati, and Cincinnati, Hamilton and Dayton, Baltimore and Cincinnati, and Cincinnati Southern Railways. With the premises, it occupies a frontage on the river of 122½ feet, extending back 530 feet to Front Street, affording ample wharf room for receiving and shipping our lumber and manufactured work. We have large yards for storing a great quantity of every description of lumber; the principal one being situated in the upper part of the City, on the river bank, with 375 feet wharf space, and extending back 500 feet, to Front Street.

We purchase and sell annually several million feet of boards, joists, framing timbers, scantling; also, shingles, lath, etc, etc. With the advantages afforded by our large yards, we are enabled to keep constantly on hand, stored up, ready for use, a full assortment of *seasoned* lumber. This we sell at wholesale or retail—unworked, or manufactured into doors, sash, blinds, etc., etc, ready to be put at once into buildings.

From our long experience in this business, and the facilities afforded us by the most improved machinery, and workmen skilled in every branch of their trade, we can manufacture and finish up work of the best quality in a style not surpassed in any other factory, nor by hand-made work, either as regards accuracy, perfection of finish, or durability.

We invite your attention to the facilities we offer for furnishing stairs. There is nothing inside a dwelling, or any other house, more ornamental than a properly constructed flight of stairs. (For plans and illustrations of this article, we refer the reader to pages 29 and 30.)

We also call your attention to the importance of obtaining a good plan of your building, and drawing of all the mechanical work, with the bill of items. (See page 7.)

Persons desirous of securing all the modern improvements in building, heating, lighting, and furnishing dwelling-houses, churches, stores, etc., will do well to visit Cincinnati, where they can have an opportunity of seeing them brought to the highest perfection. The architecture of many of our buildings in the city and country-seats around Cincinnati, is equal if not superior to any in the United States, and will afford you a good opportunity to select a plan.

The extensive scale on which the different branches of manufacturing are carried on in Cincinnati, enables the proprietors to furnish them cheaper than any of the Eastern or Western cities.

Such, also, are our arrangements with manufacturers in this city, that we can furnish any of the following articles, used in the building line, at manufacturer's prices—such as Bell Trimmings, Hardware and Nails, Iron Castings, Verandah Railings, Marble, Iron or Slate Mantels, Coal Grates, French and American Window Glass, Tin Spouting and Gutters, Iron Columns, Caps and Bases, Outcalt's Portable Iron Roofing.

In our business we have had two objects in view: first, to produce a superior article of work; secondly, to make our charges moderate. All know from experience that this rule will create a great demand in any business. The large amount of our sales enables us to sell at small profits.

Respectfully,

HINKLE & CO.

HINKLE & CO., BUILDERS' WAREROOMS,

DOOR, SASH, VENETIAN SHUTTER FACTORY, PLANING MILL & LUMBER YARD,

No. 365 WEST FRONT ST., CINCINNATI, O.

(ADJOINING GAS WORKS.)

Our Warehouse and Factory is 60 by 250 feet, four stories high. We manufacture and keep constantly on hand, Panel Doors, Sash, Venetian and Panel Shutters, Mantels, Door and Window Frames, Base, Pilaster, Weatherboarding, White and Yellow Pine Flooring, Shelving for Stores, Planed Boards, and Moldings of various patterns, suitable for the finish of Frame or Brick Houses of every description. All kinds of Stairs, with Mahogany or Cherry rail, plain or fancy Newel. (See pages 29-30.) Sash, painted and glazed, constantly on hand. In the Lumber Yard connected with this establishment, we have an extensive assortment of Lumber, for building purposes.

Orders filled for Boards, Plank, Shaved and Sawed Shingles, Joist, Lath, Framing and Cornice Timber of every description. Also—Paints, Oils, Glass and Hardware, including Locks, Bolts, Hinges, Sliding Door Trimmings, Screws, Nails, &c.

FLOORING.

We only measure the Face of the board and not the tongue, as is customary in many other cities In some places they measure the board in the rough, allowing nothing for waste in working; in this way the purchaser pays cost and freight on 1000 feet Flooring, while he only gets from 700 to 800 feet.

CINCINNATI BILL OF PRICES, 1862.

Price of Sash, Venetian Shutters, Box & Com. Window Frames for 12 Light Windows.

Size of Lights.	Thickness.	Price of Sash per Light.	Price of Venetian Shutters per pair.	Price of Window Frames—Sash Pulleys included. Box.	Common.	Size of Sash for 12 Light Windows. Shutters 1¼ inch longer. Width.	Length
Inches.	in.	cts.	$ cts.	$ cts.	$ cts.	ft. in.	ft. in.
8 by 10	1⅛	4½	1 50	2 00	1 20	2 4	3 9½
8 by 10	1⅜	5½	1 75	2 00	1 20	2 4	3 9½
9 by 12	1⅛	5½	1 75	2 50	1 30	2 7½	4 6½
9 by 12	1⅜	6½	2 00	2 50	1 30	2 7½	4 6½
10 by 12	1⅛	5½	1 75	2 50	1 30	2 10½	4 6½
10 by 12	1⅜	6½	2 00	2 50	1 30	2 10½	4 6½
10 by 14	1⅜	7½	2 25	2 75	1 40	2 10½	5 2½
10 by 15	1⅜	8	2 37½	2 75	1 40	2 10½	5 6½
10 by 16	1⅜	8½	2 50	3 20	1 50	2 10½	5 10½
10 by 18	1⅜	9	2 75	3 75	1 80	2 10½	6 6½
10 by 20	1⅜	10	3 12½	4 00	1 90	2 10½	7 2½
11 by 15	1⅜	8½	2 50	3 20	1 50	3 2	5 6½
11 by 16	1⅜	9	2 62½	3 35	1 60	3 2	5 10½
11 by 17	1⅜	9	2 75	3 50	1 70	3 2	6 2½
11 by 18	1⅜	9½	2 90	3 75	1 80	3 2	6 6½
11 by 19	1⅜	10	3 12½	4 00	1 90	3 2	6 10½
11 by 20	1⅜	10½	3 25	4 12½	2 00	3 2	7 2½
11 by 21	1⅜	11	3 37½	4 25	2 12½	3 2	7 6½
11 by 22	1⅜	11½	3 50	4 37½	2 25	3 2	7 0½
12 by 16	1⅜	9	2 75	3 75	1 80	3 5	5 10½
12 by 18	1⅜	10	3 12½	4 00	1 90	3 5	6 6½
12 by 20	1⅜	11	3 37½	4 25	2 12½	3 5	7 2½
12 by 22	1⅜	12	3 62½	4 50	2 30	3 5	7 10½
12 by 24	1⅜	13	3 87½	4 75	2 50	3 5	8 6½

All 1⅜ inch Sash are made with Hook Meeting Rails.
Sash over 1⅜ inch thick, extra price.
Sash Ploughed and Bored, or under 6 Lights, extra price.
Venetian Shutters over 1⅜ inch thick, extra price.
Pivot Shutters extra price. Shutters are made 1¼ inch longer than Sash.
Flat Panel Shutters same price as Venetian with Stationary slats; for Raised Panel Shutters, or Bead and Butt, and Flat, add 12½ cents per pair to price of Venetian with Stationary Slats. Raised and Beveled Panel Shutters, add 37½ cents per pair to price of Venetian with Stationary Slats. Raised and Molded Panel Shutters, add 75 cents per pair to price of Venetian with Stationary Slats.

PRICE OF DOORS WITH 4 PANELS.

Size of Doors. Width.	Length.	Flat, 1⅛ inches thick.	Flat, 1⅜ inches thick	Flat and beveled 1⅜ thick.	Flat and molded 1⅜ thick.	Raised 1⅜ thick.	Raised & beveled 1⅜ thick.	Raised & molded 1⅜ thick.
ft. in.	ft. in.	$ cts.	$ cts.	$ cts.	$ cts.	$ cts.	$ cts.	$ cts.
2 6	6 6	2 00	2 25	2 75	3 00	2 50	3 00	3 25
2 8	6 8							
2 10	6 6	2 25	2 50	3 00	3 25	2 75	3 25	3 50
2 10	6 10							
3	6 6							
3	7							
3 2	7 6	2 75	3 00	3 50	3 75	3 25	3 75	4 00
3 6	8	3 25	3 50	4 00	4 25	3 75	4 25	4 50

Doors over 1⅜ inches thick, extra price.

ALL KINDS OF CIRCULAR, GOTHIC AND FANCY DOORS. SASH, ETC., MADE TO ORDER.

Price of Sash Store Doors, for Open Fronts, with Shutters, Trimmed with Shutter Locks, Stubs and Lifts.

1⅜ inches thick, 2 fold, 30 cents per foot superficial
2⅜ do do 2 fold, 36 do do do.
2⅜ do do 3 fold, 40 do do do.
2⅜ do do 4 fold, 44 do do do.

Price of Door Frames, 3 by 7 feet, and Under.

For Brick Houses,	9 inch wall, no sill, poplar,	$1 50
For do	9 inch do do with impost, do.	2 00
For do	12 inch do no sill, do.	2 00
For do	12 inch do do with impost, do.	2 50
For Frame Houses, with sill	- - - - - -	1 50
For do	with sill and impost - -	2 00

Frames of Pine, extra price.

PRICE OF MANTELS.---See Designs, p. 37.

Plain Pilaster,	(Figure 1,) - - - -	$3 00
Plain Box,	do 2, - - - -	4 00
Box Molded,	do 3, - - - -	5 00
Circular Box, Molded,	do 4, - - - -	7 00

CIRCULAR WORK.

☞ Circular Window Frames, Sash Blinds, Doors, etc., extra price.

☞ Orders for Doors, Sash, and Venetian Shutters, should give Size, Thickness and Finish. Odd sizes extra price.

☞ PARTICULAR ATTENTION given to the making of inside Venetian, Pivot and Panel Shutters in any number of folds desired, and in most improved manner. Boxing and Drayage extra.

Directions in Sending Orders.

☞ It is important that you should make your Window Frames to suit the size given in our Circular; then your orders for Doors, Sash and Blinds can be filled immediately, as we have them always on hand.

☞ For odd sized work we charge extra price. It also requires longer time to fill such orders, as we have to manufacture the work.

☞ Orders for Sash, when the frames are made, should give width and hight of frame in clear; also, thickness of Sash, and the number and size of lights in each window.

☞ Orders for Doors, and Venetian or Panel Shutters, should give width, hight, thickness, and finish.

☞ Orders for Door and Window Frames should give thickness of wall, and state if for Frame or Brick House, and whether Outside or Partition Door frames.

☞ In the Lumber Yard connected with this establishment we have an extensive assortment of Lumber for building purposes.

☞ We advise that doors, blinds, &c., be painted one coat before being shipped, as it will preserve them from swelling, if exposed to the weather.

Office of HINKLE & CO.,

CINCINNATI, OHIO, 1869.

TO THE PUBLIC:

Owing to the advance in labor, and all kinds of building materials, we are compelled to make an advance on the Cincinnati Bill of Prices of 1862, *contained in this book on the preceding and following pages.*

If persons wishing to build, or wanting any thing in our line, will send us a bill of items, giving SIZE, QUALITY, and QUANTITY, we will send them the cost by return mail.

Our Factory is in full operation, and with a good stock of seasoned lumber on hand, we are prepared to fill orders for lumber or manufactured carpenter work at short notice.

DRAWINGS AND SPECIFICATIONS.

It is no uncommon thing for persons to consider plans and drawings unnecessary, and when about to build a house, take upon themselves to be the architects; the consequence is, they get up an ill-proportioned, odd-looking building, and when too late for remedy, they find they have paid dear for the experiment.

Remember, the first thing when about to build, is to obtain a good plan, and drawings of all the different mechanical work and bill of items, giving the sizes, quantities, and qualities of materials; with them you will be enabled to make intelligent contracts for work and material, and save ten times the cost, by avoiding the alterations made when working without them, which frequently causes law-suits. If persons wishing to build houses, will send us by mail a plan and bill of items, we will give the cost, or they can have the plans and bill of items made in Cincinnati at reasonable prices, by sending us a sketch of their building, giving size of rooms, and height of stories, stating the amount they wish to expend; this will enable the architect to make the plans accordingly.

Important for your Interest.

Send your orders direct to **HINKLE & CO., Cincinnati, Ohio,** *THEN you will be sure of receiving work manufactured by them, and they will inform you how to send pay for the same.*

REFERENCE given in your neighborhood if desired. Any information connected with their business furnished on application.

PRICE LIST OF MOLDINGS, &C.

1862.

☞ Price of Moldings, Architraves and Base, is per 100 feet lineal, in 12 or 16 feet lengths. Brackets, Modillions, and Braces, price each.

Number.	From Machine.		Smoothed off.		Number.	From Machine.		Smoothed off.		Number.	From Machine.		Smoothed off.		Number.	From Machine.		Smoothed off.		Brackets.	Number.	From Machine.	
	$	c	$	c		$	c	$	c		$	c	$	c		$	c	$	c			$	c
1		40		48	73	2	20	2	46	144		70		80	215	2	40	2	69		286		50
2		45		53	74	1	25	1	47	145		90	1	06	216	2	75	3	08		287		50
3		50		59	75	2	25	2	59	146	2	40	2	69	217	7	00	7	84		288	2	25
4		55		65	76	1	60	1	84	147	1	00	1	18	218	2	25	2	52		289	1	95
5		65		77	77	3	15	3	53	148	1	70	1	95	219	4	75	5	22		290	1	75
6		65		77	78	1	70	1	95	149	1	70	1	95	220	5	50	6	32		291	1	65
7		70		83	79	4	00	4	48	150	1	00	1	18	221	4	00	4	40		292	1	60
8		75		89	80	1	30	1	46	151	1	25	1	47	222	5	00	5	60		293	2	75
9		80		95	81	1	40	1	61	152	2	55	2	86	223	10	00	11	50		294	2	67
10		80		95	82	1	65	1	90	153	1	40	1	61	224	7	00	8	00		295	2	25
11		90	1	06	83	2	30	2	58	154	1	25	1	47	225	6	00	6	90		296	1	50
12	1	00	1	18	84	1	30	1	46	155	1	25	1	47	226	3	25	3	64		297	2	00
13	1	10	1	30	85	2	70	3	02	156	2	00	2	24	227		10		16	1¾ in. thick	298	1	30
14	1	20	1	38	86		90	1	06	157	2	20	2	46	228		50		65	3¾ in. thick	299	2	20
15	1	35	1	55	87	3	70	4	14	158	2	20	2	46	229		25		35	2¾ in. thick	300	2	00
16	1	50	1	72	88	1	40	1	61	159	1	75	2	01	230		10		16	1¾ in. thick	301	1	35
17	1	65	1	90	89	4	10	4	59	160	1	65	1	90	231		14		20	3¾ in. thick	302	1	15
18	1	30	1	49	90	1	00	1	18	161	3	25	3	64	232		30		42	3¾ in. thick	303	4	20
19	3	15	3	53	91	1	15	1	32	162	1	05	1	24	233		15		23	1¾ in. thick	304	2	10
20	2	10	2	35	92	2	10	2	35	163		35		41	234		17		25	3¾ in. thick	305	3	75
21		80		95	93		80		95	164		30		36	235		35		48	1¾ in. thick	306	3	75
22	1	35	1	55	94		90	1	06	165		25		30	236	3	75	4	2[illegible]		307	2	50
23	1	00	1	18	95		50		59	166		65		77	237		09		15	3¾ in. thick	308	2	00
24	1	90	2	13	96		50		59	167		65		77	238						309	1	50
25	1	30	1	49	97		70		83	168		55		65	239						310	2	37
26	2	00	2	24	98		75		89	169		85	1	00	240	2	15	2	47		311	1	70
27	1	45	1	63	99		70		83	170		85	1	00	241	1	70	1	95		312	2	90
28	1	25	1	47	100	1	30	1	49	171		70		83	242	1	50	1	[illegible]2		313	1	00
29		70		83	101	1	05	1	24	172		90	1	06	243	2	25	2	59		314		70
30	1	40	1	61	102		80		95	173	1	10	1	30	244						315		70
31	2	10	2	35	103	1	75	2	01	174	1	30	1	49	245						316	5	00
32	1	00	1	18	104		70		83	175		80		95	246						317	6	00
33	2	35	2	63	105	1	50	1	72	176	1	40	1	61	247	3	00	3	30		318	4	75
34		90	1	06	106		50		59	177	2	00	2	24	248	14	00	15	68		319	4	75
35	1	15	1	32	107	1	70	1	95	178	3	00	3	30	249	9	00	10	00		320	4	00
36	2	50	2	80	108	2	85	3	20	179	2	35	2	63	250	10	00	11	00		321	7	50
37	2	10	2	35	109		95	1	12	180	3	50	3	92	251	9	00	10	08		322	4	00
38	2	00	2	24	110	1	40	1	61	181	2	00	2	24	252	6	85	7	67		323	8	00
39	1	80	2	07	111		90	1	06	182	2	75	3	08	253	6	35	7	11		324	7	75
40	4	10	4	59	112	1	80	2	07	183	3	30	3	70	254	5	10	5	75		325	2	00
41	1	50	1	72	113	1	95	2	24	184	3	00	3	30	255	7	25	8	12		326	2	00
42	3	70	4	14	114	1	90	2	13	185	3	75	4	20	256	9	50	10	64		327	3	50
43	1	40	1	61	115	1	25	1	47	186	1	80	2	07	257	10	00	11	20		328	6	00
44	2	00	2	24	116	2	15	2	47	187	1	85	2	14	258	2	30	2	58		329	5	50
45	3	25	3	64	117	1	35	1	55	188	3	50	3	92	259	1	50	1	72		330	8	00
46		70		83	118		80		95	189	2	50	2	80	260	1	75	2	01		331	2	50
47	1	25	1	47	119	2	50	2	80	190	3	25	3	64	261	1	75	2	01		332	2	25
48	1	25	1	47	120	2	40	2	69	191	3	50	3	92	262	3	00	3	30		340	2	67
49	2	35	2	63	121		75		89	192	3	75	4	20	263	9	00	10	08		340½	2	25
50	1	10	1	36	122	2	55	2	86	193	1	85	2	14	264	3	25	3	64		341	2	75
51	3	05	3	42	123	1	15	1	32	194	3	75	4	20	265	6	00	6	72		341½	2	50
52	1	05	1	24	124	3	00	3	30	195	5	00	5	60	266	2	25	2	59		342	2	15
53	2	90	3	25	125	1	85	2	14	196	5	25	5	88	267		30		36		342½	1	75
54	1	15	1	32	126	3	15	3	53	197	3	75	4	20	268		35		41		343	1	50
55	2	70	3	02	127	1	80	2	07	198	3	35	3	75	269		40		48		343½	1	15
56	1	35	1	55	128	3	30	3	70	199	3	75	4	20	270		45		53		344	2	10
57	2	25	2	59	129		95	1	12	200	4	25	4	75	271		50		59				
58	1	35	1	55	130		75		89	201	3	15	3	53	272		55		65				
59	2	00	2	24	131	2	00	2	24	202	3	25	3	64	273		60		71				
60	1	45	1	63	132	1	25	1	47	203	7	00	7	70	274		70		83				
61	2	35	2	63	133	1	90	2	13	204	6	40	7	04	275		80		95				
62	1	15	1	32	134	1	90	2	13	205	6	00	6	60	276		90	1	06				
63	2	50	2	80	135	4	20	4	70	206	7	00	7	70	277	1	00	1	18				
64	1	10	1	30	136	1	00	1	18	207	8	75	9	62	278	1	10	1	30				
65	2	50	2	80	137	4	50	5	04	208	3	20	3	59	279	1	20	1	38				
66	1	30	1	46	138		70		80	209	3	20	3	59	280	1	35	1	55				
67	2	90	3	25	139	3	90	4	37	210	3	00	3	30	281	1	90	2	13				
68	1	05	1	24	140	1	15	1	32	211	5	50	6	16	282	2	10	2	35				
69	4	20	4	70	141		40		48	212	8	00	8	64	283	3	00	3	30				
70		90	1	06	142		50		59	213	4	25	4	75	284		50		65	3¾ in. thick			
71	1	35	1	55	143	3	50	3	92	214	4	00	4	48	285		70		90	3¾ in. thick			
72	2	10	2	35																			

Valuable Information on Building.

We invite attention to the following suggestions, addressed to those about to erect or improve buildings, on the importance of procuring Plans and Bill of Items.

We are in frequent receipt of letters asking at what price we will furnish a building of a given size, at some distant city or plantation, ready for occupation. The writers seem to suppose that the cost of a house can be as readily estimated as that of a suit of clothes.

We do not undertake to build or finish houses. Our business is to furnish the lumber and other materials, including carpenter or joiner work, ready made for brick or frame houses; but in order to estimate for them, it is necessary that we be furnished with plan and bill of items, and that persons may understand what we mean by these, we give an example below.

The Plans show how a plain frame dwelling is to be constructed, with the arrangement of the foundations, chimneys, doors, windows, stairs, etc.

The Bill of Items gives the size, quality, and quantity of the materials.

Plans.

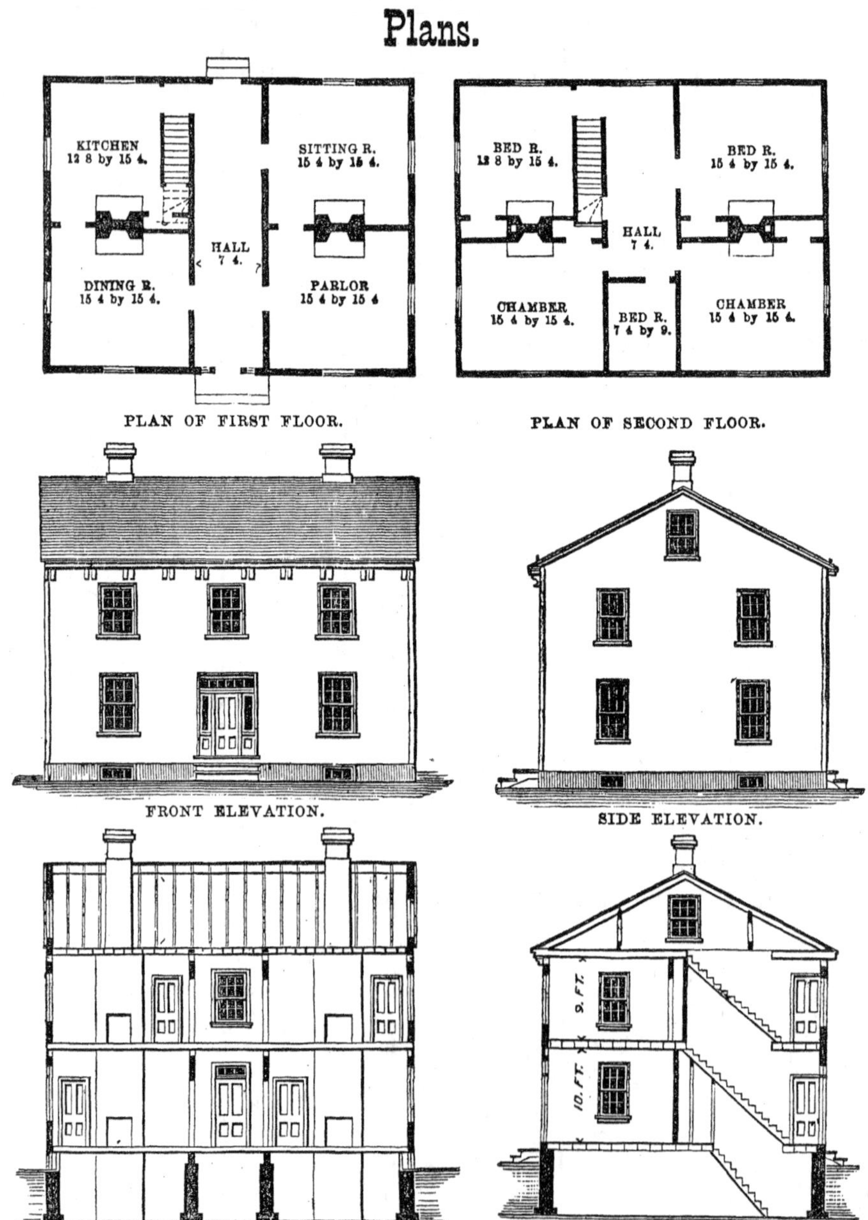

PLAN OF FIRST FLOOR.

PLAN OF SECOND FLOOR.

FRONT ELEVATION.

SIDE ELEVATION.

LONGITUDINAL SECTION.

TRAVERSE SECTION.

Dwelling House 39 ft. 4 in. long, 31 ft. 8 in. wide; first story contains 4 rooms and hall, 10 ft. high; second story, 5 rooms 9 ft. high in clear; 1 garret room, and cellar 7 ft. deep.

Bill of Items.

FRAMING TIMBER, JOISTS, RAFTERS, BRIDGING, ETC.

2 sills 4 by 10 in., 39 ft. 4 in. long.
4 sills 4 by 10 in., 31 ft. 8 in. long.
8 posts 4 by 6 in., 21 ft. long.
2 plates 4 by 6 in., 39 ft. 4 in. long.
4 plates 4 by 6 in., 33 ft. 6 in. long.
1 girder 4 by 6 in., 39 ft. 4 in. long.
14 joists 3 by 10 in., 16 ft. long.
103 joists $1\frac{1}{2}$ by 10 in., 16 ft. long. } First and second floors.
10 joists 1 by 10 in., 16 ft. long. }
54 joists $1\frac{1}{2}$ by 10 in., 17 feet long. Third floor.
10 purlins 3 by 4 in., 16 feet long.
42 rafters $1\frac{1}{2}$ by 5 in., 19 ft. long.
150 studs 2 by 4 in., 21 ft. long.
112 studs 2 by 4 in., 10 ft. long.
100 ft. braces $2\frac{3}{4}$ by 4 in.
12 pieces 1 by 4 in., 16 ft. long, to cut in studs to receive joists.
80 ft. raising plate 1 by 8 in.
600 ft. bridging 1 by $2\frac{1}{2}$ in.

WEATHER BOARDS, SHINGLES, CORNICE, FLOORING, AND MANUFACTURED WORK.

4500 ft. weather boards, white pine, 2d common dressed.
1800 ft. sheathing and scaffolding, 1 in. pine, 3d common.
15000 shingles, pine No. 1, 16 in. long.
96 ft. lineal cornice planceer, dressed, $\frac{7}{8}$ by 10 in.
96 ft. lineal cornice drop fascia, dressed, $\frac{7}{8}$ by $6\frac{1}{2}$ in.
96 ft. lineal cornice crown moulding, No. 209 Hinkle & Co.'s Book.
80 ft. lineal barge board, dressed, $\frac{7}{8}$ by 5 in.
90 ft. lineal corner strip, dressed, $1\frac{3}{8}$ by 4 in.
20 brackets, $9\frac{3}{4}$ in. projection, 12 in. high, $1\frac{3}{4}$ thick, No. 232 Hinkle & Co.'s Book.
96 ft. bed mold, No. 100 Hinkle & Co.'s Book.
80 ft. stop, to form gutter on roof, $1\frac{3}{4}$ by 3 in.
3600 ft. flooring white pine, 2d common, dressed one side, tongued and grooved.
500 ft. pine boards, dressed, $\frac{7}{8}$ in., for shelving, grounds, etc.
672 ft. lineal beveled base, as No. 247 Hinkle & Co.'s Book.
48 ft. lineal plinth, $1\frac{1}{8}$ and $1\frac{3}{8}$ rebated for base, and molded.
912 ft. lineal band molding, No. 277 Hinkle & Co.'s Book.
90 ft. lineal window sill, $\frac{7}{8}$ by $2\frac{3}{4}$ in.
90 ft. lineal window facia, $\frac{7}{8}$ by 4 in.
80 ft. lineal carpet sill, $\frac{1}{2}$ by $3\frac{1}{2}$ in., beveled.
1 side light and impost door frame, with door side light and transom; frame 6 ft. by 8 ft. 3 in., jambs $6\frac{1}{4}$ wide, door posts $3\frac{3}{4}$ in. thick; panel door 3 by 7 ft. raised and beveled, $1\frac{3}{8}$ thick; side lights panel below raised and beveled, and transom all glazed.
1 impost door frame with door and transom; frame 2 ft. 10 in. by 8 ft. 1 in., jambs $6\frac{1}{4}$ wide; door 2 ft. 10 in. by 6 ft. 10 in., raised and beveled $1\frac{3}{8}$ in.; transom glazed.
16 partition door frames 2 ft. 10 in. by 6 ft. 10 in., jambs $5\frac{3}{4}$ in. wide, rebated $1\frac{3}{8}$ in.
2 partition door frames 2 ft. 3 in. by 6 ft. 10 in., jambs $5\frac{3}{4}$ in., rebated $1\frac{3}{8}$ in.
16 doors 2 ft. 10 in. by 6 ft. 10 in., flat and beveled $1\frac{3}{8}$ in.

2 doors 2 ft. 3 in. by 6 ft. 10 in., flat and beveled 1⅝ in.
8 cellar window frames 10 by 12 in., 3 lights.
2 common window frames 12 by 16 in., 12 lights 1⅝ in.
6 " " " 10 by 16 in., 12 lights 1⅝ in.
3 " " " 12 by 14 in., 12 lights 1⅝ in.
7 " " " 10 by 14 in., 12 lights 1⅝ in.
2 " " " 10 by 12 in., 12 lights 1⅝ in.
2 pair sash 12 by 16 in., 12 lights, primed and glazed, 1⅝ in.
6 " 10 by 16 in., 12 lights, primed and glazed, 1⅝ in.
3 " 12 by 14 in., 12 lights, primed and glazed, 1⅝ in.
7 " 10 by 14 in., 12 lights, primed and glazed, 1⅝ in.
2 " 10 by 12 in., 12 lights, primed and glazed, 1⅝ in.
8 sash 10 by 12 in., 3 lights, primed and glazed, 1 in.
2 pair venetian shutters 12 by 16 in., 12 lights, 1⅝ in.
6 " " 10 by 16 in., 12 lights, 1⅝ in
3 " " 12 by 14 in., 12 lights, 1⅝ in.
7 " " 10 by 14 in., 12 lights, 1⅝ in.
2 " " 10 by 12 in., 12 lights, 1⅝ in.
8 mantels, plain pilaster, 4 ft. high, 5 ft. 2 in. breast.
2 flight of box stairs, as plan, carriages gained and beveled, steps and risers prepared.
1 flight of stairs to cellar, carriages and step undressed.
1 scuttle door and frame in roof 22 in. wide 3 ft. long.
Outside steps, and platform in front, as plan.

The style of finish can be selected from Hinkle & Co.'s Book of Moldings, etc., and reference be made to the number or figure on bill of items. It contains a great variety of cornice, moldings, base or washboard, architraves, stairs, rails, newels, balusters, brackets, mantels, doors, windows, columns, veranda posts, etc. If anything not found in this book is wanted, it will be necessary to give working drawings.

Remember, the first thing when about to build or alter is to obtain a good plan, bill of items, and specifications. By so doing, you invite competition, as each branch is brought within the comprehension of ordinary mechanics, enabling them to estimate, in a short time, intelligently. Starting thus with a definite plan, you ascertain the whole cost before commencing, and avoid alterations and disputes.

If plans, bills of items, and specifications, can not be procured in your vicinity, you can obtain them in Cincinnati at a reasonable price, by sending us the outside length and width of building, hight of story, hight of first floor above ground, depth of cellar, if wanted, and a sketch of rooms, giving size, and places for doors and windows marked, and state the amount wished to be expended in the building; with this information the architect can furnish the required plans, etc.

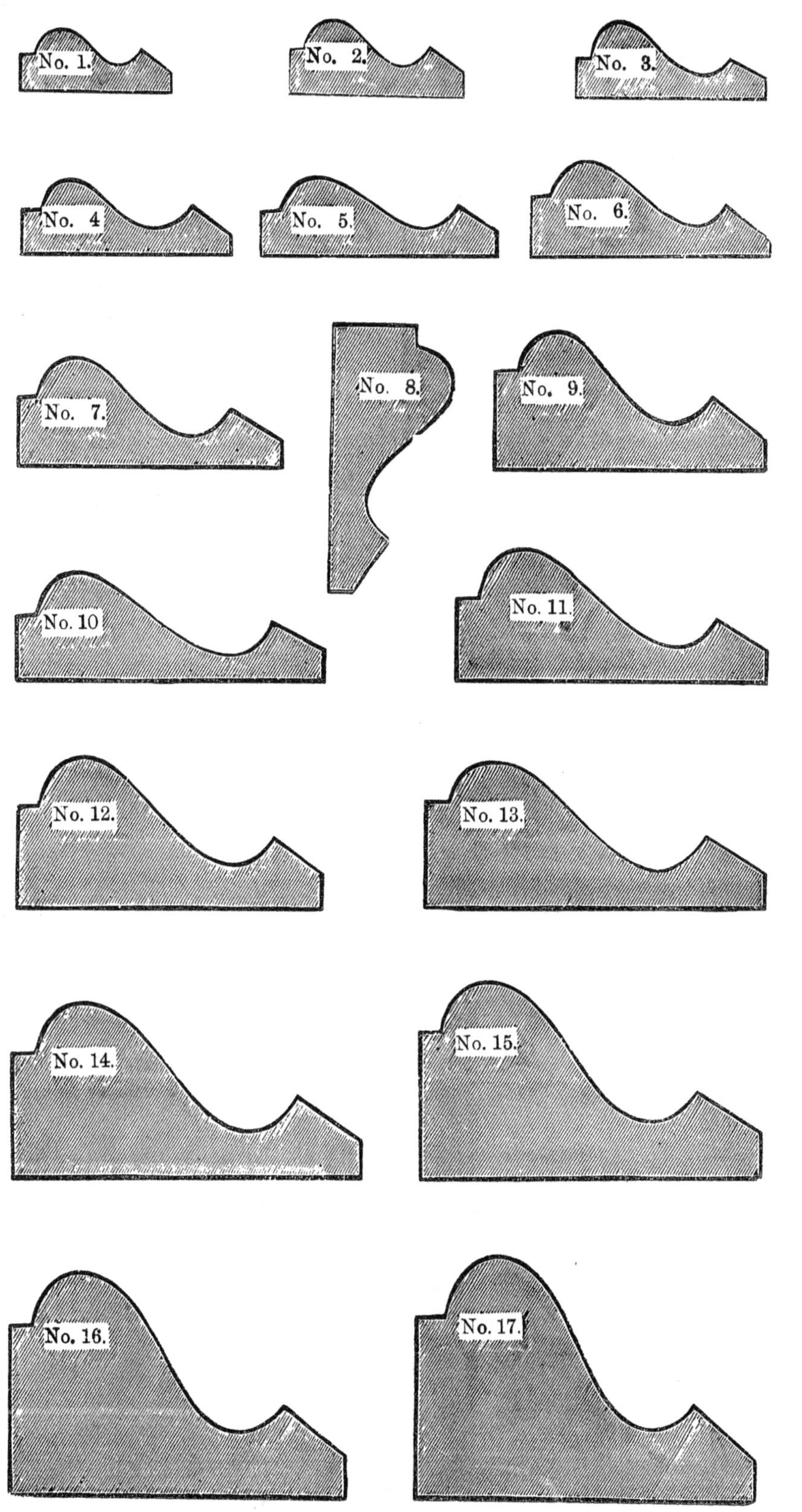
No. 1.
No. 2.
No. 3.
No. 4
No. 5.
No. 6.
No. 7.
No. 8.
No. 9.
No. 10
No. 11.
No. 12.
No. 13.
No. 14.
No. 15.
No. 16.
No. 17.

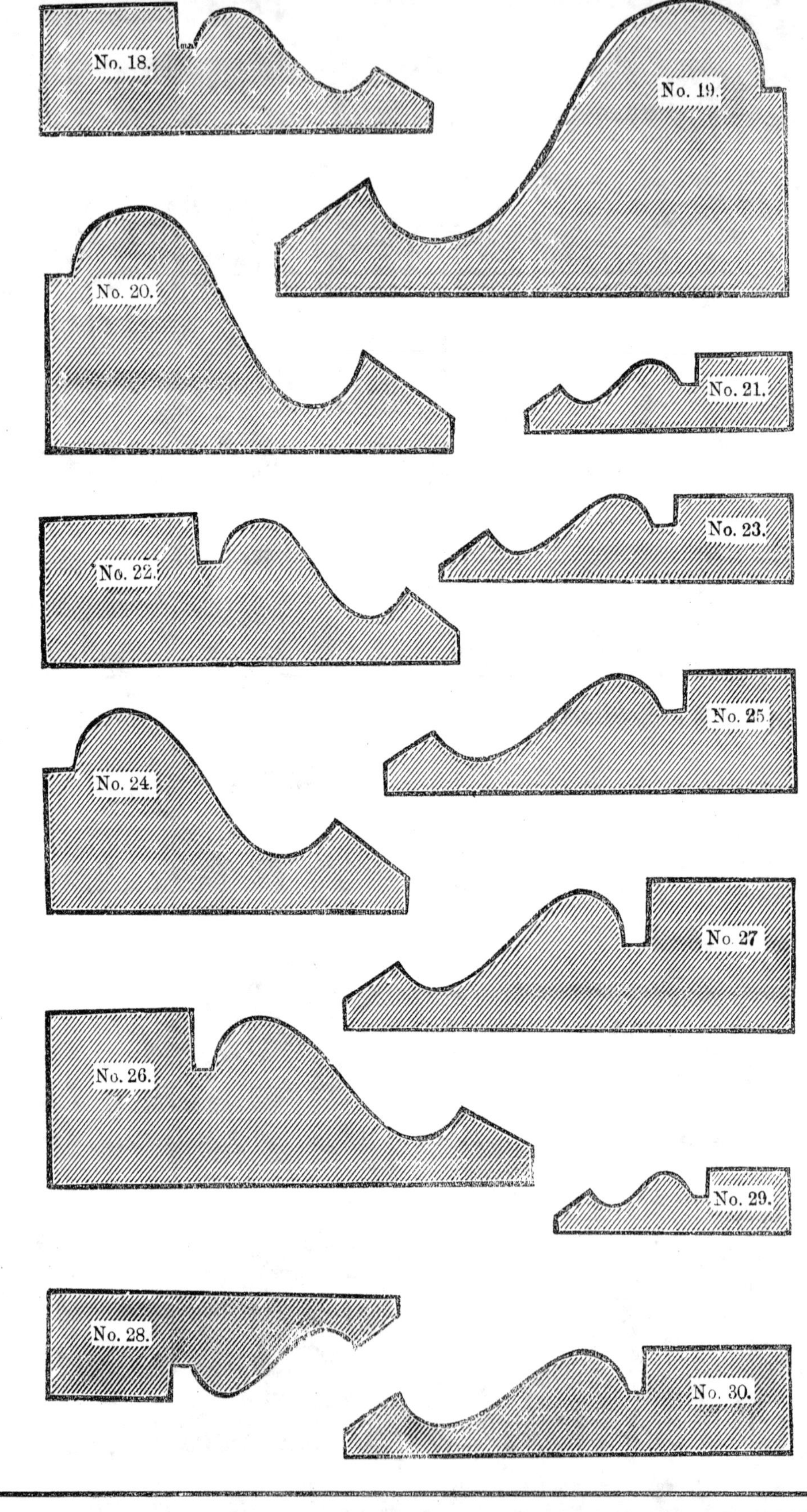
No. 18.
No. 19.
No. 20.
No. 21.
No. 22.
No. 23.
No. 24.
No. 25.
No. 26.
No. 27
No. 28.
No. 29.
No. 30.

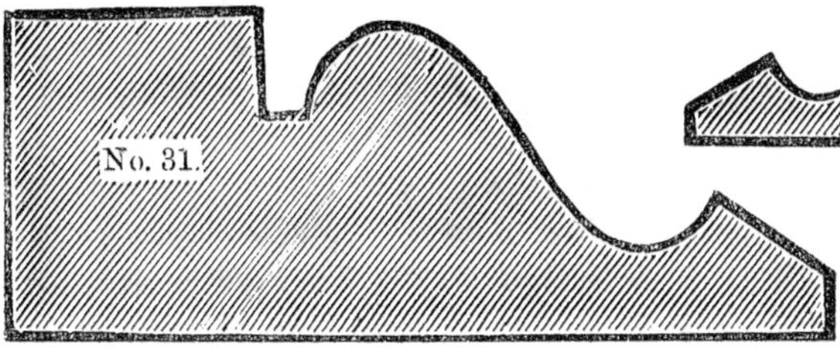

No. 31.

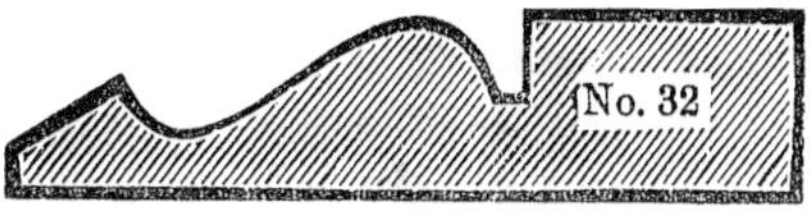

No. 32

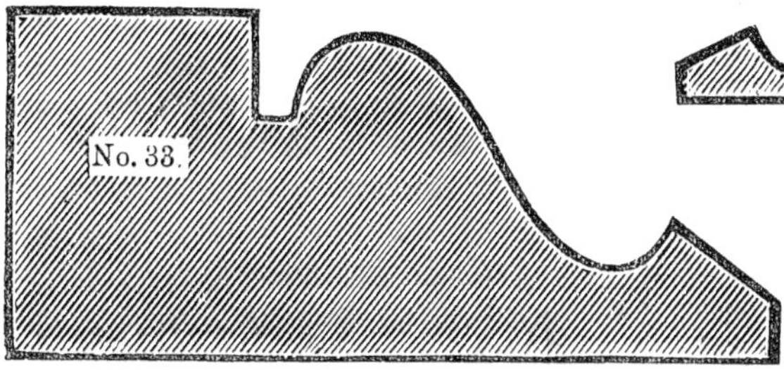

No. 33.

No. 34.

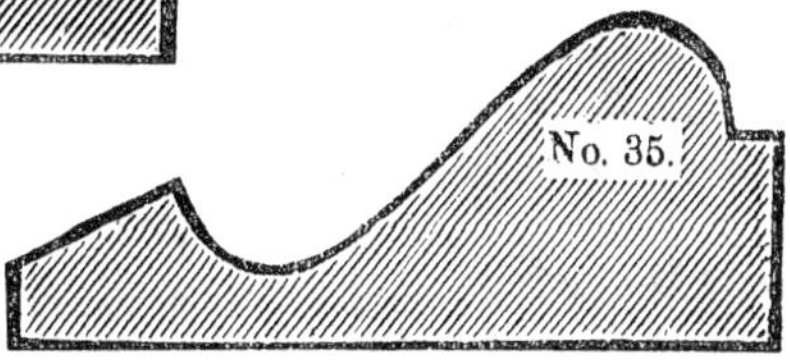

No. 35.

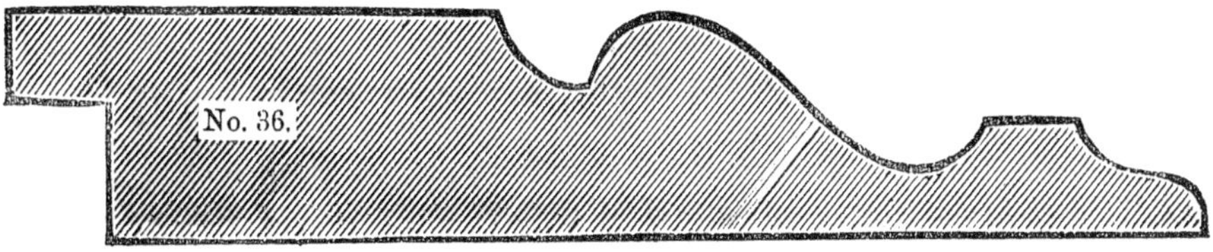

No. 36.

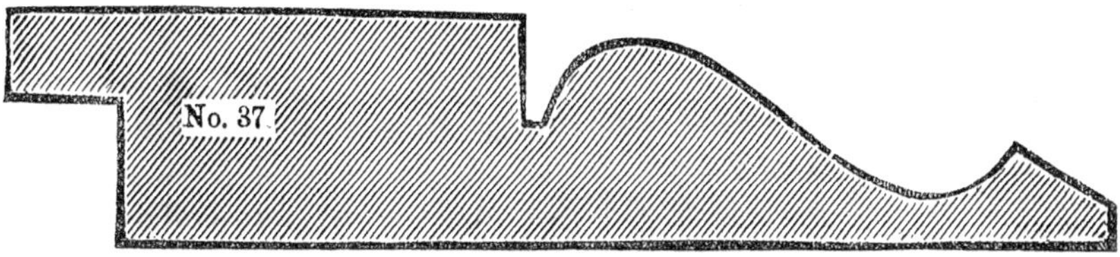

No. 37

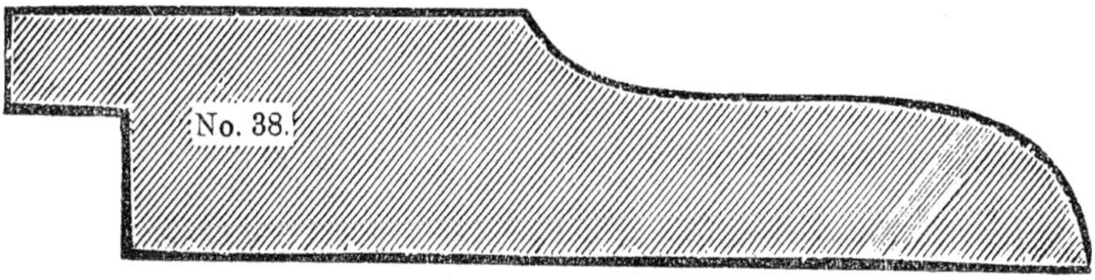

No. 38.

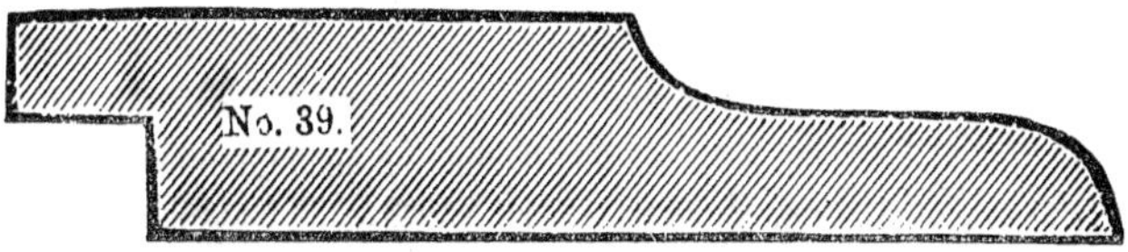

No. 39.

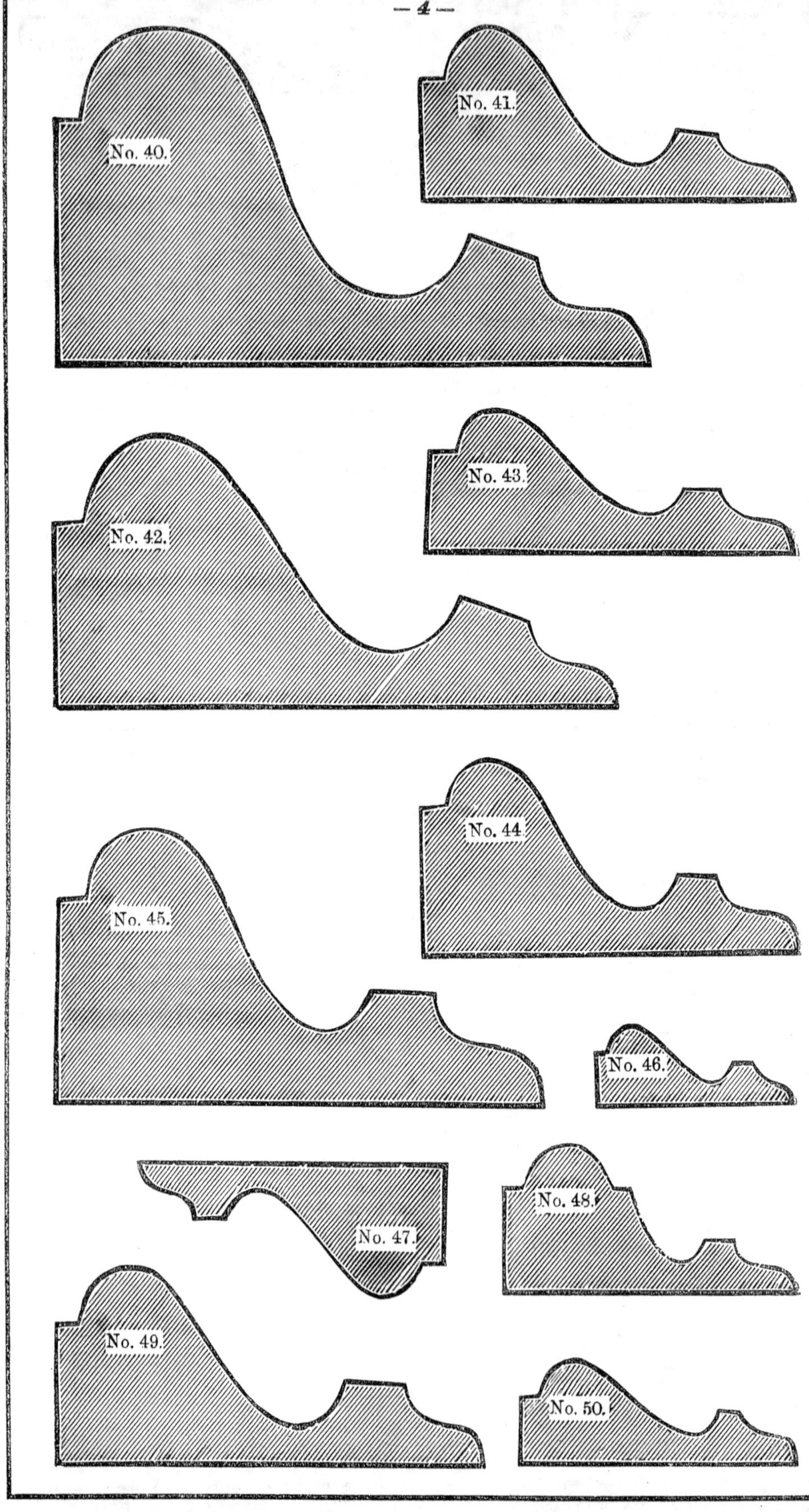
No. 40.
No. 41.
No. 42.
No. 43.
No. 44.
No. 45.
No. 46.
No. 47.
No. 48.
No. 49.
No. 50.

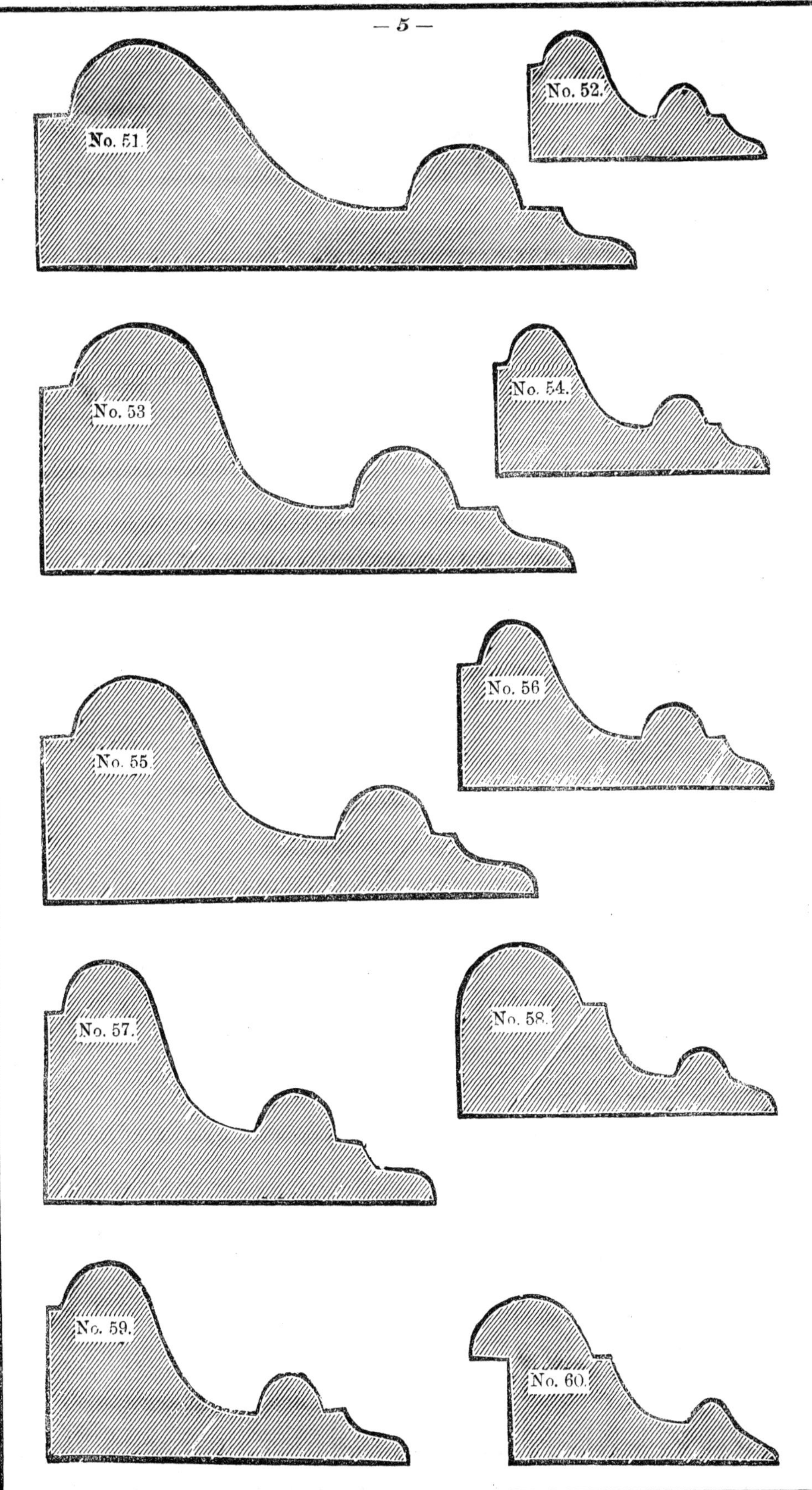
No. 51.
No. 52.
No. 53
No. 54.
No. 55.
No. 56
No. 57.
No. 58.
No. 59.
No. 60.

No. 61.
No. 62.
No. 63.
No. 64.
No. 65.
No. 66.
No. 67.
No. 68.
No. 69.
No. 70.

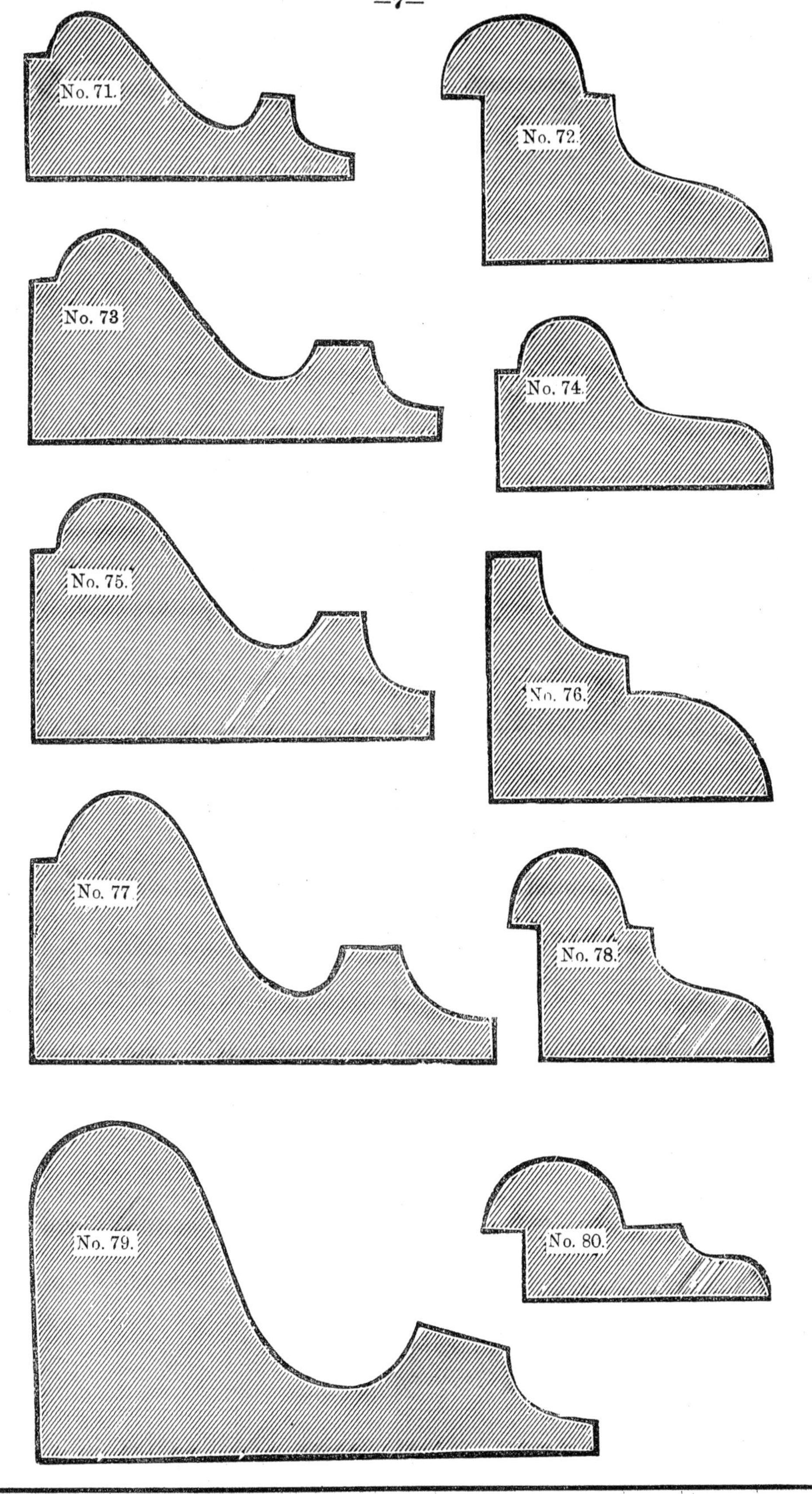
No. 71.
No. 72.
No. 73
No. 74.
No. 75.
No. 76.
No. 77
No. 78.
No. 79.
No. 80.

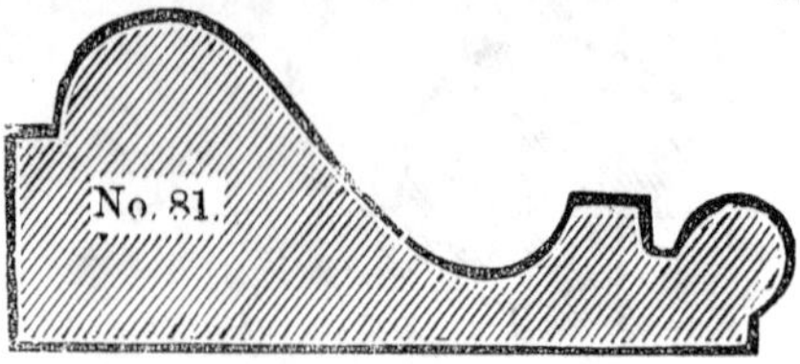

No. 81.

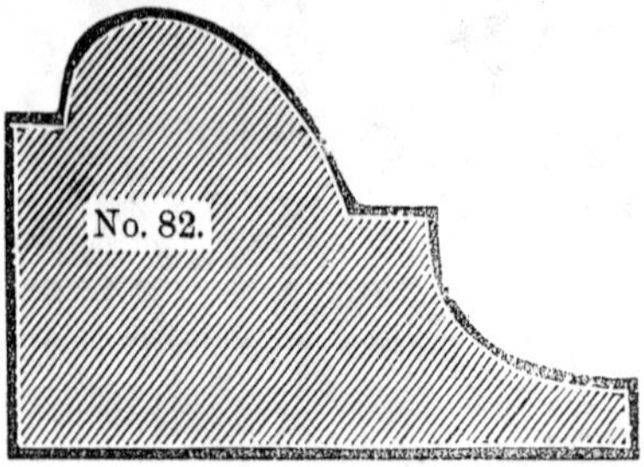

No. 82.

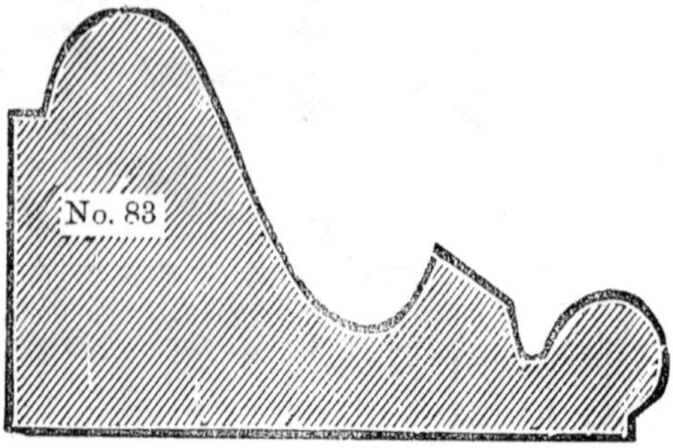

No. 83

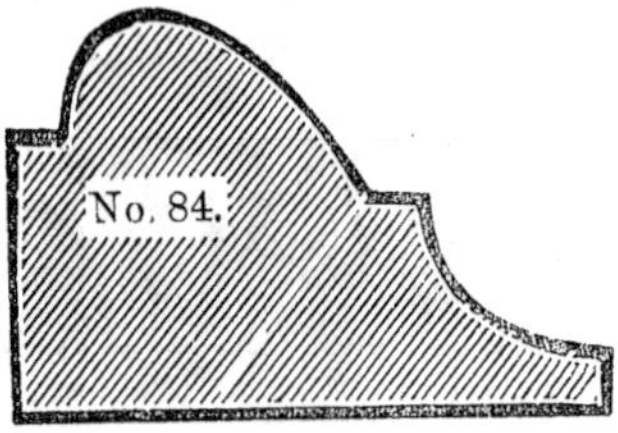

No. 84.

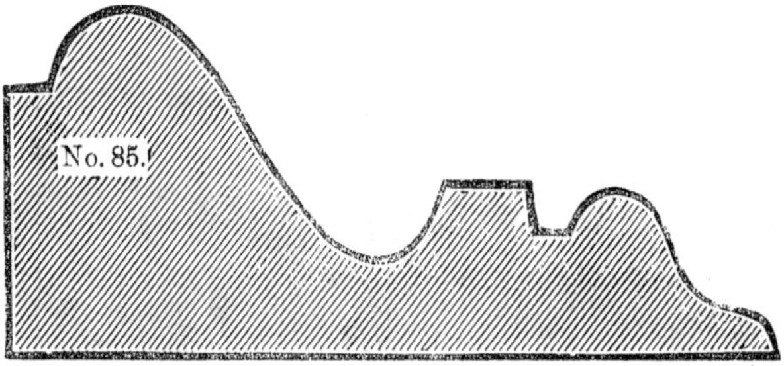

No. 85.

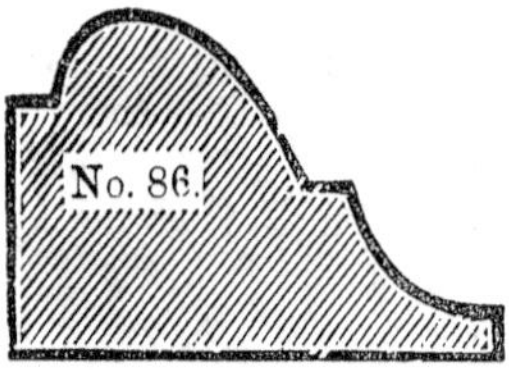

No. 86.

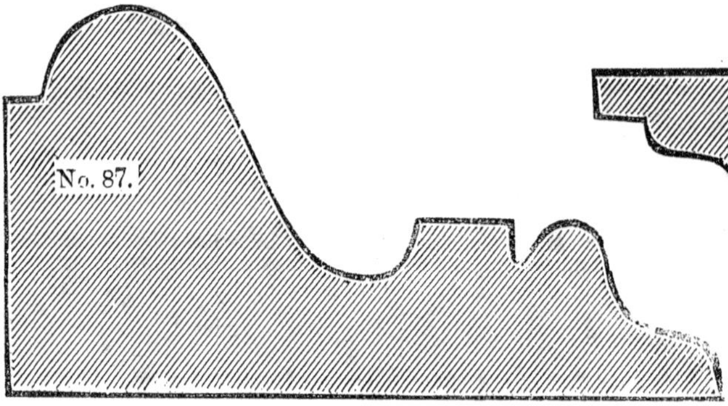

No. 87.

No. 88.

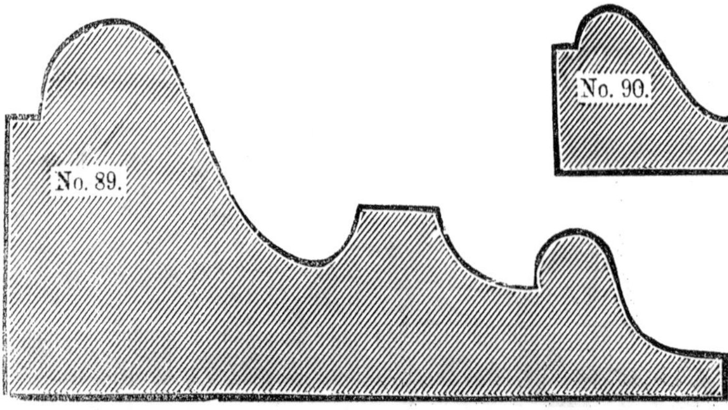

No. 89.

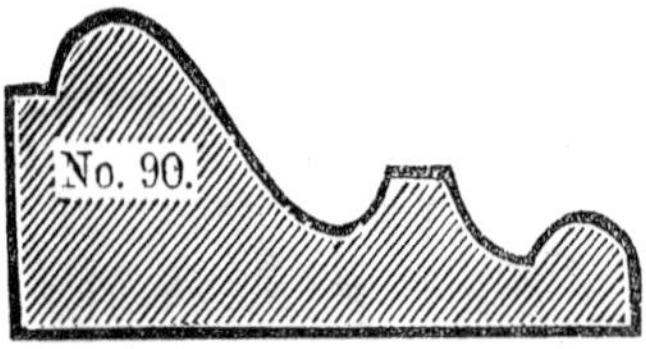

No. 90.

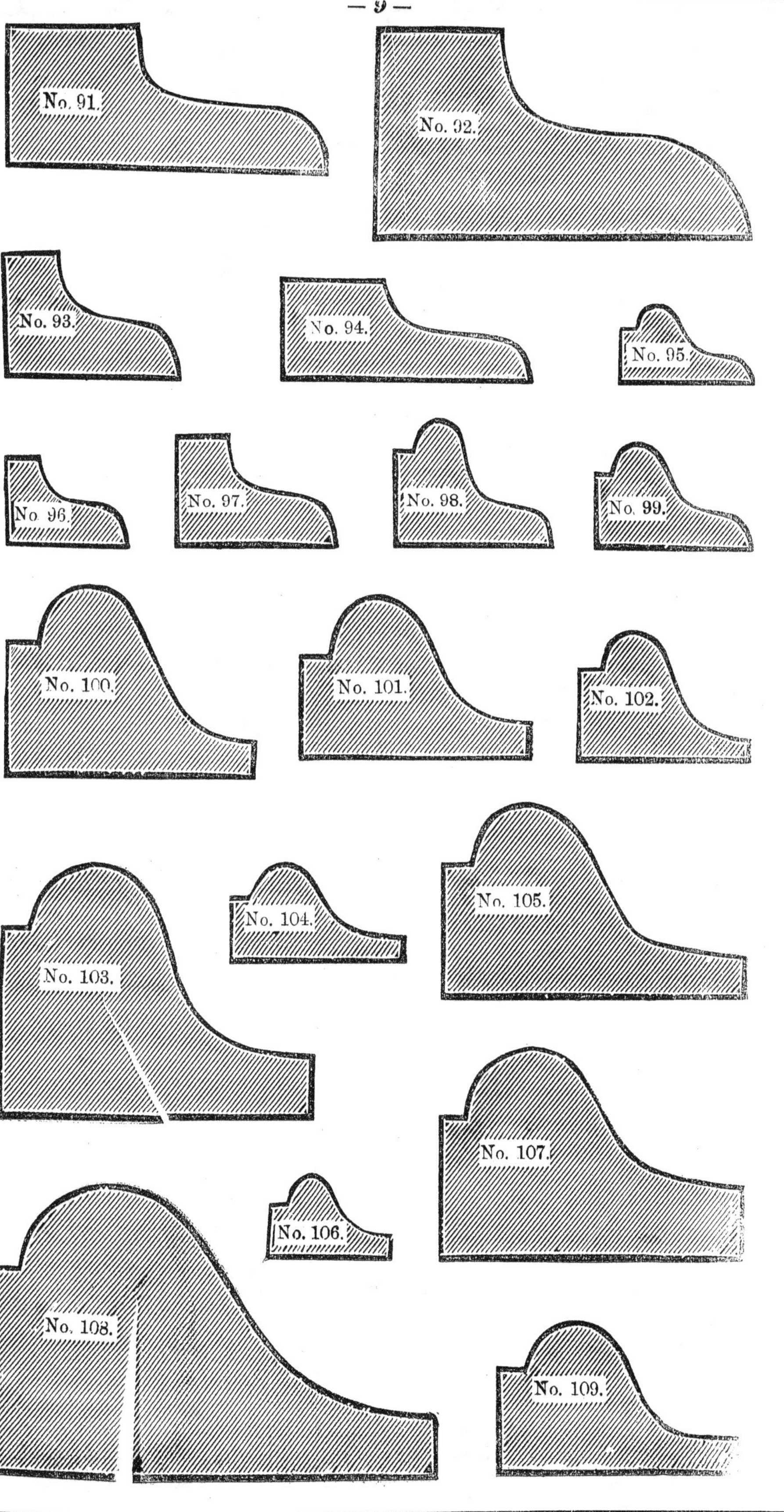
No. 91.
No. 92.
No. 93.
No. 94.
No. 95.
No. 96.
No. 97.
No. 98.
No. 99.
No. 100.
No. 101.
No. 102.
No. 103.
No. 104.
No. 105.
No. 106.
No. 107.
No. 108.
No. 109.

No. 110.

No. 111.

No. 112.

No. 113.

No. 114.

No. 115.

No. 116.

No. 117.

No. 118.

No. 119.

No. 120.

No. 121.

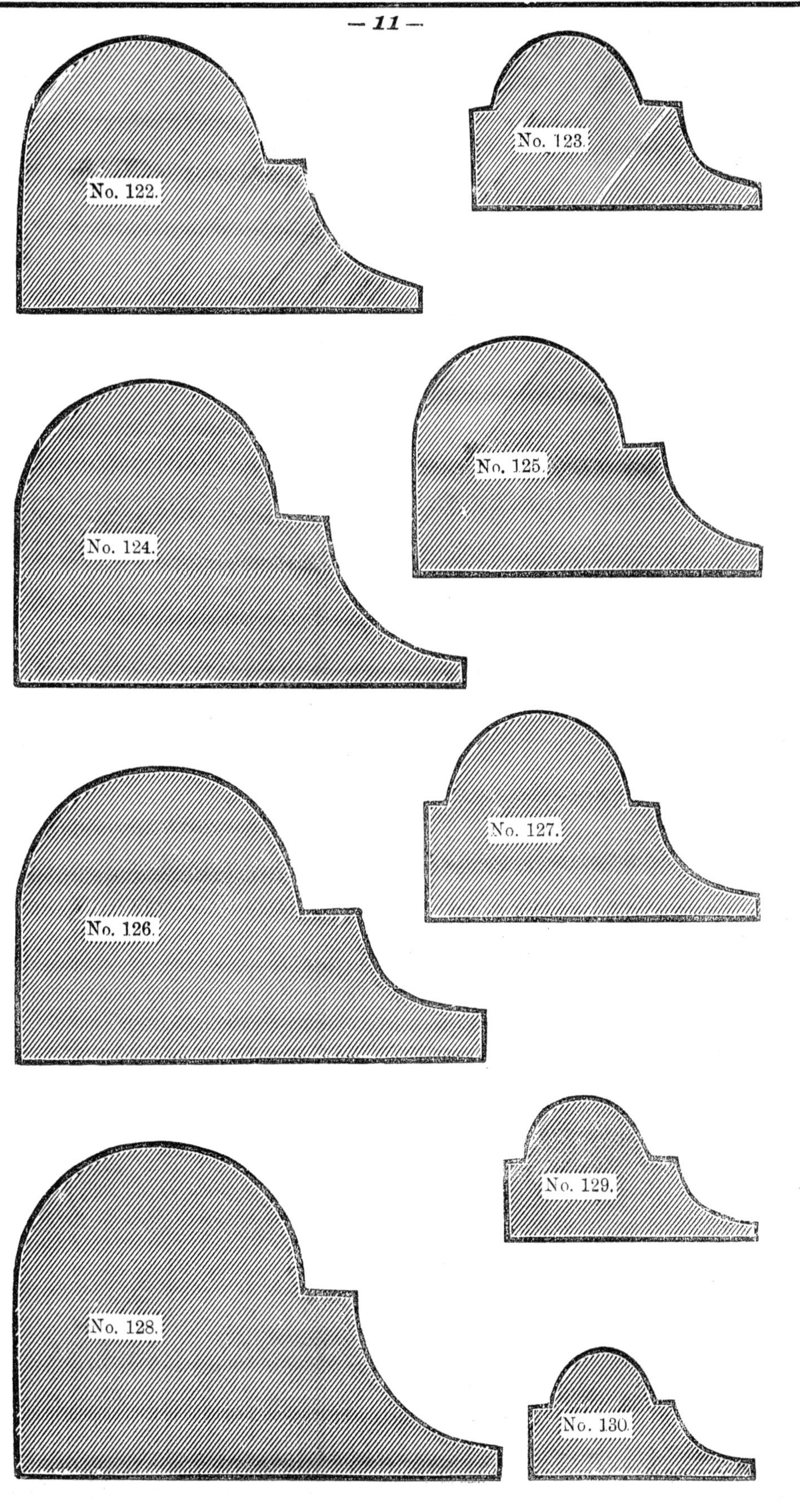
No. 122.
No. 123.
No. 124.
No. 125.
No. 126.
No. 127.
No. 128.
No. 129.
No. 130.

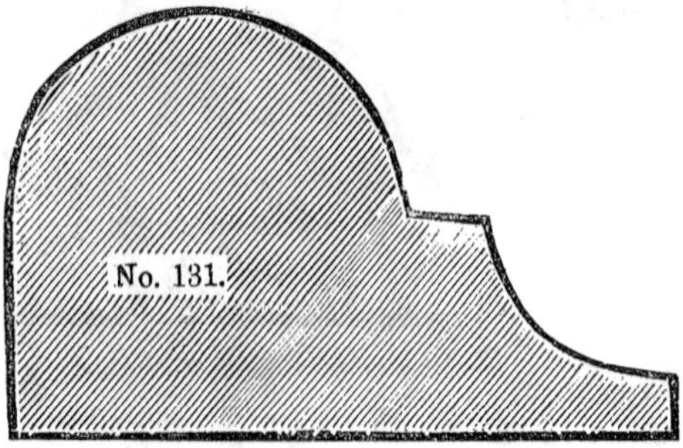

No. 131.

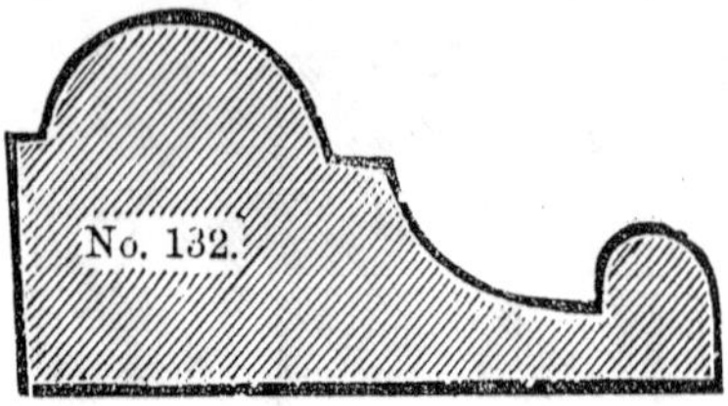

No. 132.

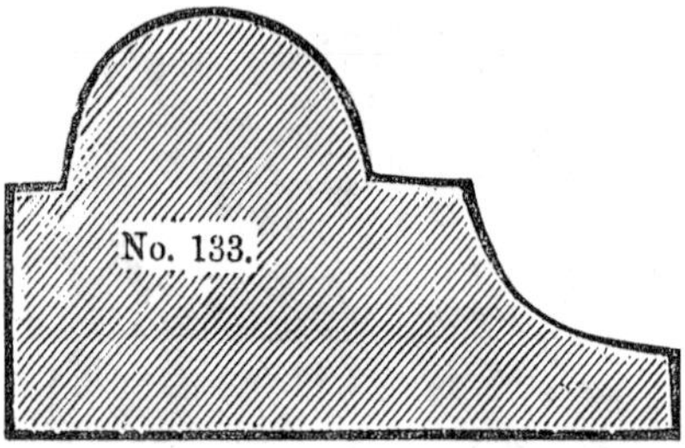

No. 133.

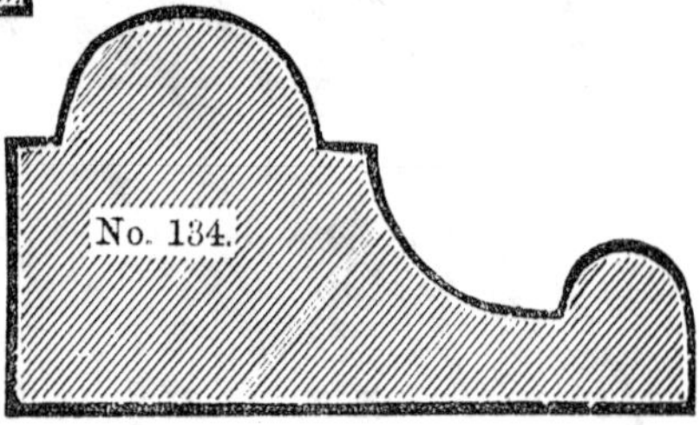

No. 134.

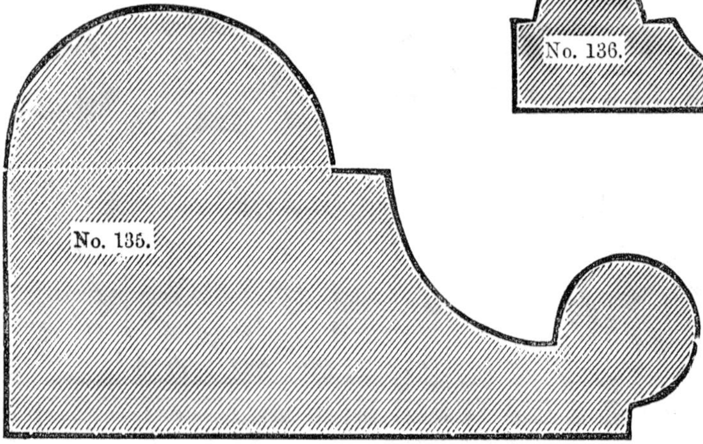

No. 135.

No. 136.

No 137.

No. 138.

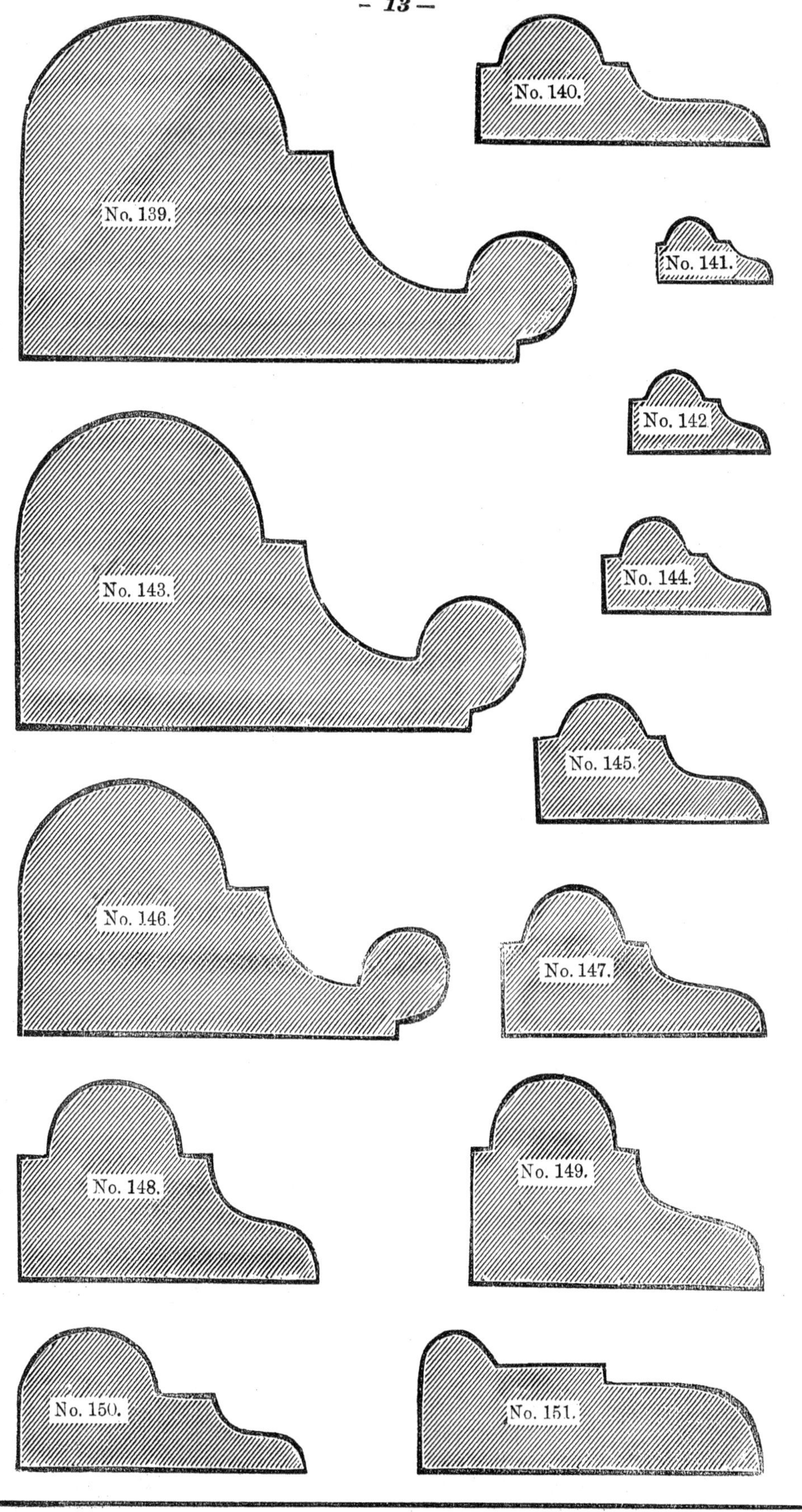
No. 139.
No. 140.
No. 141.
No. 142.
No. 143.
No. 144.
No. 145.
No. 146.
No. 147.
No. 148.
No. 149.
No. 150.
No. 151.

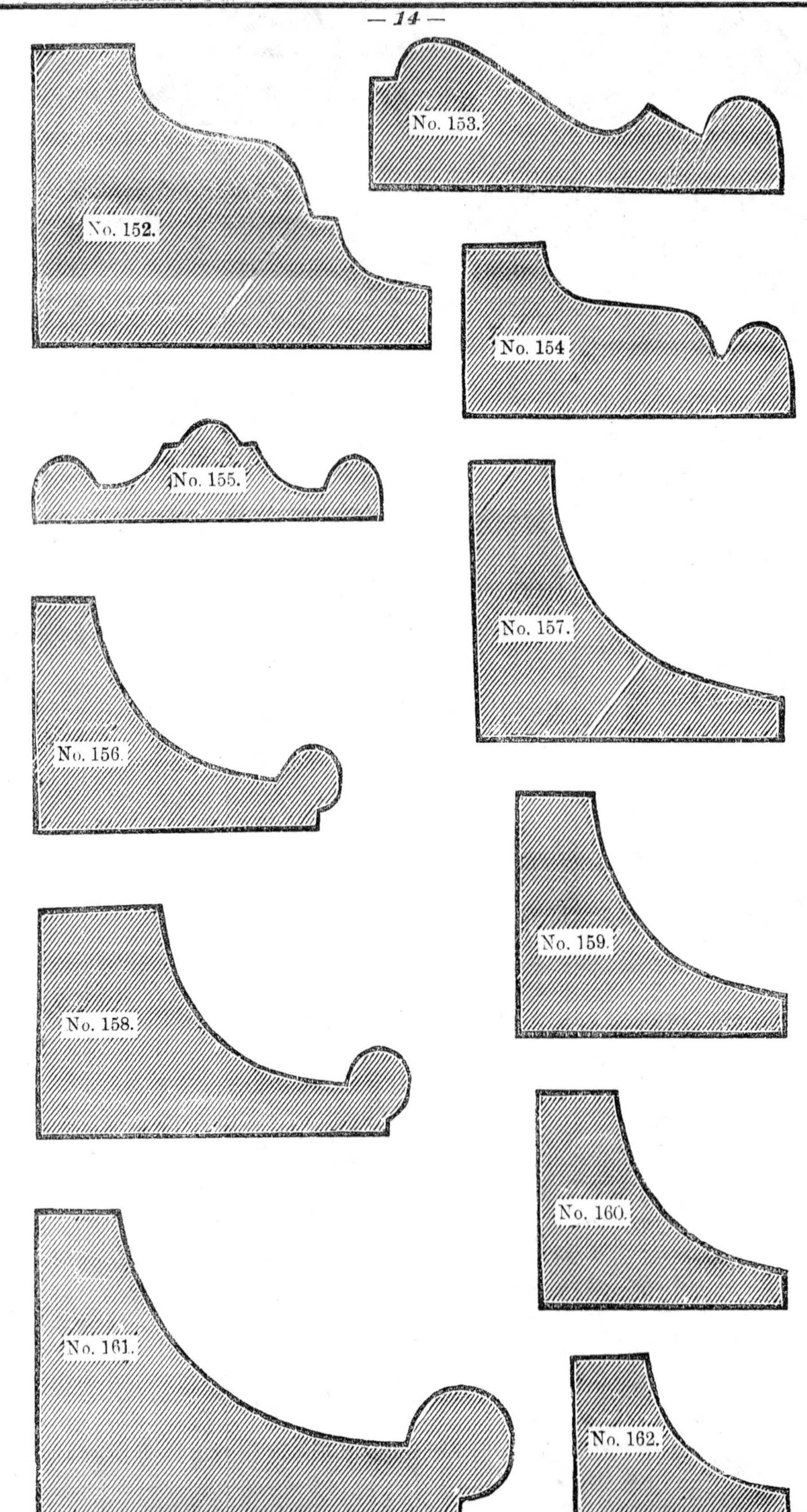
No. 152.
No. 153.
No. 154
No. 155.
No. 156.
No. 157.
No. 158.
No. 159.
No. 160.
No. 161.
No. 162.

No. 163. No. 164. No. 165.

No. 166. No. 167. No. 168.

No. 169. No. 170. No. 171.

No. 172. No. 173. No. 174.

No. 175. No. 176. No. 177.

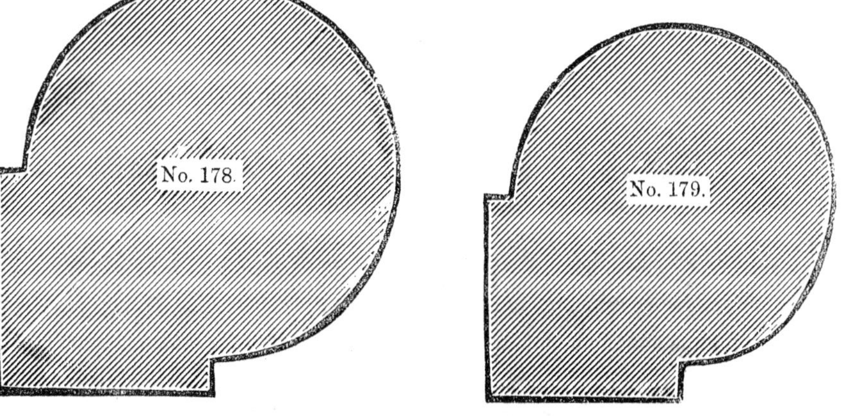

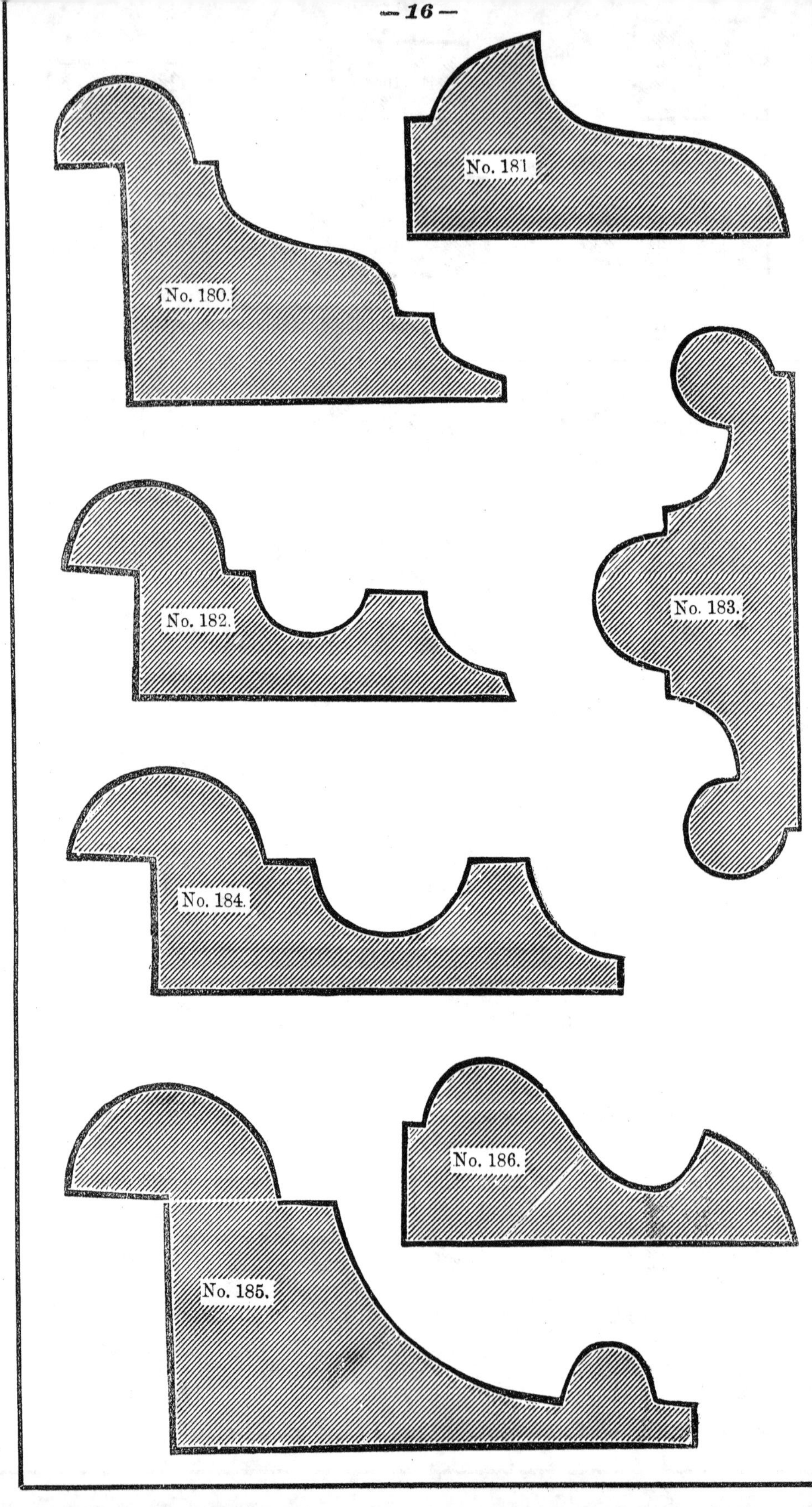
No. 180.
No. 181
No. 182.
No. 183.
No. 184.
No. 185.
No. 186.

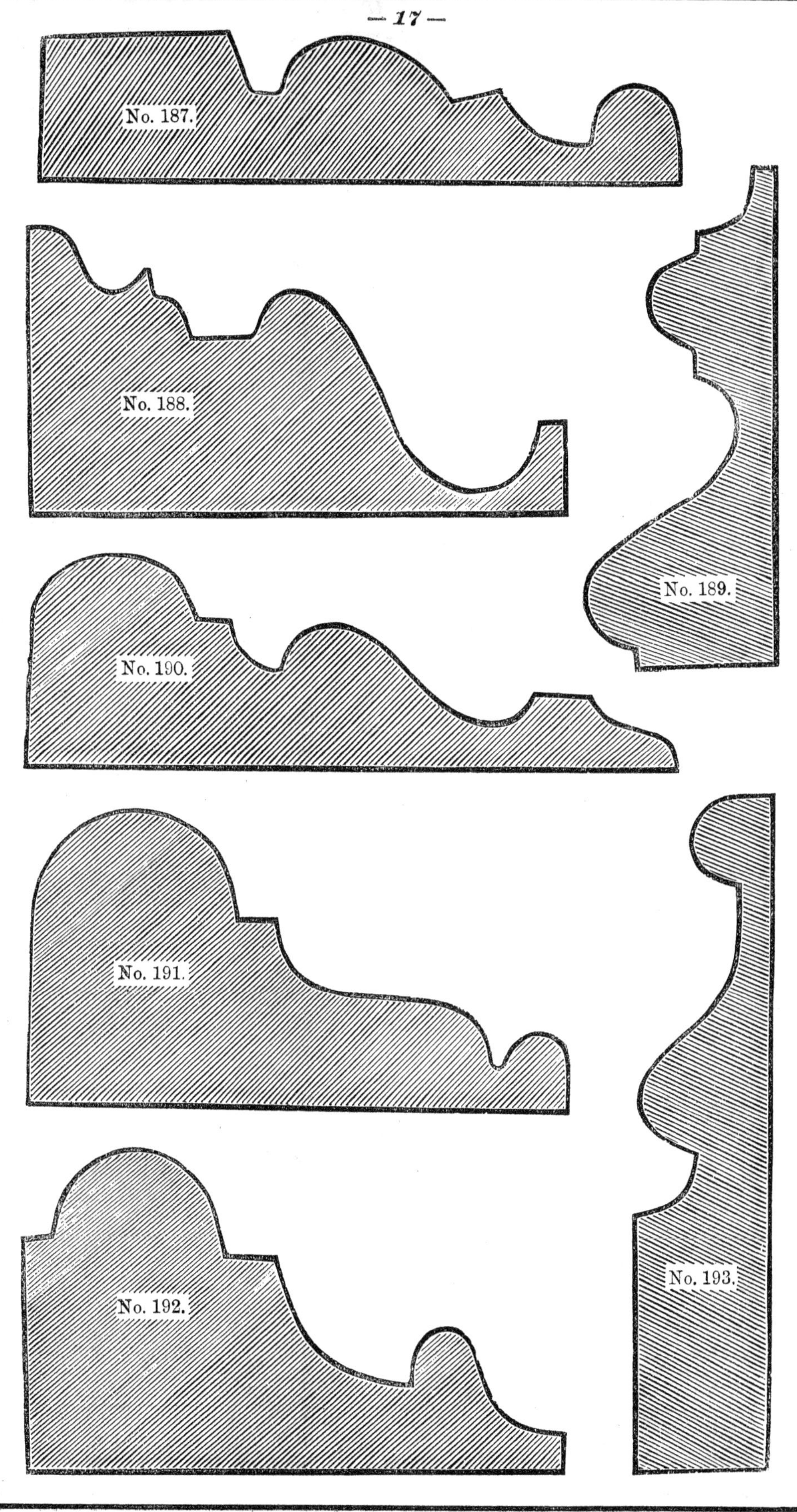
No. 187.
No. 188.
No. 189.
No. 190.
No. 191.
No. 192.
No. 193.

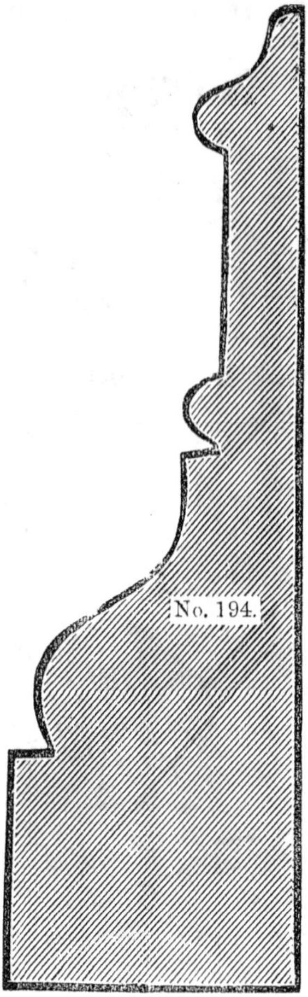

No. 194.

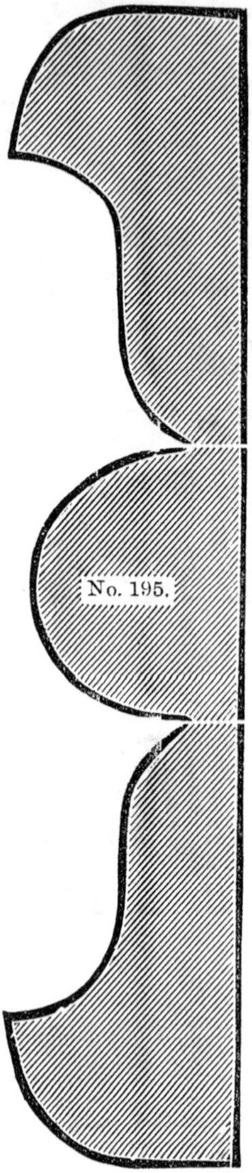

No. 195.

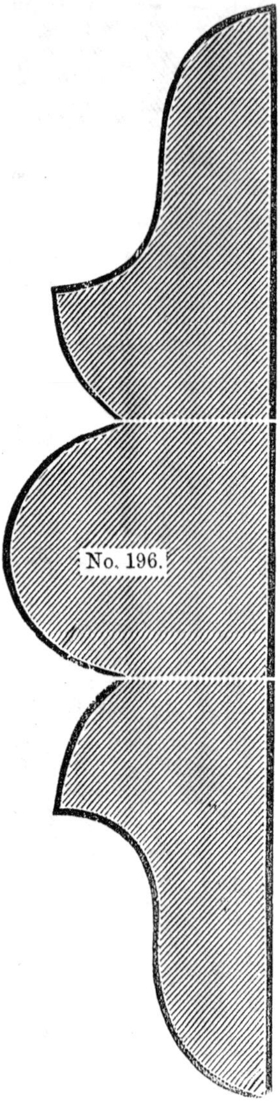

No. 196.

No. 197.

No. 198.

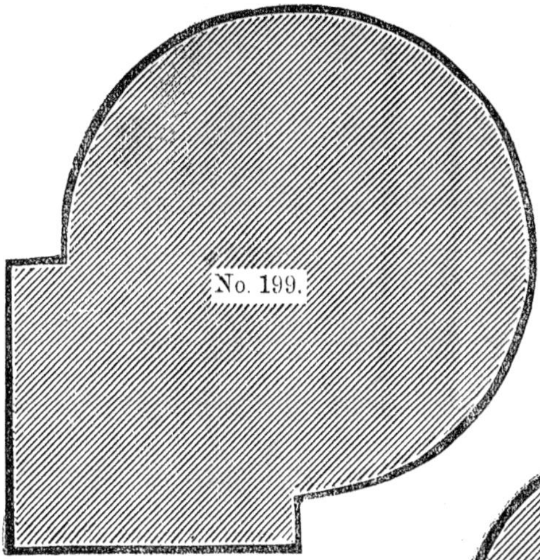

No. 199.

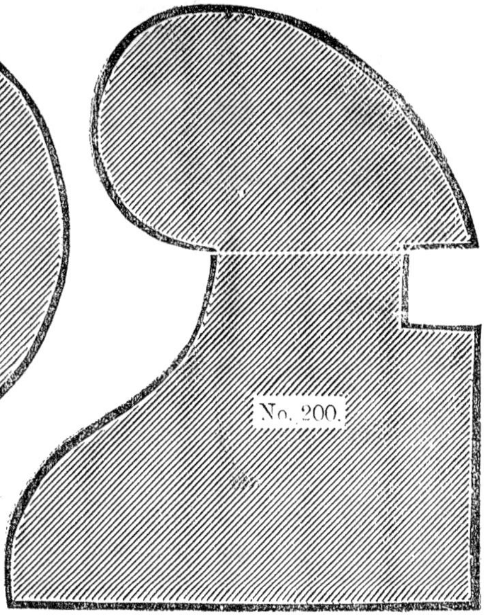

No. 200.

No. 201.

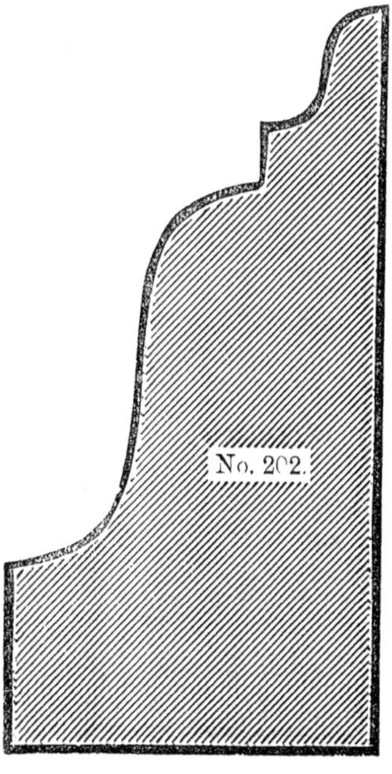

No. 202.

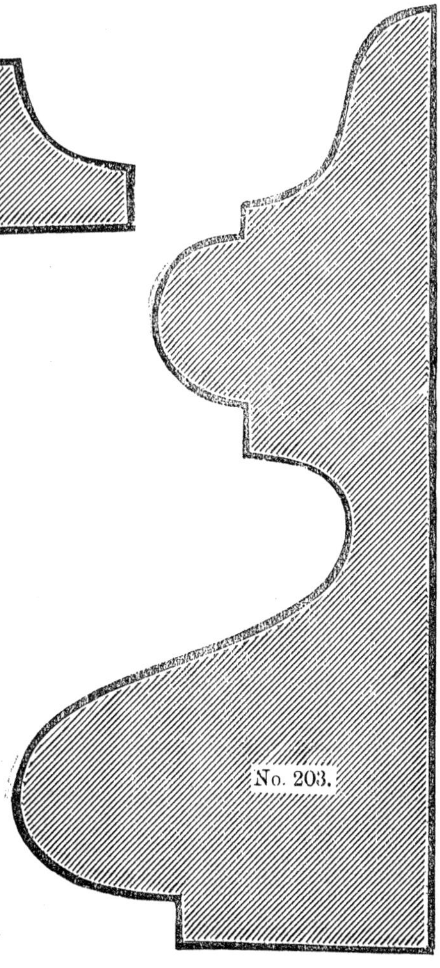

No. 203.

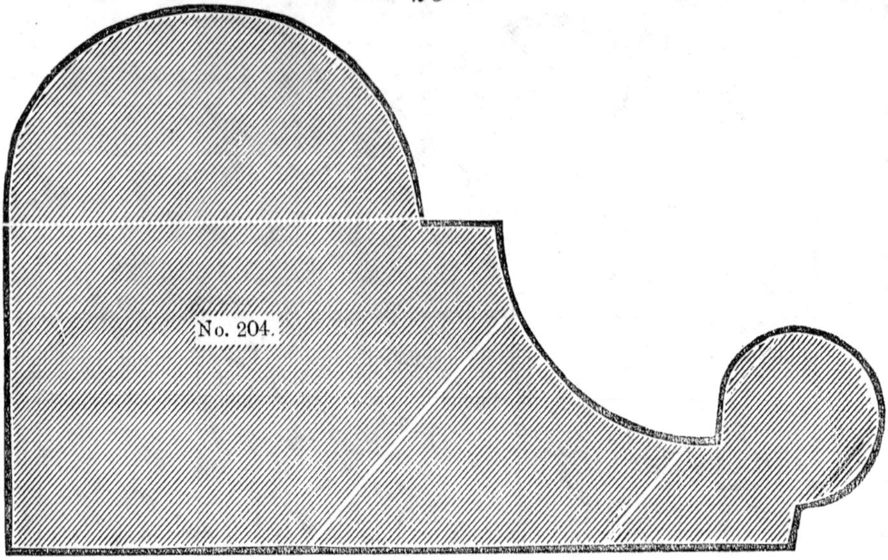

No. 204.

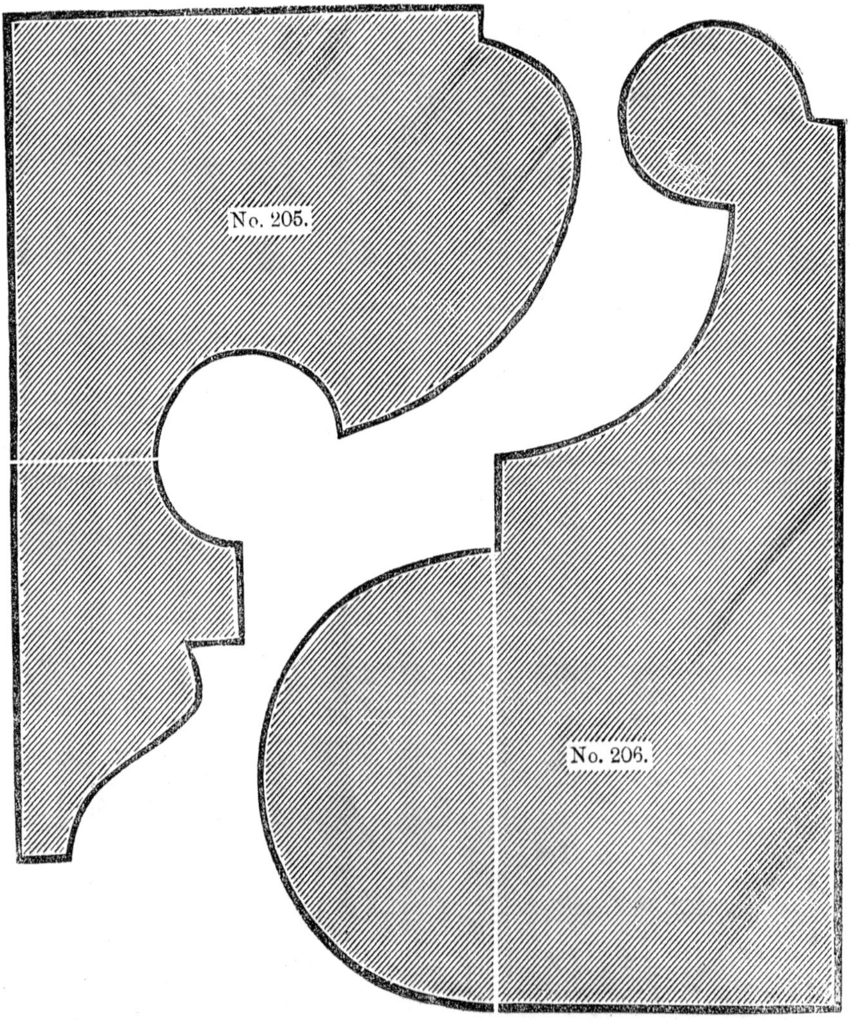

No. 205.

No. 206.

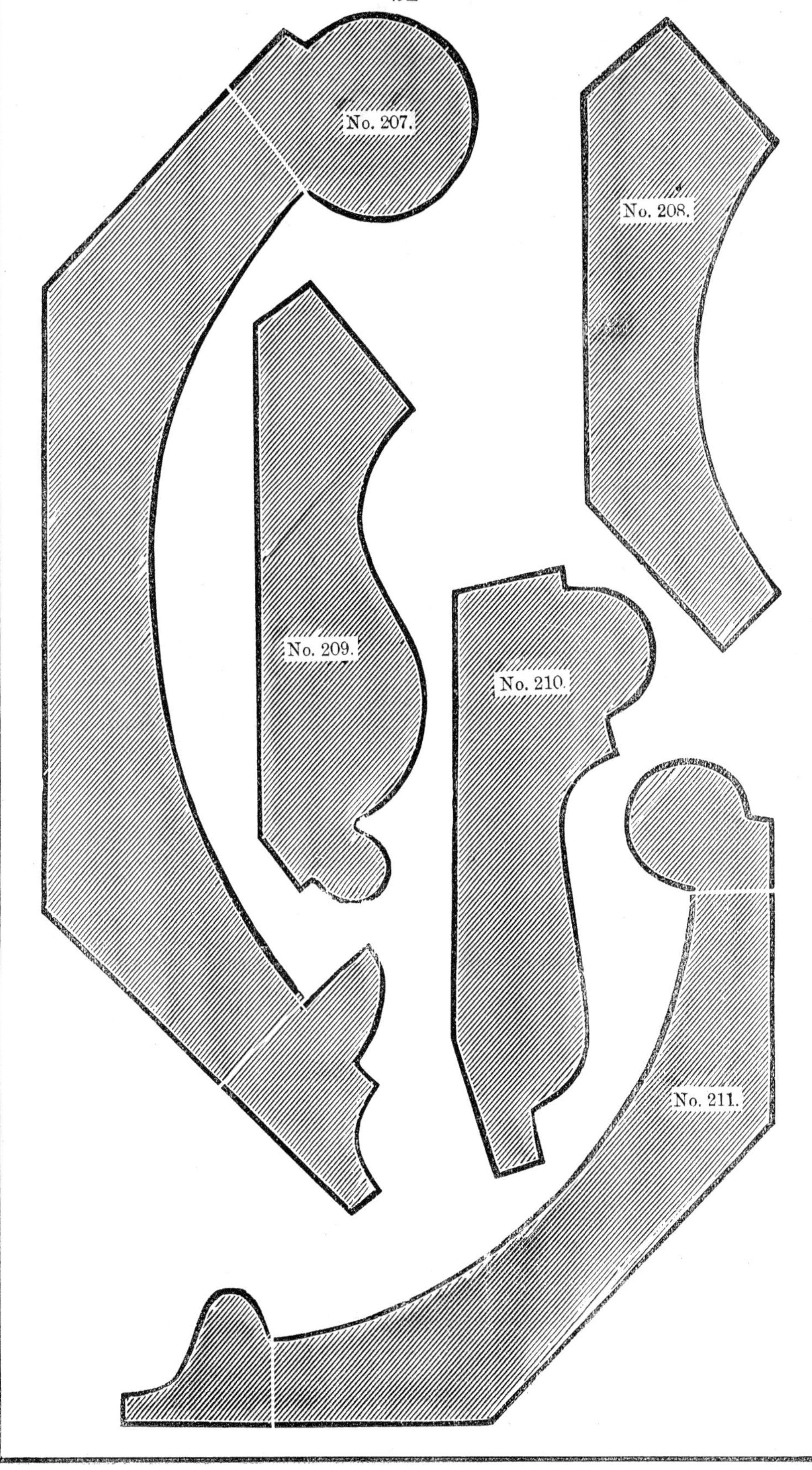
No. 207.
No. 208.
No. 209.
No. 210.
No. 211.

No. 212.
No. 213.
No. 214.
No. 215.
No. 216.

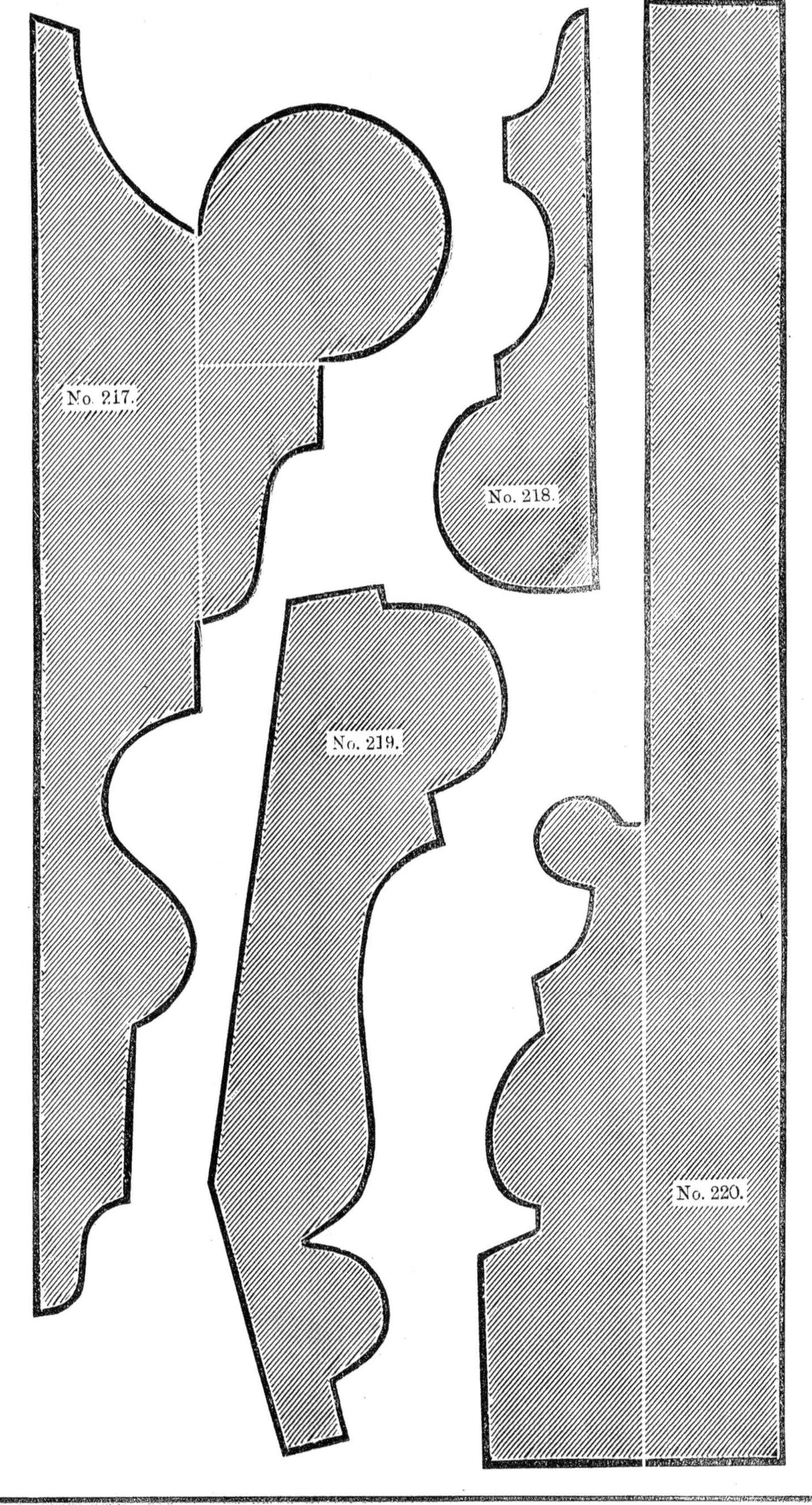
No. 217.
No. 218.
No. 219.
No. 220.

No. 221

No. 222.

No. 223.

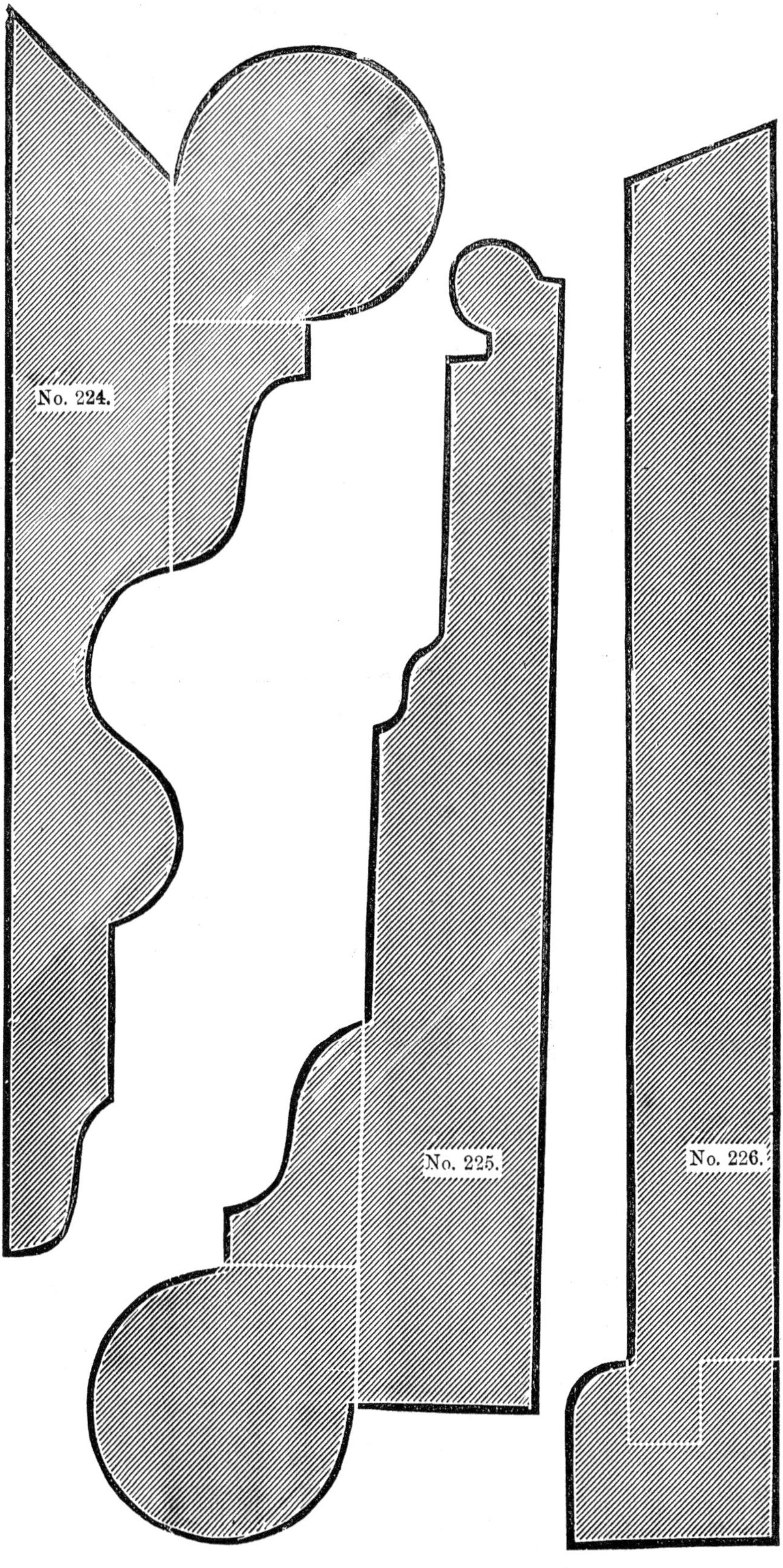

No. 224.

No. 225.

No. 226.

BRACKETS, MODILLIONS, AND BRACES, SCALE 1½ INCH TO THE FOOT.

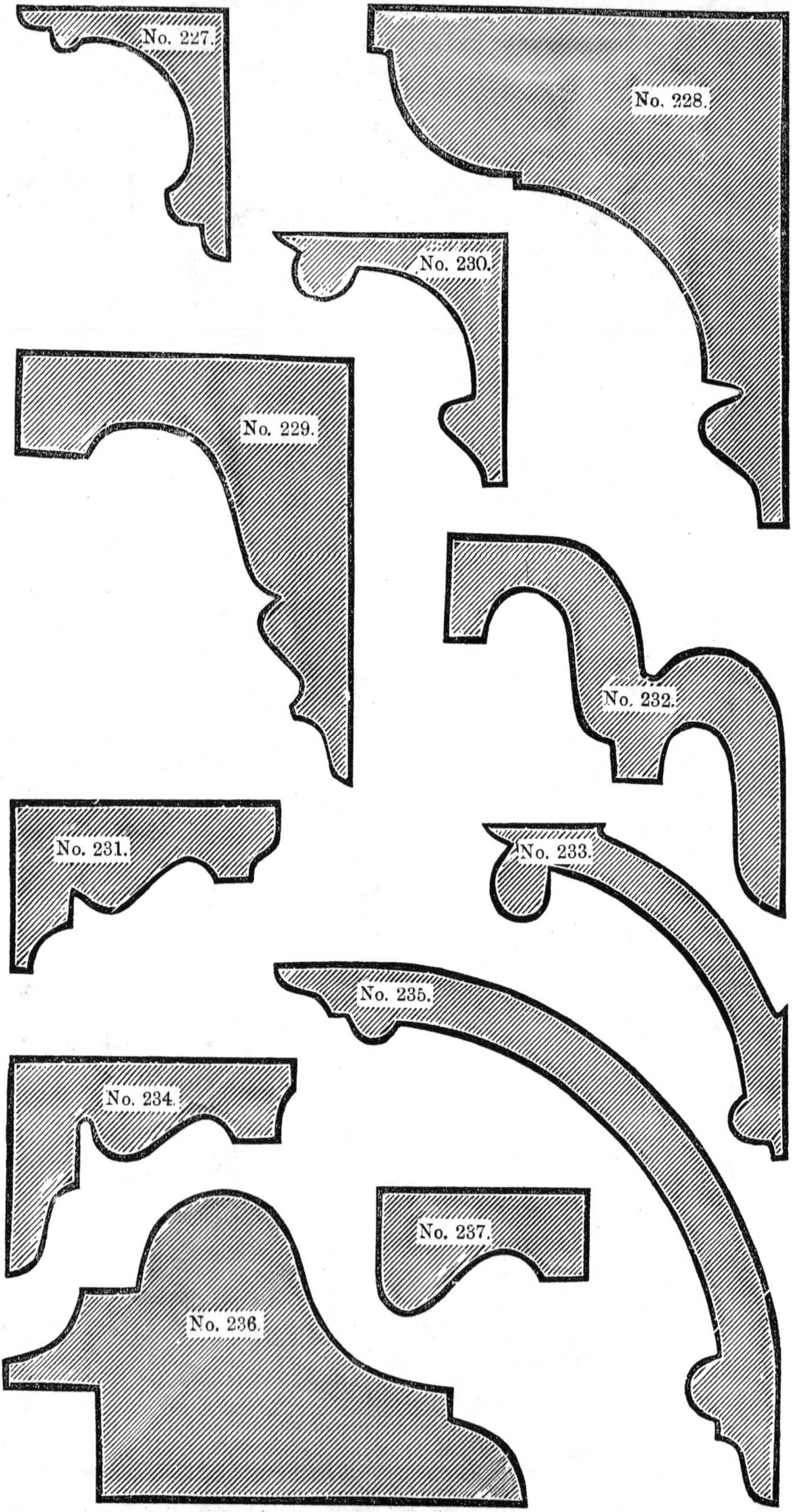

No. 227.

No. 228.

No. 230.

No. 229.

No. 232.

No. 231.

No. 233.

No. 235.

No. 234.

No. 237.

No. 236.

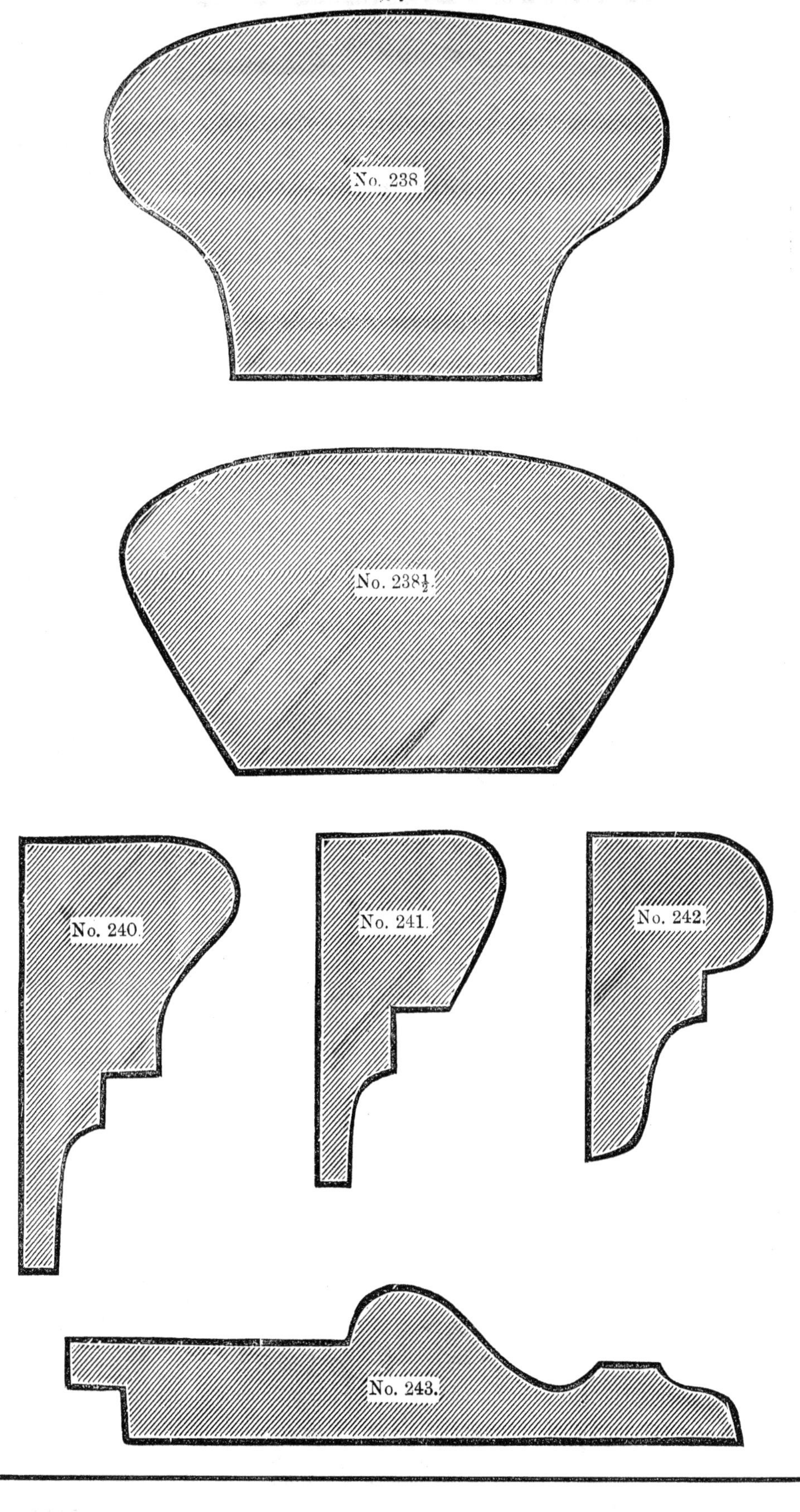
No. 238
No. 238½.
No. 240.
No. 241.
No. 242.
No. 243.

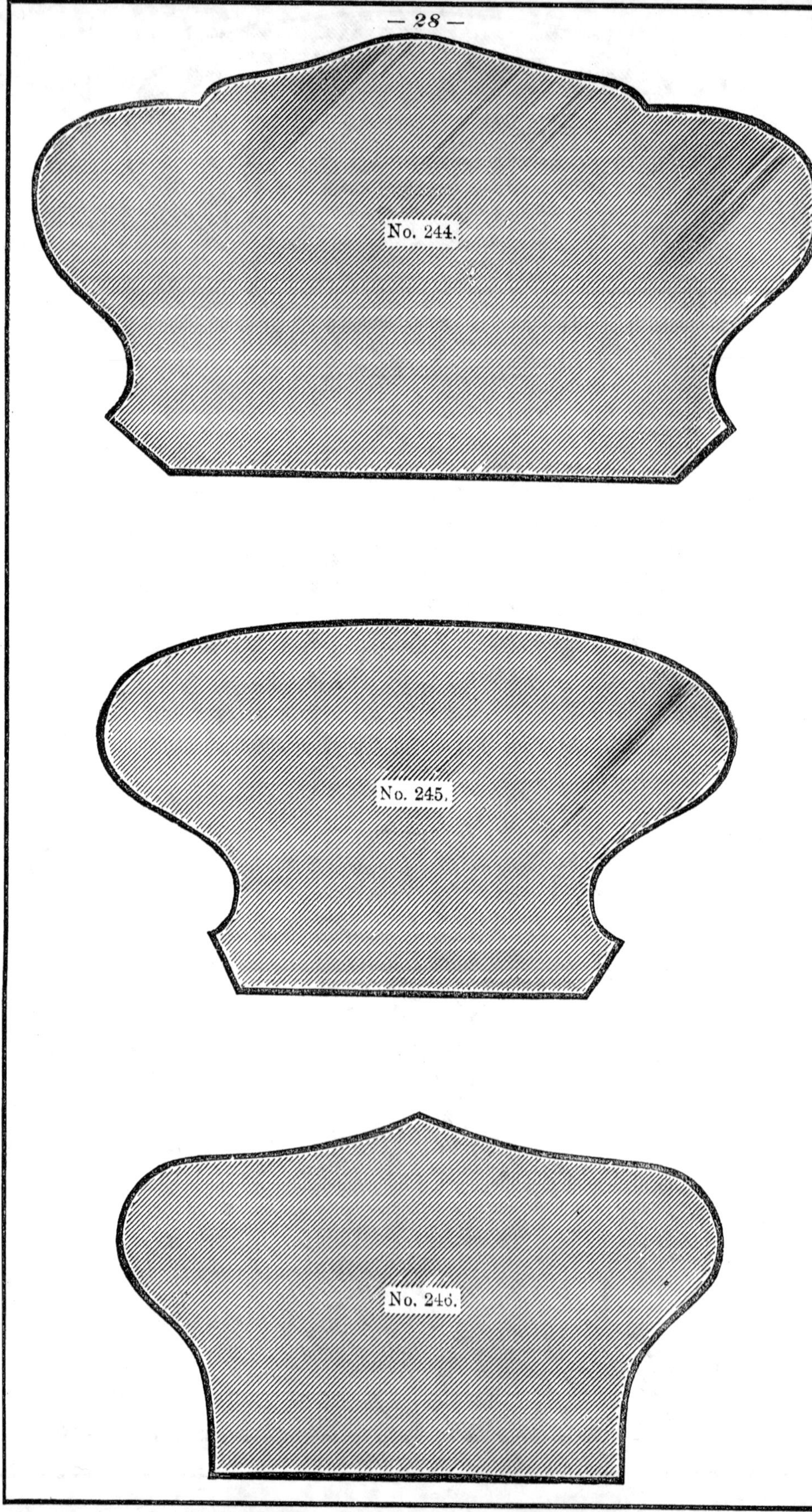
No. 244.
No. 245.
No. 246.

STAIRS.

We are prepared to furnish Stairs all ready to put up. Steps and Risers blocked, glued and housed into wall strings; Newel Posts fitted to carriages; Banisters turned, cleaned off and dove-tailed; Rails all fitted up with screws bored for banisters, and cleaned off, with the drawing and written directions for putting up in building, which can be done by any carpenter.

Orders for stairs should give the width of hall, height of story from top to top of floor; width of Joist on landing or second floor should be accompanied with a drawing, or one selected from annexed figures; also the size and finish of rail. Say if cherry or mahogany; give the length and width of Steps; the size of Banisters and Newel, and kind of wood—cherry, oak, walnut or mahogany; give drawing of base in hall, that the molding on stairs may be the same pattern. Say if circular corners are wanted, as dotted on Nos. 2, 3 and 9.

SCALE, ⅛ OF AN INCH TO THE FOOT.

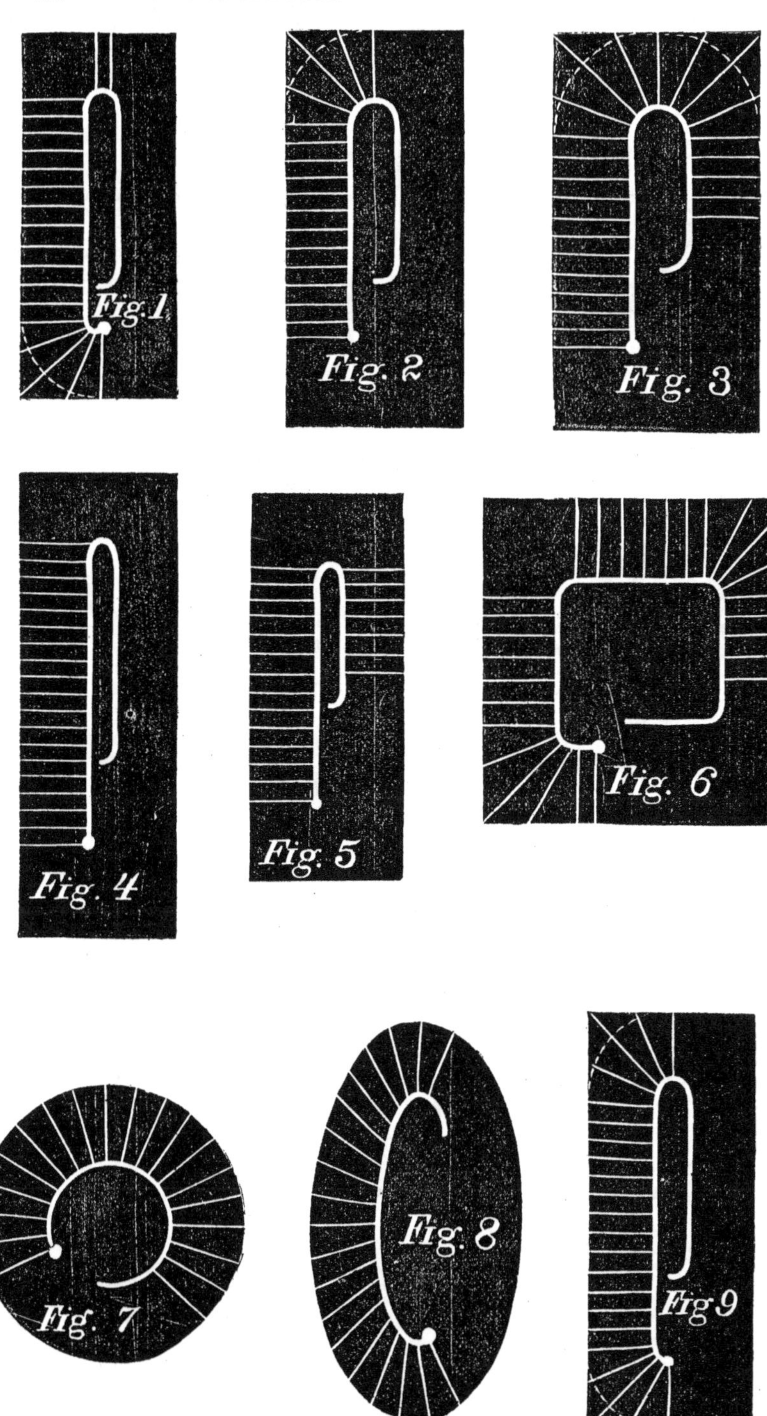

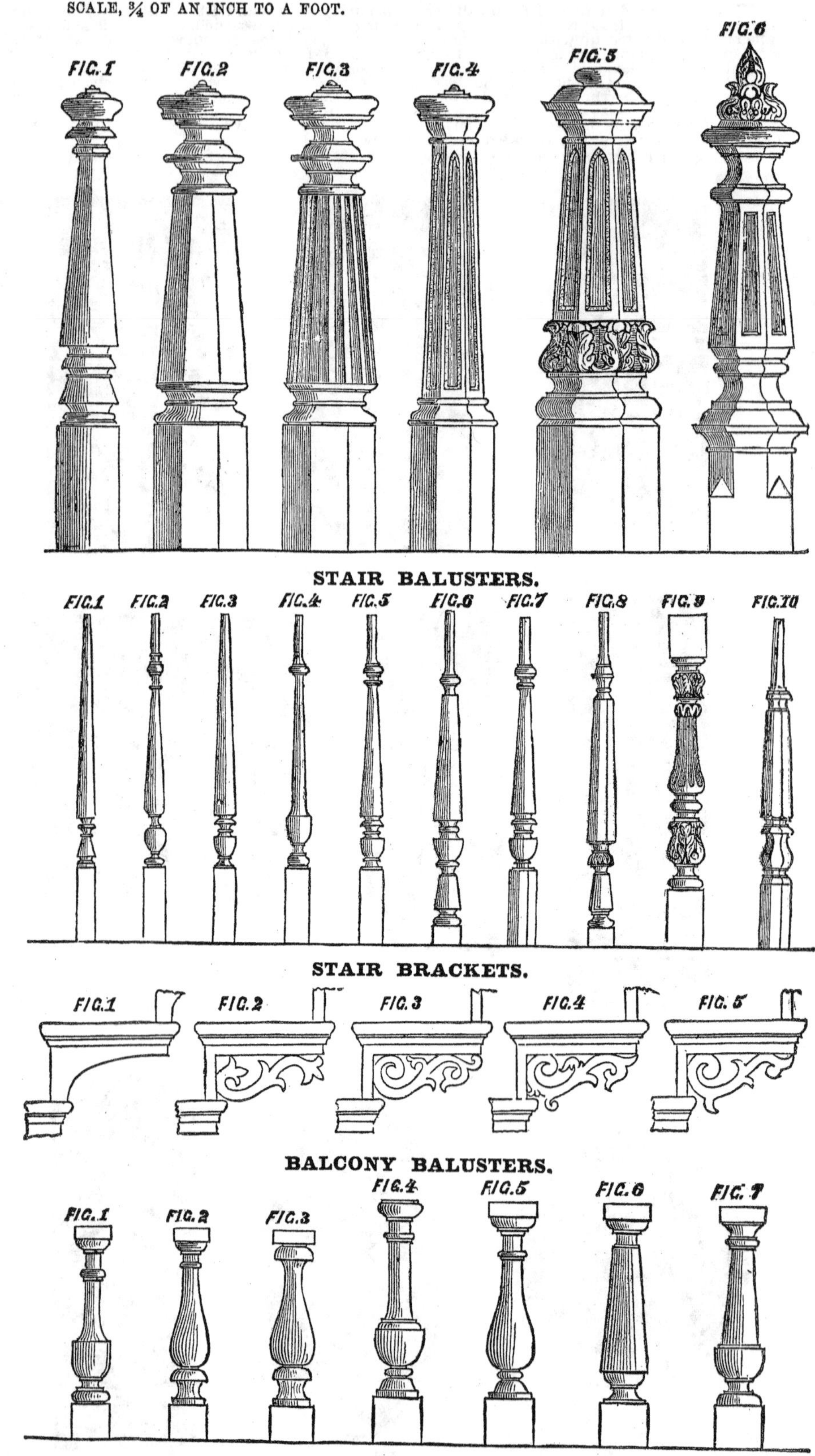
STAIR NEWELS.
SCALE, ¾ OF AN INCH TO A FOOT.
FIG. 1
FIG. 2
FIG. 3
FIG. 4
FIG. 5
FIG. 6
STAIR BALUSTERS.
FIG. 1
FIG. 2
FIG. 3
FIG. 4
FIG. 5
FIG. 6
FIG. 7
FIG. 8
FIG. 9
FIG. 10
STAIR BRACKETS.
FIG. 1
FIG. 2
FIG. 3
FIG. 4
FIG. 5
BALCONY BALUSTERS.
FIG. 1
FIG. 2
FIG. 3
FIG. 4
FIG. 5
FIG. 6
FIG. 7

No. 247½
No. 248
No. 219.
No. 245½

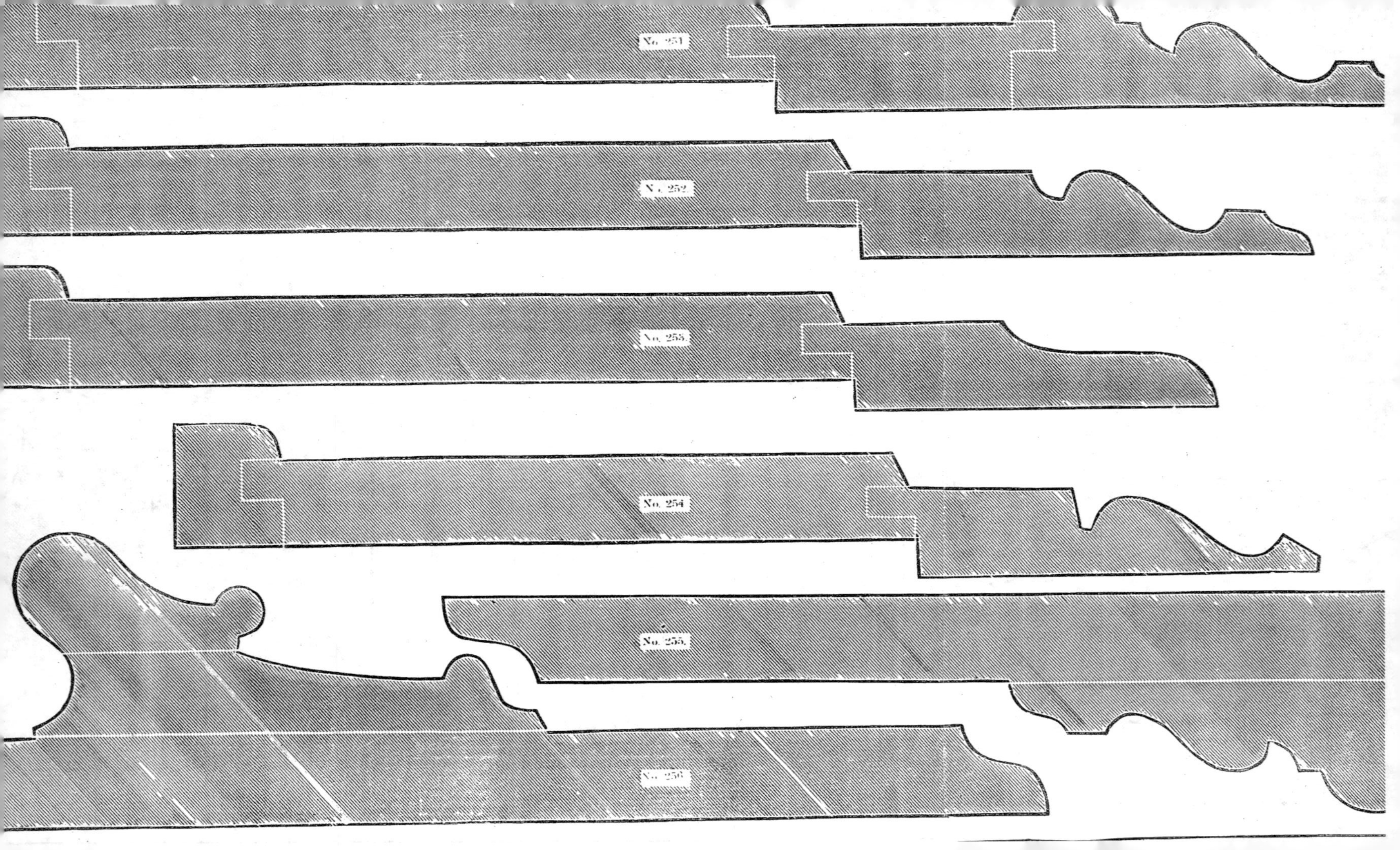
No. 251.
No. 252.
No. 253.
No. 254.
No. 255.
No. 256.

No. 258.

No. 259.

No. 260.

No. 261.

No. 257.

No. 262.

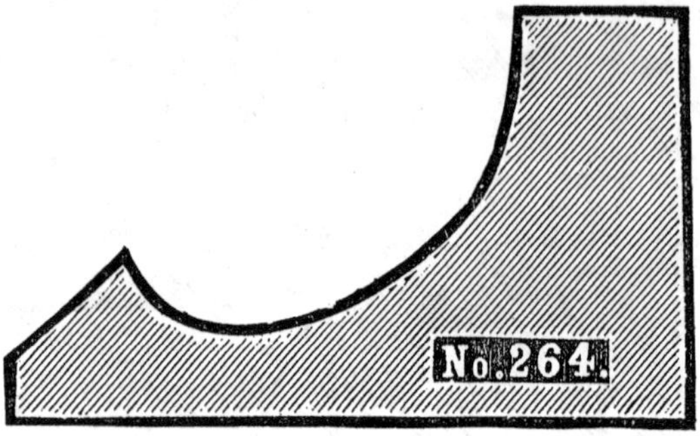

No. 264.

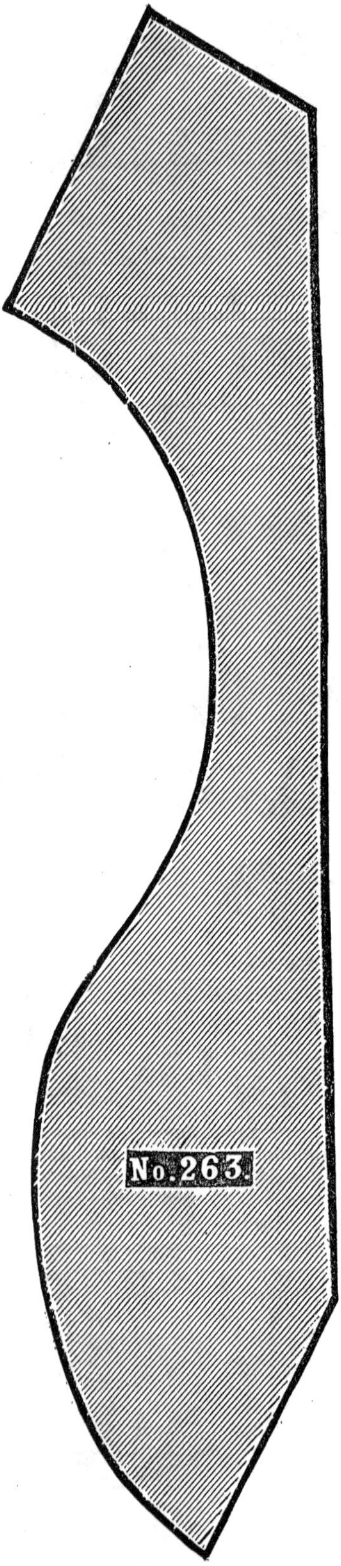

No. 263.

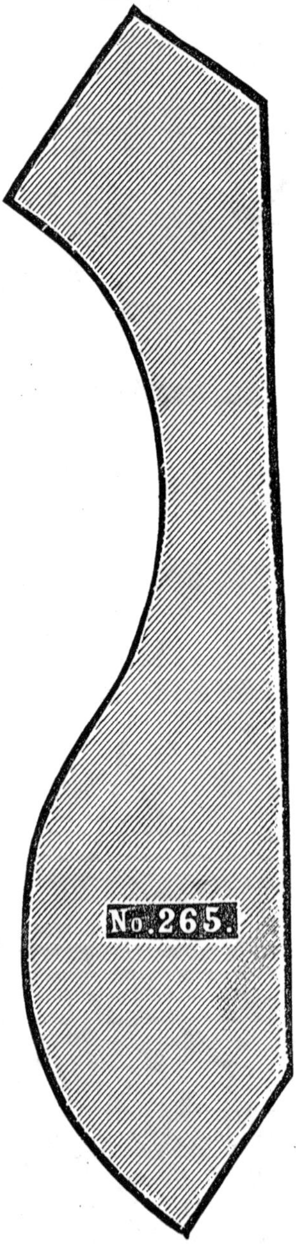

No. 265.

No. 266.

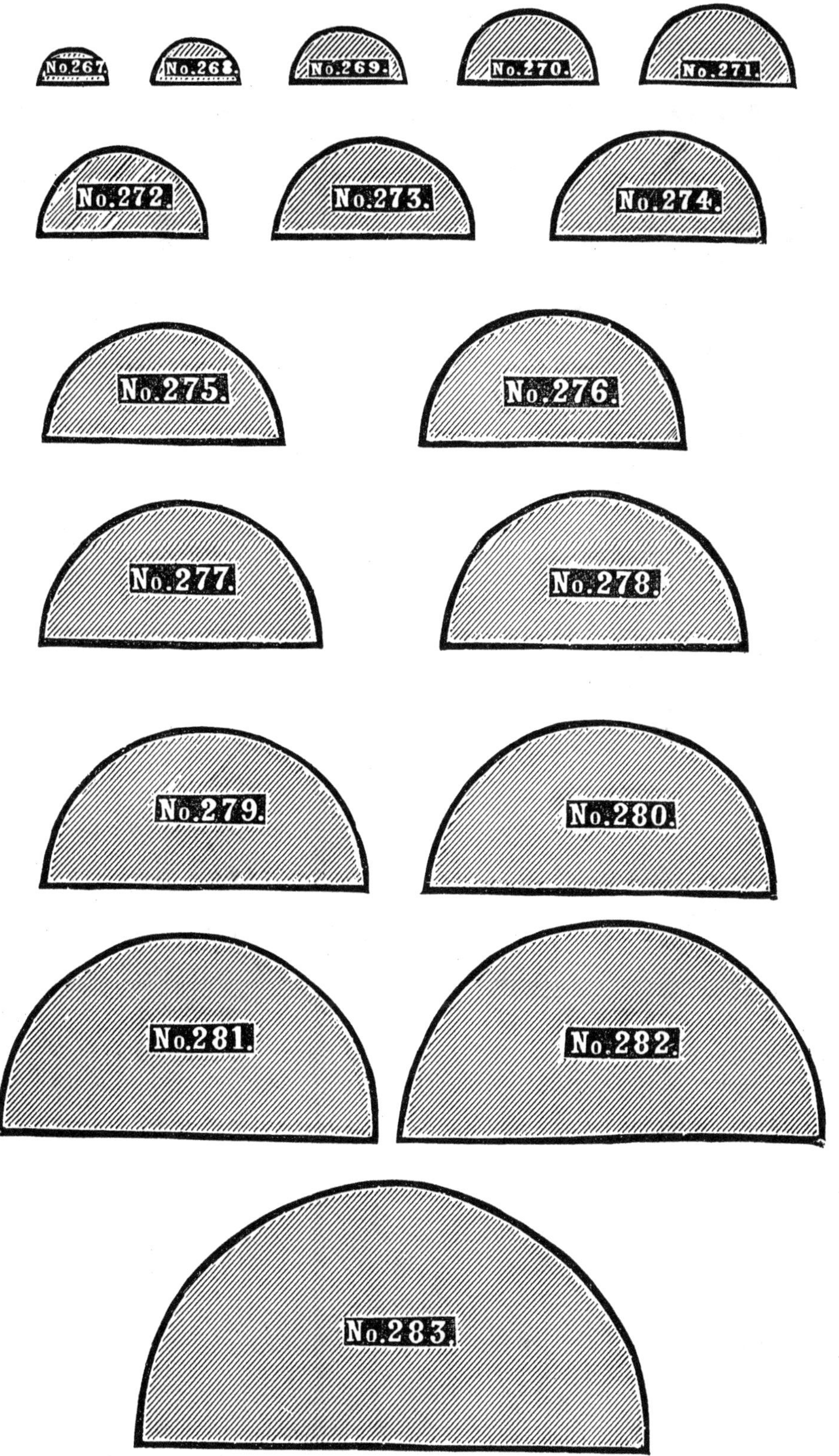
No.267.
No.268.
No.269.
No.270.
No.271.
No.272.
No.273.
No.274.
No.275.
No.276.
No.277.
No.278.
No.279.
No.280.
No.281.
No.282.
No.283.

CORNICE AND BRACKETS.

SCALE, ¾ OF AN INCH TO THE FOOT.

FIG. 1 FIG. 2

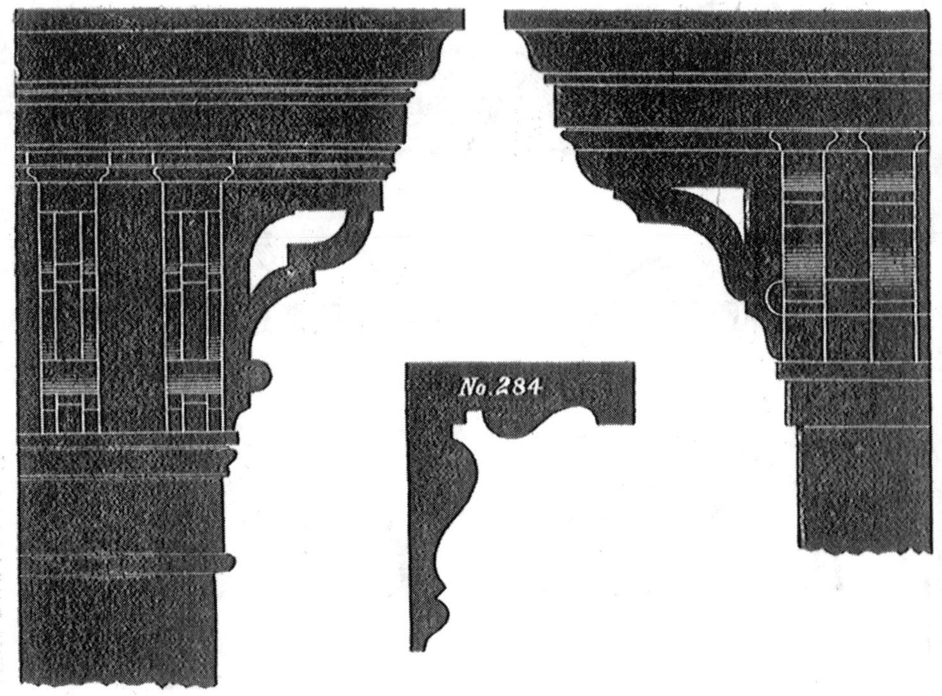

FIG. 3 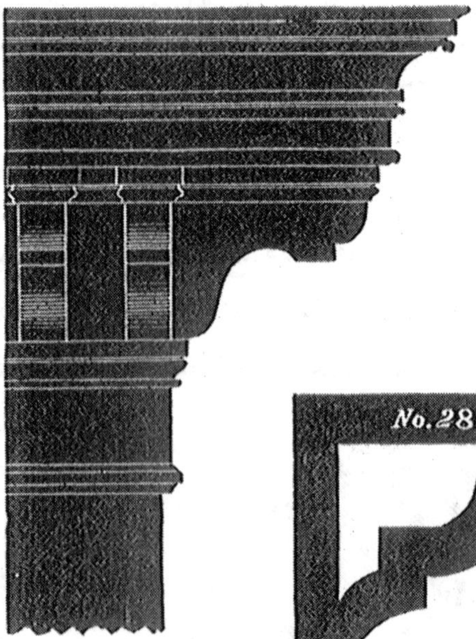 FIG. 4

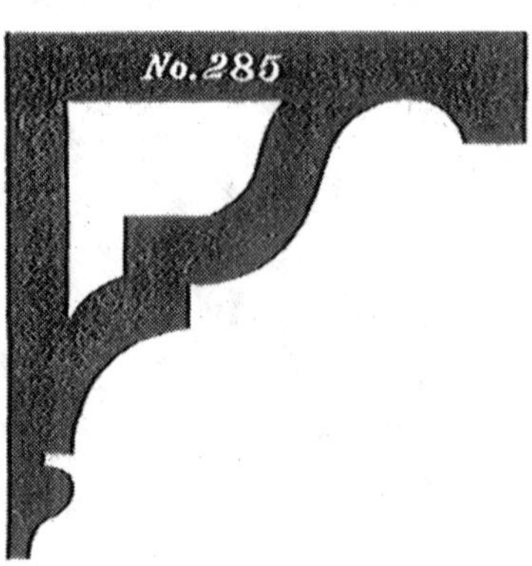

No. 285

MANTELS.

When ordering Mantels give width of Chimney Breast, height and width of Fire Place.

Scale ¼ inch to the foot.

WINDOW FRAMES AND SASH.

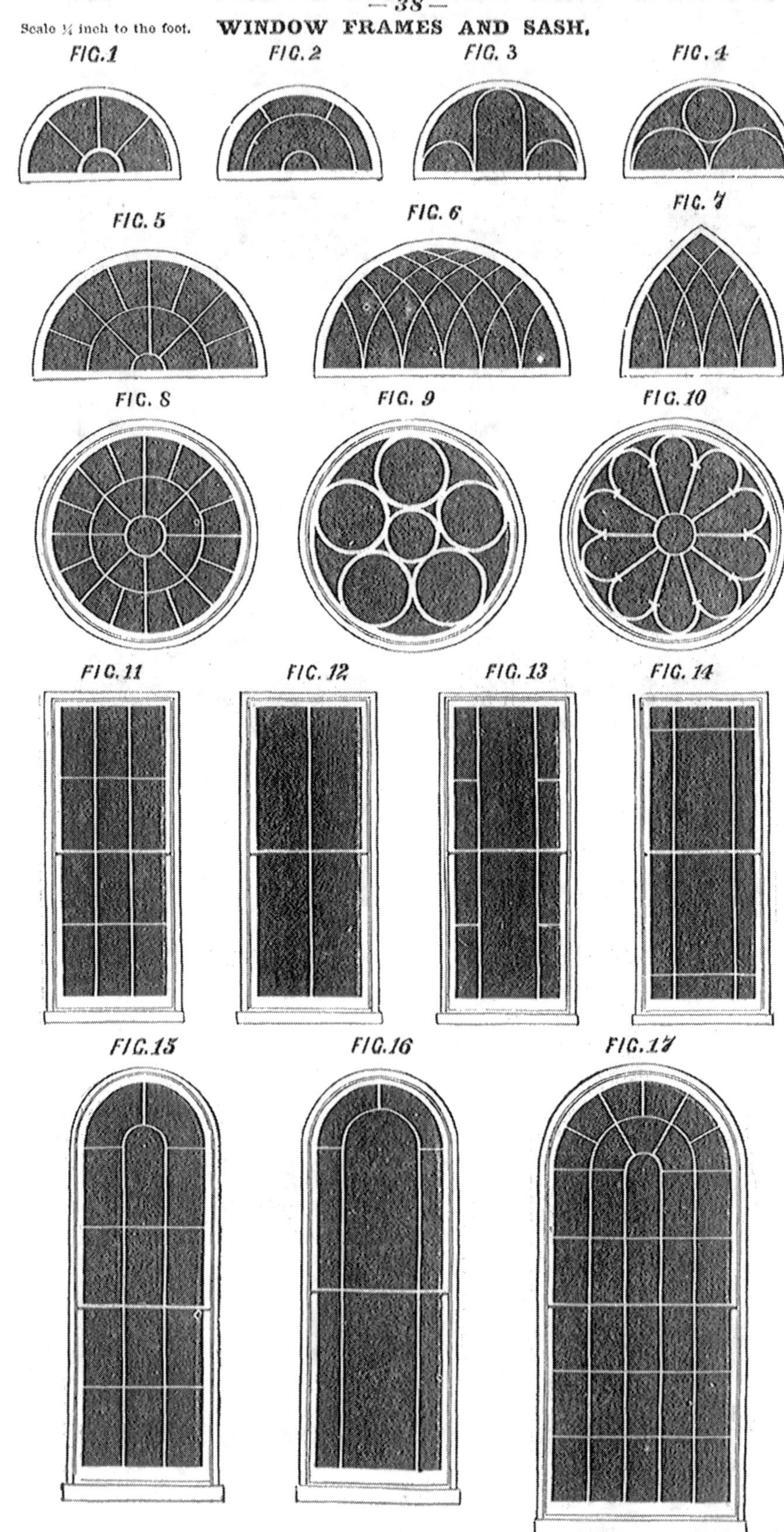

FIG. 18
Scale ¼ inch to the foot.
FIG. 19
FIG. 20
FIG. 21
FIG. 22
FIG. 23
FIG. 24
FIG. 25

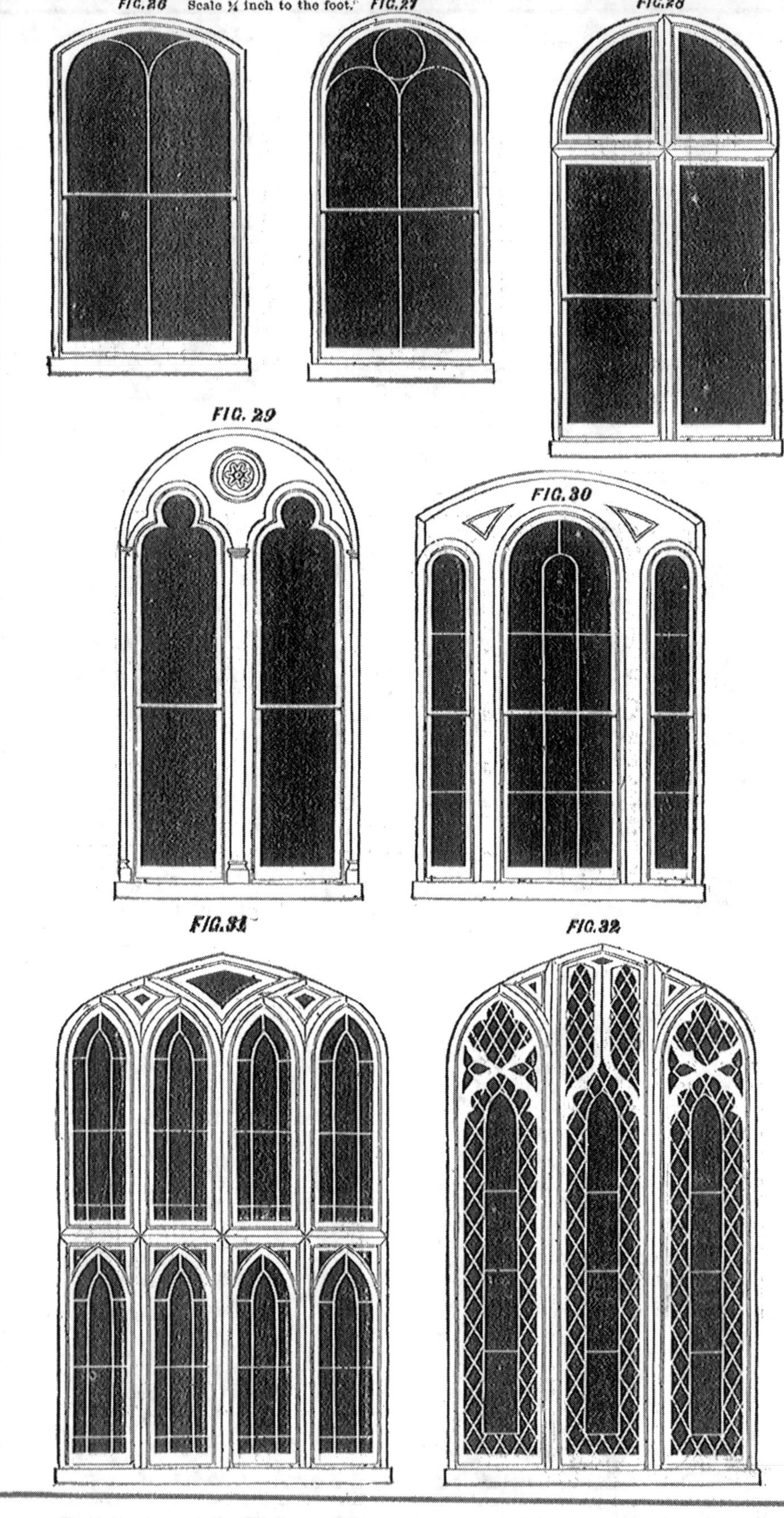
FIG. 26
Scale ¼ inch to the foot.
FIG. 27
FIG. 28
FIG. 29
FIG. 30
FIG. 31
FIG. 32

Scale ¼ inch to the foot.

DOORS AND COLUMNS.

Fig. 1. Fig. 2.

Fig. 3.

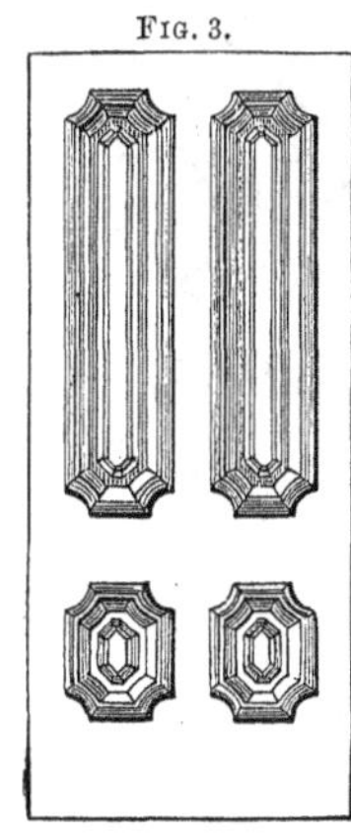

Fig. 4.

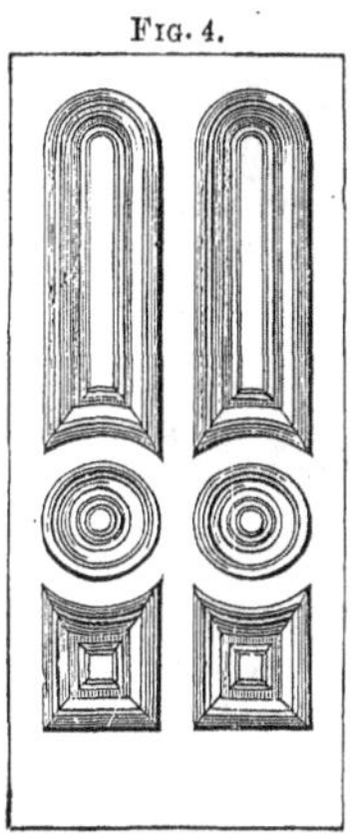

Fig. 6.

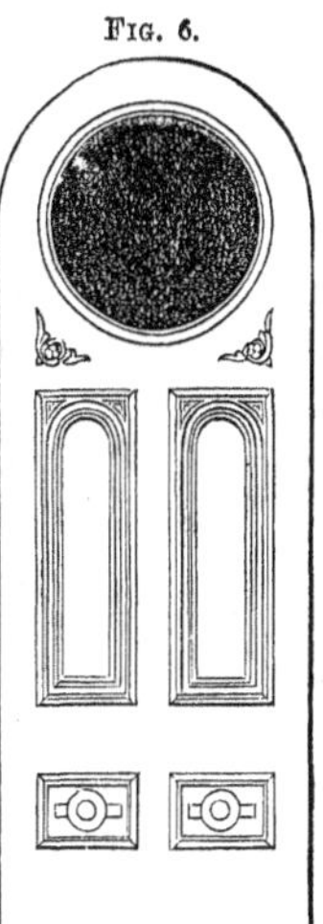

Fig. 5.

Fig. 7. Fig. 8.

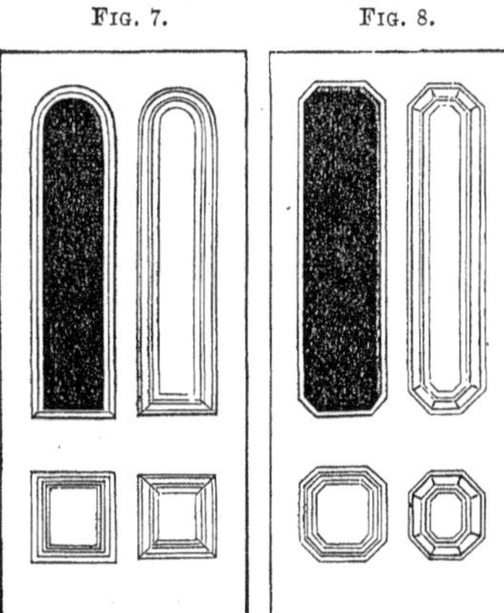

Fig. 9.

COLUMNS.

Ionic. Corinthian. Tuscan. Doric.

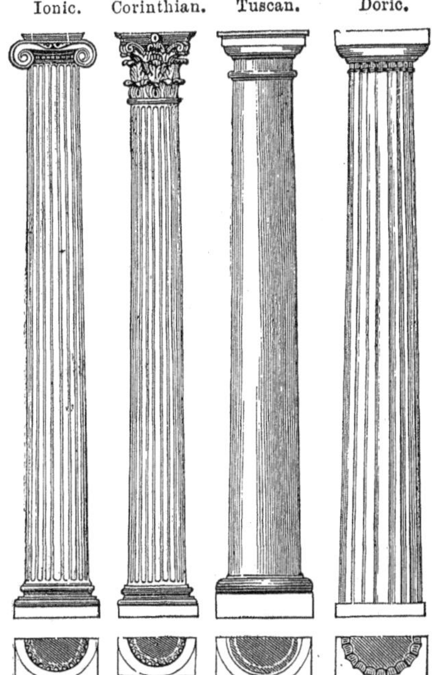

VERANDAH COLUMNS.

Fig. 1. Fig. 2. Fig. 3. Fig. 4.

COUNTERS.

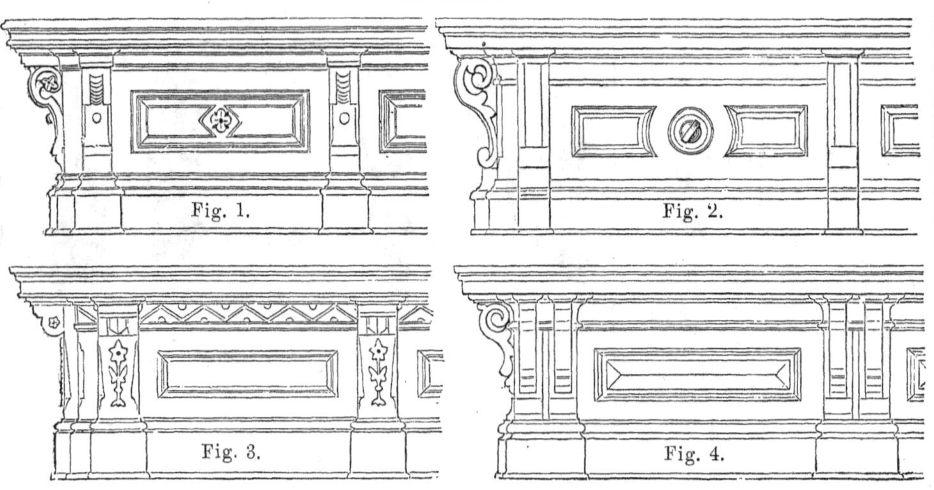

CHURCH PEWS.

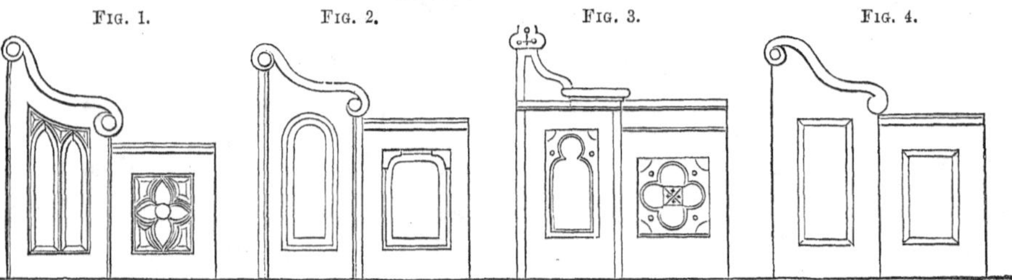

BUILDINGS

FURNISHED BY

HINKLE & CO.

On the following pages will be seen Plans of Forty-five Brick, Stone, and Frame Buildings, for which Hinkle & Co. have furnished all or part of the Wood Work, with the Location, Name of Owners, Architects, Superintendents, and Builders.

These buildings vary in cost from fifteen hundred to eighty thousand dollars. It will be seen that many of them have been erected in the extreme West and South, and some in the Middle States. The plans are adapted to the country in which they are built, and many of them possess great beauty and convenience.

Persons contemplating building will find this book valuable in assisting them to form their plans. Many of these plans are in their office on a larger scale, which can be seen at any time.

FIG. 1—210 Feet Front, 124 Deep.

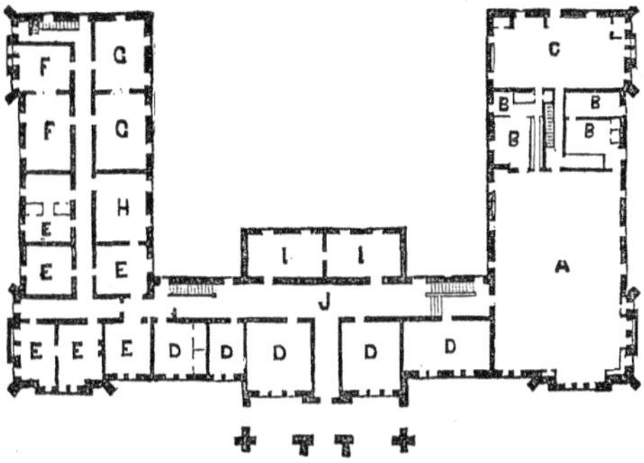

BASEMENT FLOOR.

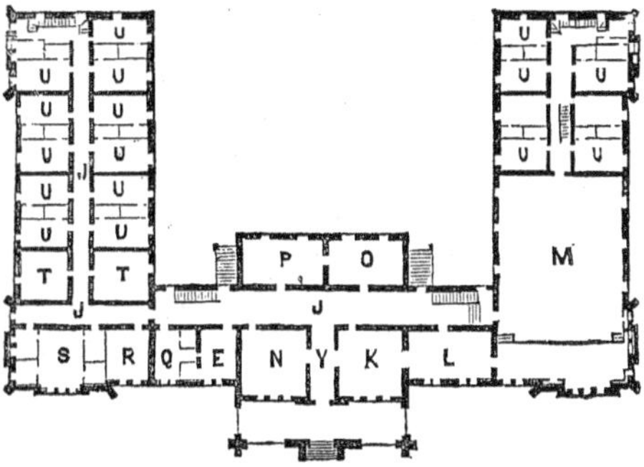

PLAN OF FIRST STORY.

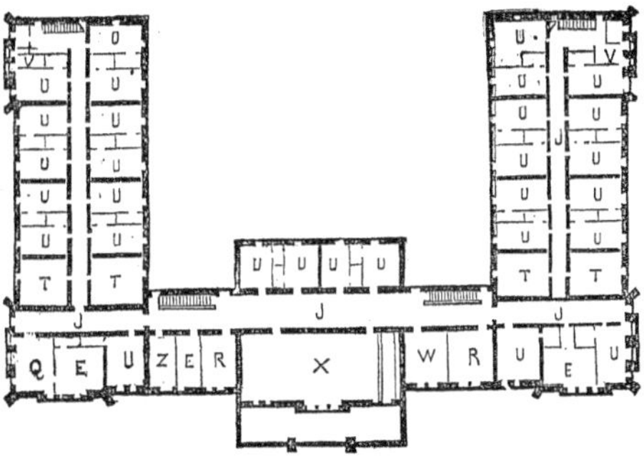

SECOND STORY.

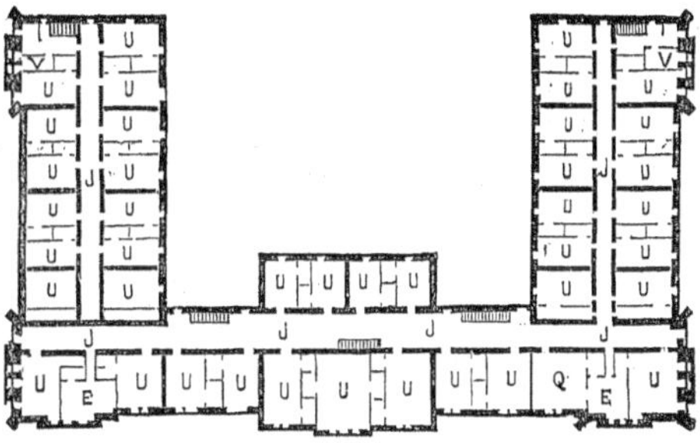

THIRD STORY.

REFERENCES TO PLANS.

A—Dining Room.
B—Store Rooms.
C—Kitchen.
D—Cellar.
E—On Basement Floor, Steward's and Assistants' Rooms.
E—On Upper Stories, Teachers' Rooms.
F—Washing Rooms.
G—Ironing Rooms.
H—Drying Room.
I—Laboratory.
J—Corridors.
K—Reception Room.
L—Parlor.
M—Chapel.
N—Principal's Room.
O—Library.
P—Reading Rooms.
Q—Teachers' Rooms.
R—Music Rooms.
S—Sick Room.
T—Recitation Rooms.
U—Students' Rooms.
V—Bath Rooms.
W—Cabinet.
X—Lecture Room.
Y—Entrance Hall.
Z—Stationery Room.

WESTERN FEMALE SEMINARY, OXFORD, OHIO.

WALTERS & WILSON, Architects, Cincinnati, Ohio. D. WAYMIRE, Dayton, and E. LOUGHEAD, Cincinnati, Superintendents.
Heated by Radiation and Ventilation, on an improved plan, by LANE & BODLEY, Cincinnati, O.

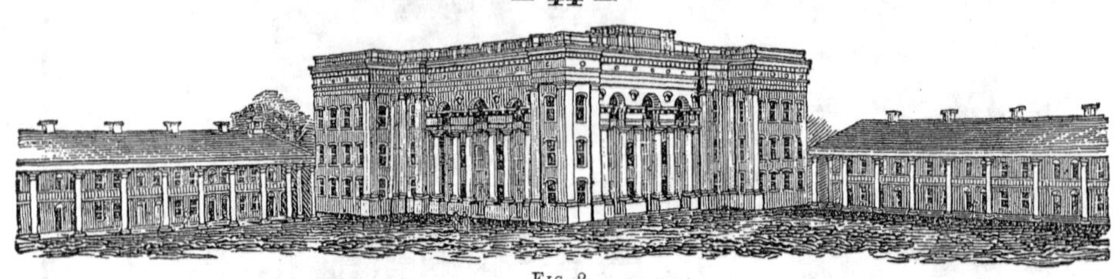

Fig. 2.

CENTENERY COLLEGE OF LOUISIANA, JACKSON, LA.

G. W. A. Simpson, Architect, Jackson, La. Thompson & Wall, Builders, Clinton, La.

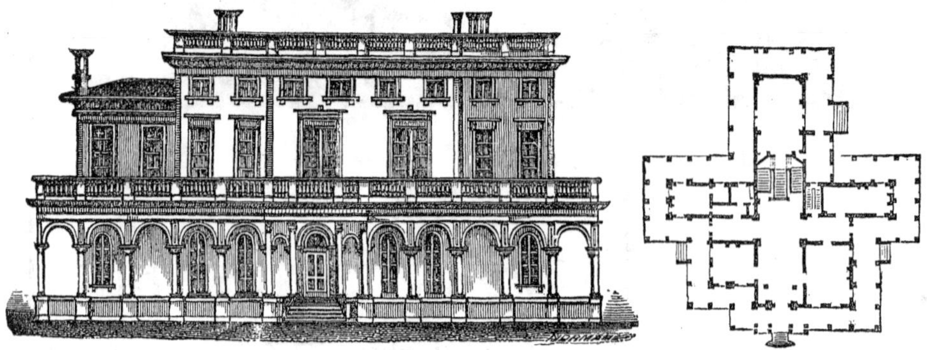

Fig. 3—129 feet Front, 133 feet Deep.

RESIDENCE OF MRS. M. L. JOHNSTON, LIVINGSTON, MISS.

J. Larmour, Superintendent, Canton, Miss.

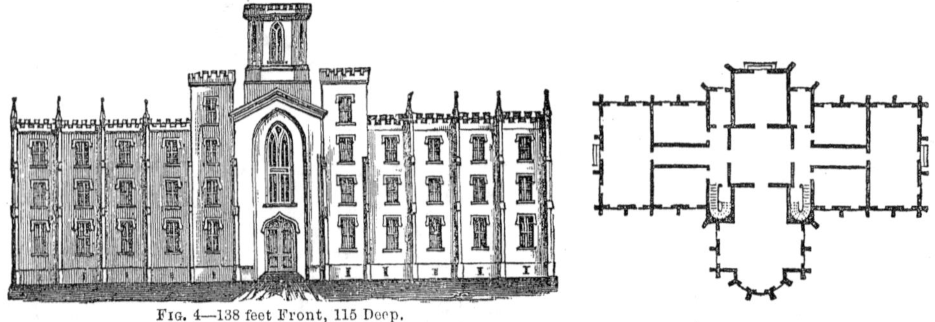

Fig. 4—138 feet Front, 115 Deep.

ST. JOHN'S COLLEGE, LITTLE ROCK, ARKANSAS.

A. Heiman, Architect, Nashville, Tenn.

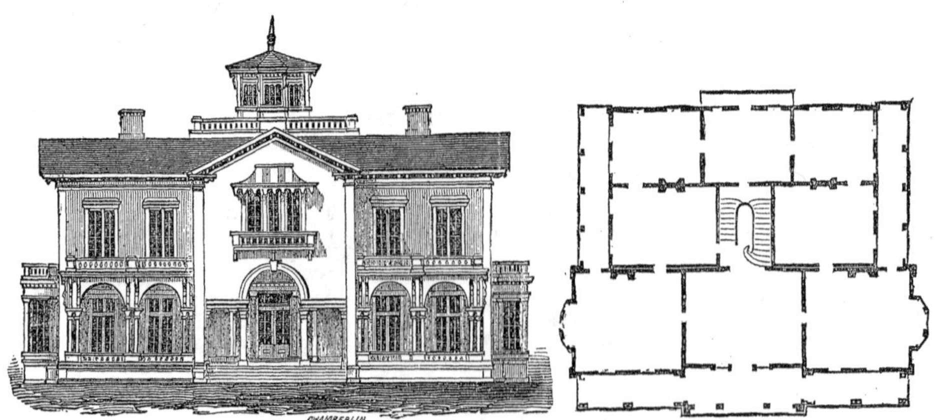

Fig. 5—79 feet Front, 64 feet Deep.

RESIDENCE OF REV. W. HOLMAN, LEXINGTON, MISS.

A. Doyle, Architect, Lexington, Miss.

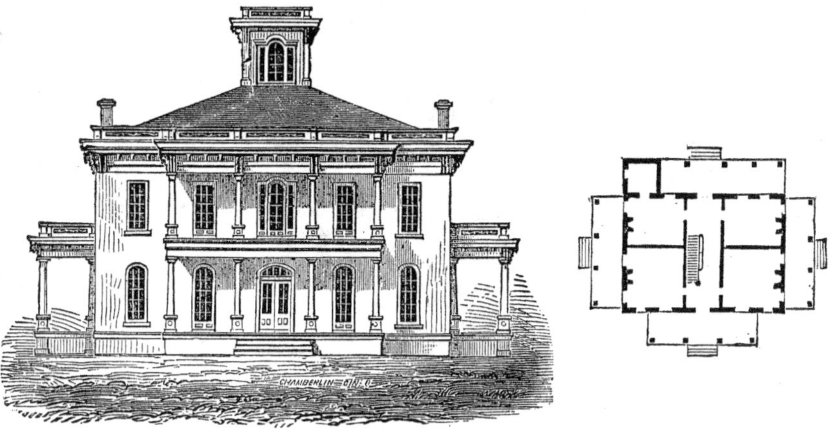

FIG. 6—76 feet Front, 64 feet Deep.
RESIDENCE OF ABNER KINNISON, FRANKLIN CO., MISS.
ROBERT TRATT, Architect, Fayette, Miss. JOHN MANIFOLD, Builder, Fayette, Miss.

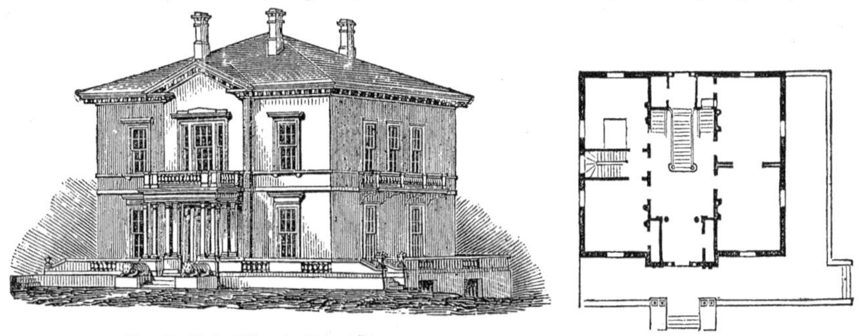

FIG. 7—52 feet Front, 48 feet Deep.
COUNTRY RESIDENCE OF P. HEIDELBACK, CLIFTON, OHIO.
WALTERS & WILSON, Architects, Cincinnati, Ohio.
JAMES BINDLEY, Superintendent and Builder.

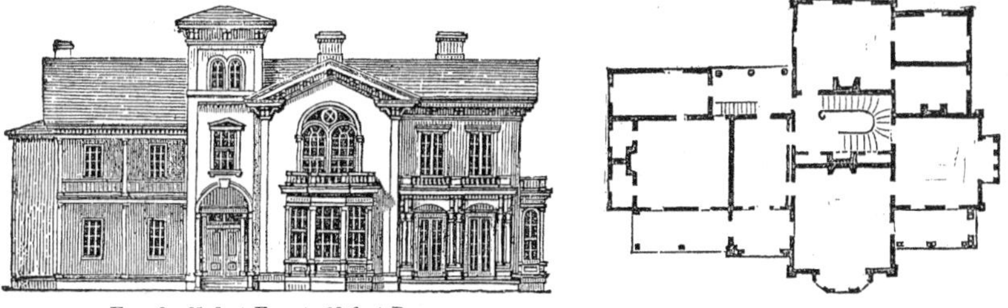

FIG. 8—81 feet Front, 60 feet Deep.
RESIDENCE OF MRS. EGGLESTON, LEXINGTON, MISS.
A. DOYLE, Architect, Lexington, Miss.

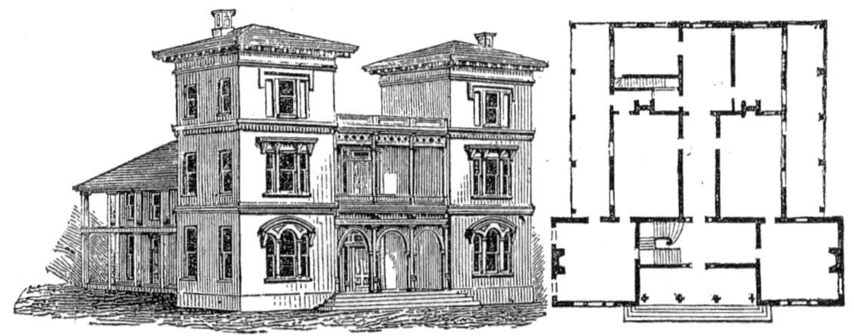

FIG. 9—75 feet Front, 70 feet Deep.
RESIDENCE OF W. C. CHAMBERLAIN, NATCHEZ, MISS.
J. EDWARD SMITH, Architect, Natchez, Miss.

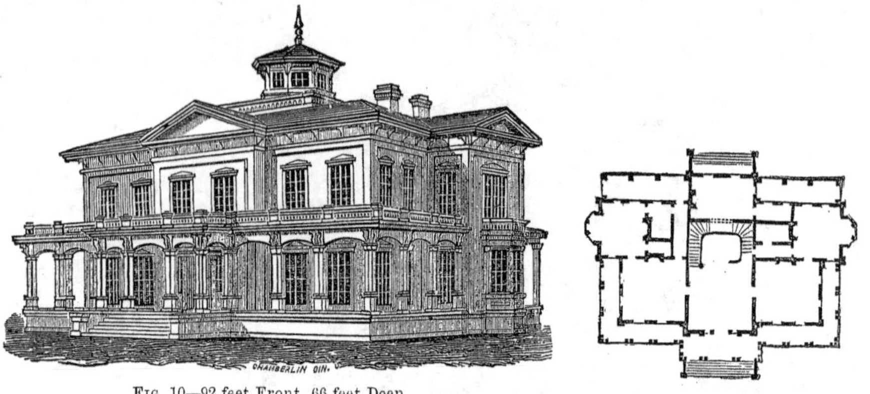

FIG. 10—92 feet Front, 66 feet Deep.
RESIDENCE OF MRS. DYER, LEXINGTON, MISS.
A. DOYLE, Architect, Lexington, Miss.

FIG. 11—60 feet Front, 100 feet Deep.
PRESBYTERIAN CHURCH, COVINGTON, KY.
J. W. MCLAUGHLIN, Architect, Cincinnati, O. J. A. WALTHALL, Contractor, Covington, Ky.

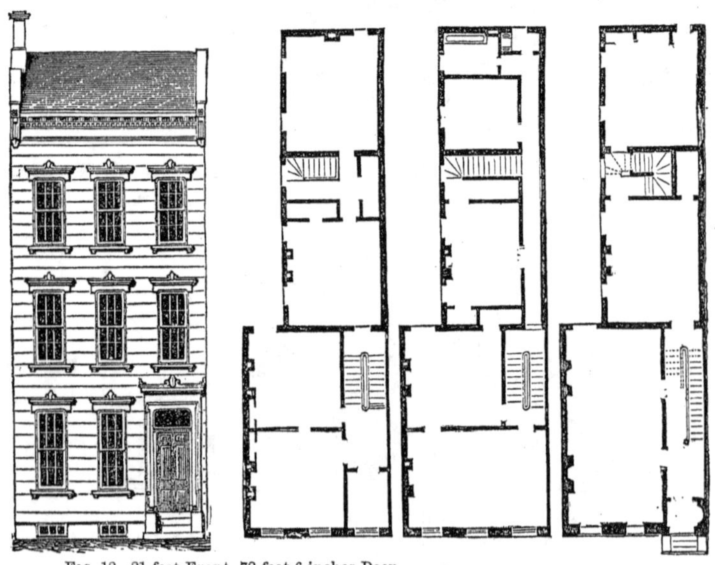

FIG. 12—21 feet Front, 72 feet 6 inches Deep.
DWELLING ON EIGHTH STREET, CINCINNATI, OHIO.
WALTERS & WILSON, Architects, Cincinnati. J. BINDLEY, Owner and Builder, Cincinnati.

Fig. 13—57 feet Front, 110 feet Deep.
BAPTIST CHURCH, CLINTON, MISS.
J. Lamour, Architect and Sup't, Canton. J. Laughlin, Contractor.

Fig. 14—50 feet Front, 115 Deep.
ST. PAUL'S CHURCH, Vicksburg, Miss.
Logan & Warner, Architects.

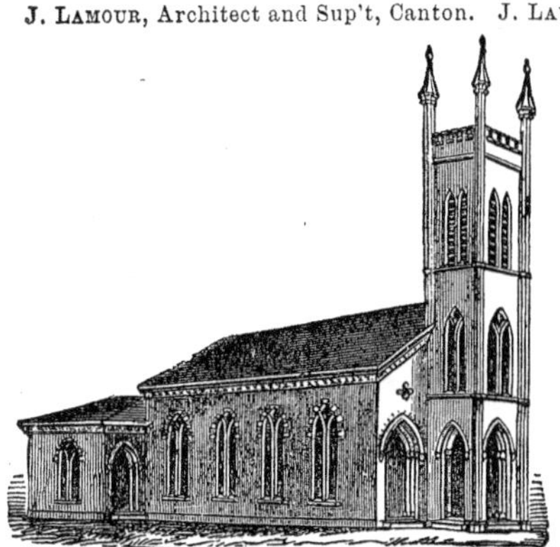

Fig. 15—43 feet Front, 80 feet Deep.
EPISCOPAL CHURCH, LITTLE ROCK, ARK.
P. C. Spaulding, Architect, Little Rock.
S. H. Smith & Co., Builders, Little Rock.

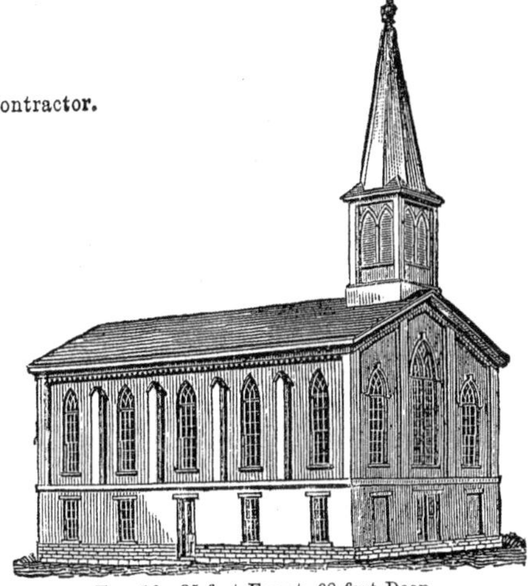

Fig. 16—35 feet Front, 68 feet Deep.
PRESBYTERIAN CHURCH, VEVAY, IND.
Alexander Edgar, Architect and Builder, Vevay.

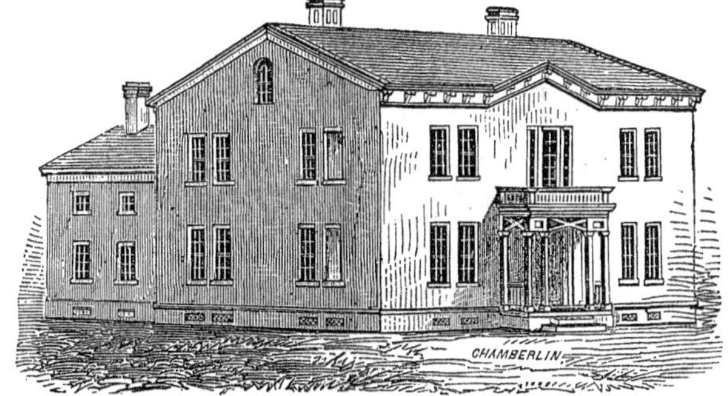

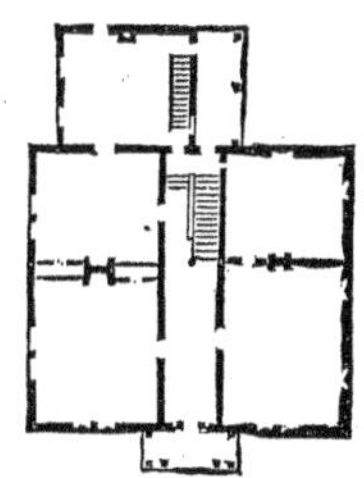

Fig. 17—42 feet Front, 50 feet Deep.
RESIDENCE OF M. L. BRETT, WASHINGTON, IND. S. Rogers & Son, Architects, Cincinnati, O.

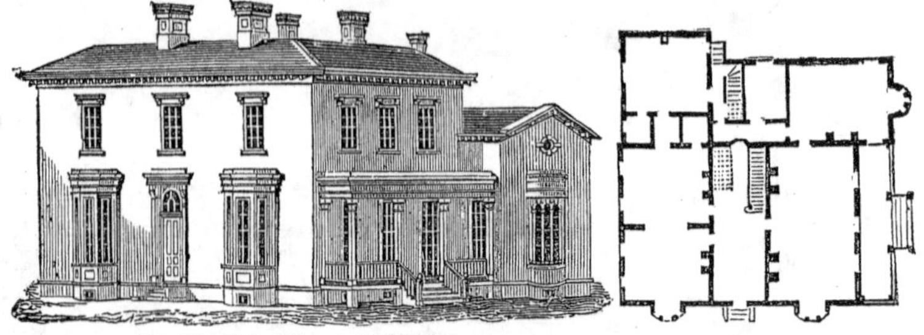

Fig. 18—52 feet Front, 46 feet Deep.

RESIDENCE OF D. S. MAJOR, LAWRENCEBURG, IND.

Hamilton & Rankin, Architects, Cincinnati, Ohio.

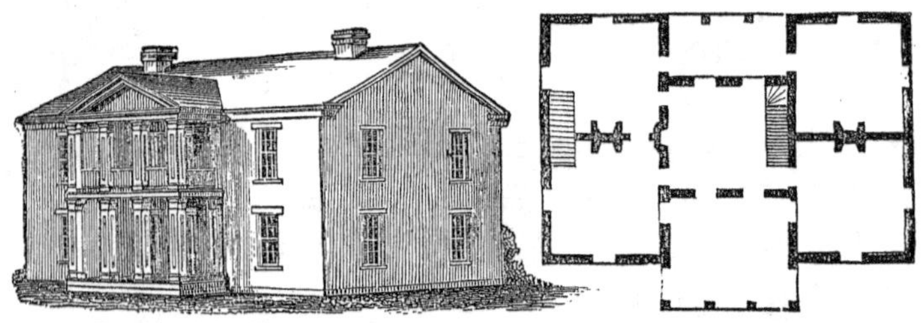

Fig. 19—62 feet Front, 48 feet Deep.

RESIDENCE OF FRANK HARDEMAN, NEAR FRANKLIN, WILLIAMSON COUNTY, TENN.

Fig. 20—90 feet Front, 62 feet Deep.

LINNEAUS FEMALE SEMINARY, LINNEAUS, MO.

T. S. Easley, Architect and Builder, Linneaus, Mo.

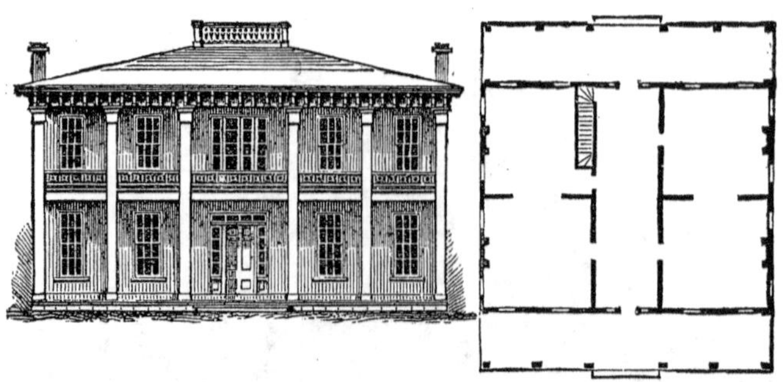

Fig. 21—50 feet Front, 60 feet Deep.

RESIDENCE OF R. SAMPLE, NEAR NATCHEZ, MISS.

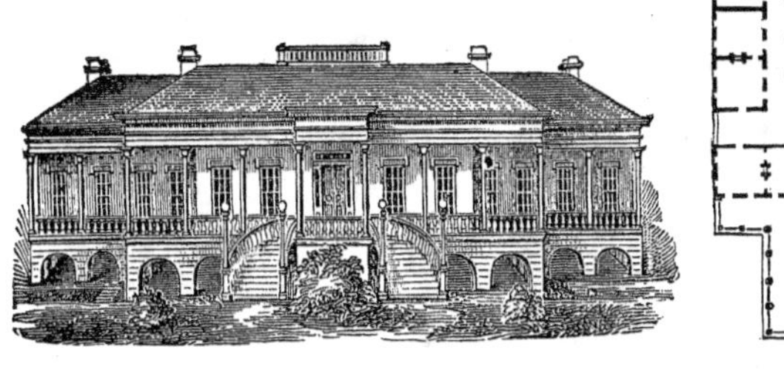
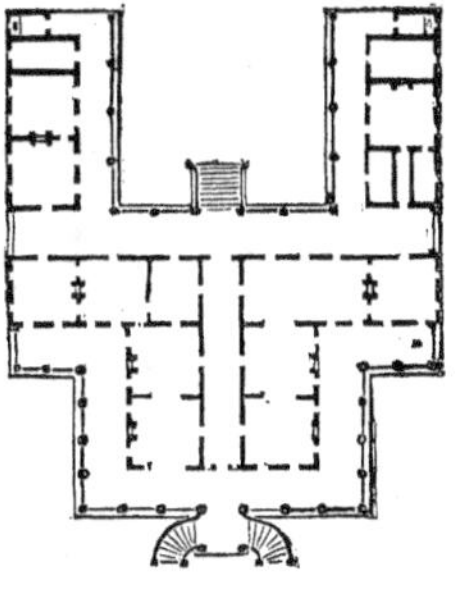

FIG. 22—130 feet Front, 148 feet Deep.

RESIDENCE OF W. S. PIKE, BATON ROUGE, LA.

L. G. FREMAUX, Architect. J. COLLINS, Builder.

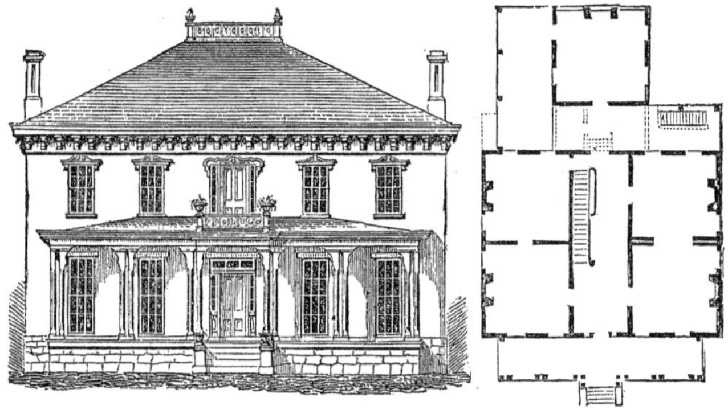

FIG. 23—52 feet Front, 70 feet Deep.

RESIDENCE OF T. L. McNARY, PRINCETON, KY.

M. L. CALDWELL, Memphis; BOWEN & MILLER, St. Louis, Architects.
PARKER JONES & JOHN BINGHAM, Builders, Princeton, Ky.

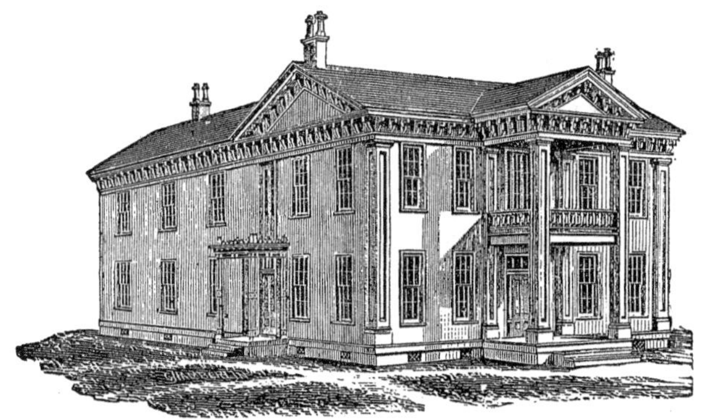

FIG. 24—52 feet Front, 59 feet Deep.

RESIDENCE OF H. P. COOLIDGE, HELENA, ARK.

F. M. MOORE, Architect, Cincinnati, O.

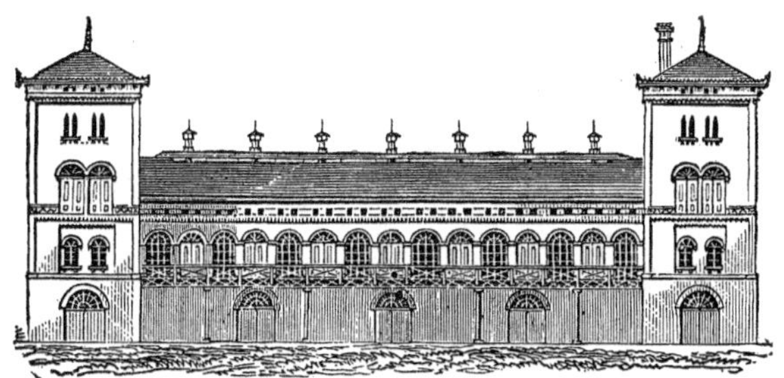

SOUTH GAS WORKS, CINCINNATI, OHIO.

JOHN JEFFREY, Engineer and Architect.

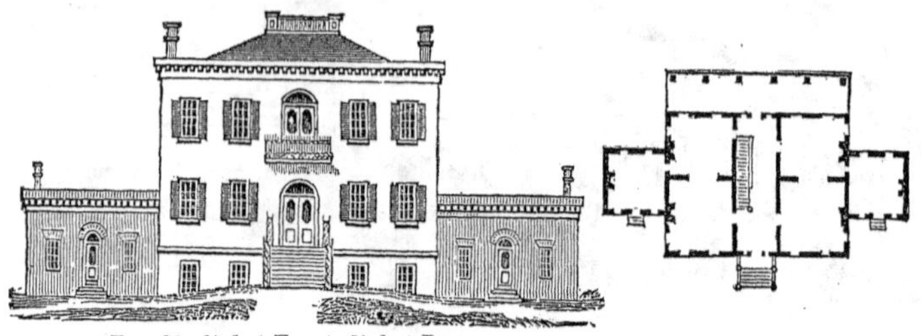

FIG. 26—88 feet Front, 50 feet Deep.

RESIDENCE OF JOHN HEBRON, LaGRANGE NURSERY, WARREN COUNTY, MISS.

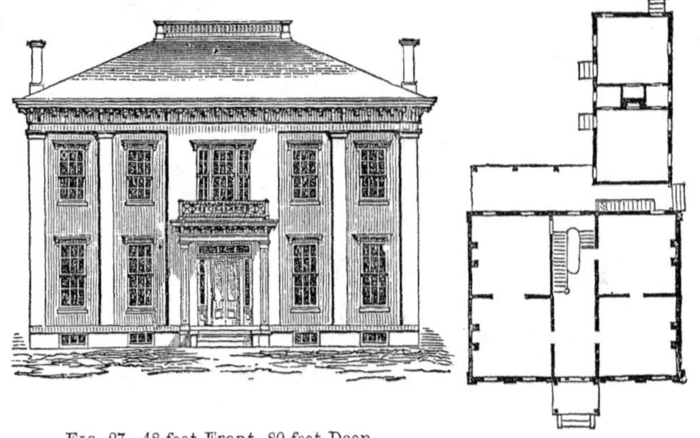

FIG. 27—48 feet Front, 80 feet Deep.

RESIDENCE OF JOHN A. GEX, GHENT, KY.

F. M. MOORE, Architect, Cincinnati, Ohio.

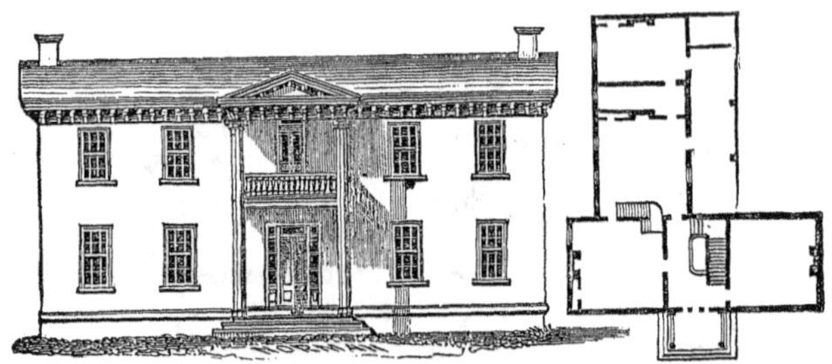

FIG. 28—52 feet Front, 60 feet Deep.

RESIDENCE OF C. BURGESS, WESTON, MO.

F. M. MOORE, Architect, Cincinnati, Ohio.
D. F. POLK, Builder, Weston, Mo.

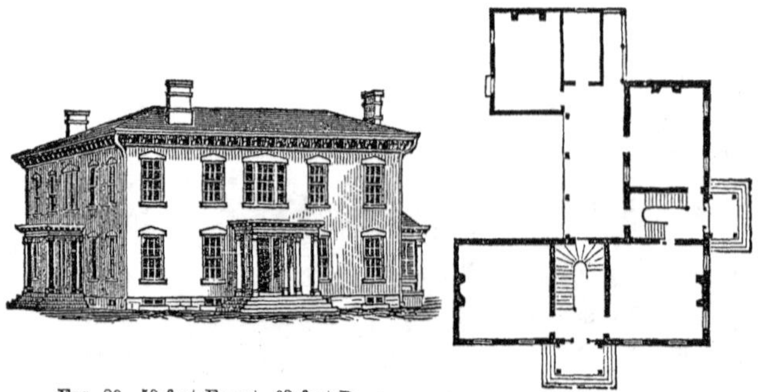

FIG. 29—50 feet Front, 63 feet Deep.

RESIDENCE OF F. A. LYON, GEORGETOWN, KY.

JAMES BAILEY, Architect and Builder, Georgetown, Ky.

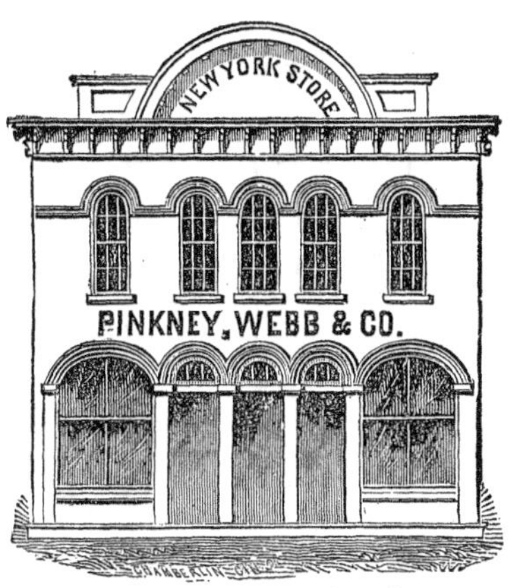

FIG. 30—37 feet Front, 144 feet Deep.
PINKNEY, WEBB & CO., FRANKLIN, IND.

FIG. 31—30 feet Front, 60 feet Deep.
MASONIC LODGE, SMITHLAND, KY.
J. M. LAYMAN, Architect and Builder, Smithland.

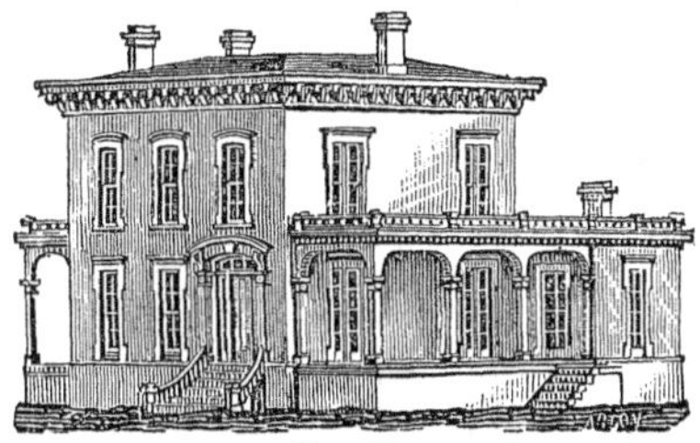

FIG. 32.
RESIDENCE OF DR. W. A. CANTRELL, LITTLE ROCK, ARK
P. C. SPAULDING, Architect, Little Rock, Ark.

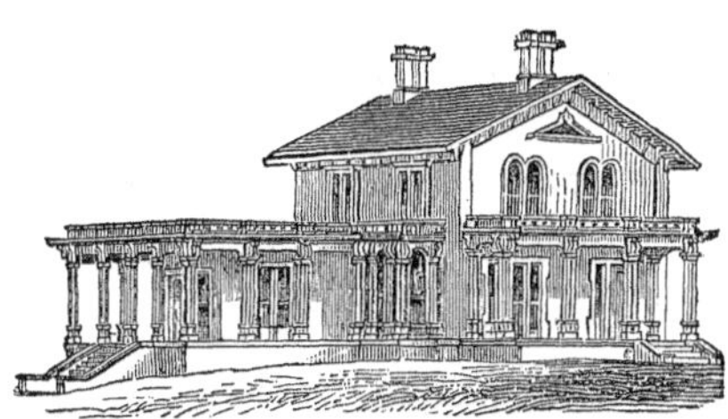

FIG. 33.
RESIDENCE OF HON. E. H. ENGLISH, LITTLE ROCK, ARK.
P. C. SPAULDING, Architect, Little Rock, Ark.

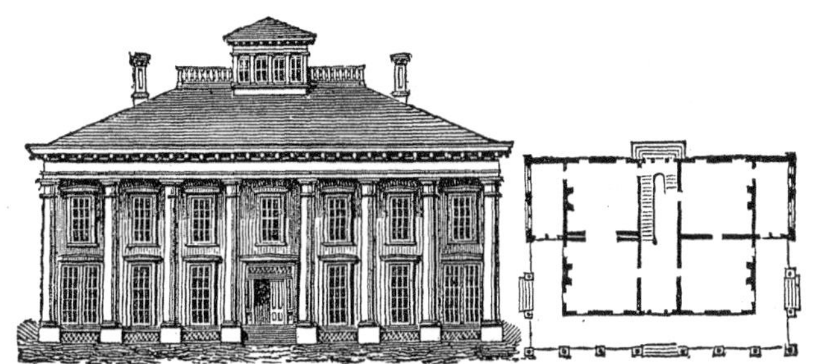

FIG. 34—78 feet Front, 54 feet Deep.
RESIDENCE OF WM. B. LOTT, NEAR SHARON, MADISON COUNTY, MISS.

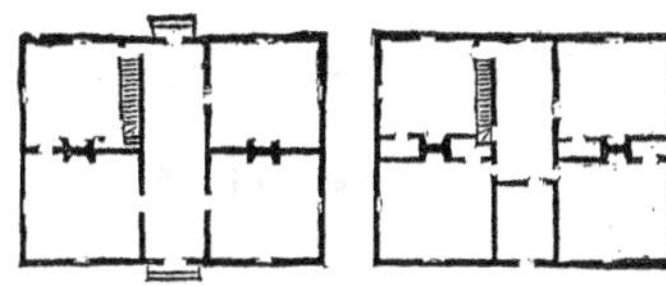

FIG. 35—40 feet Front, 32 feet Deep.
RESIDENCE OF REV. F. A. GRAY, HEMPLAND, MO.
F. M. MOORE, Architect, Cincinnati, Ohio.

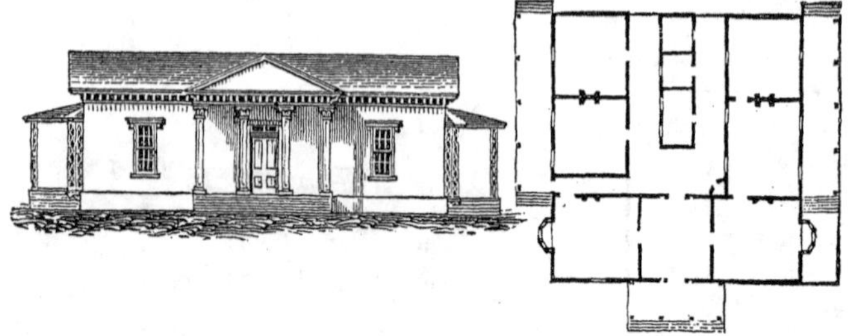

FIG. 36—60 feet Front, 66 feet Deep.

RESIDENCE OF DR. WM. L. WILSON, YAZOO CO., MISS.

JACOB VOGT, Builder, Cincinnati. Ohio.

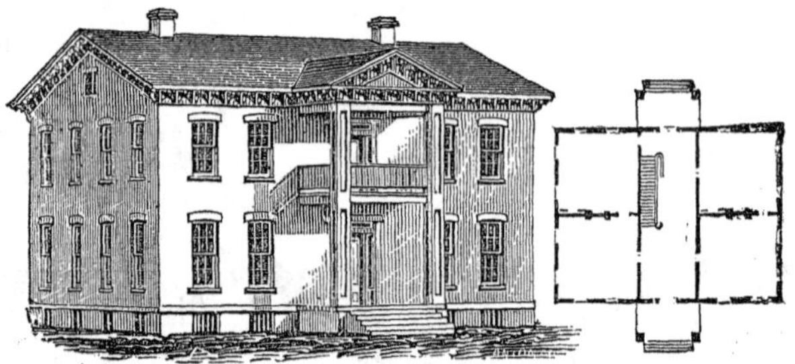

FIG. 37—56 feet Front, 42 feet Deep.

RESIDENCE OF ROBERT MULLAN, TROY, MISS.

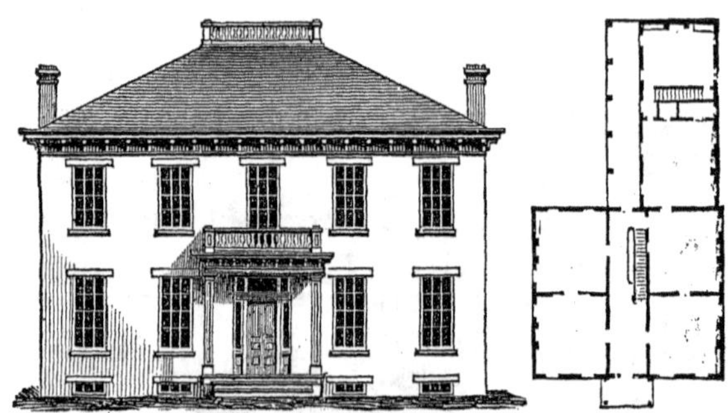

FIG. 38—44 feet Front, 76 feet Deep.

RESIDENCE OF THOMAS M. GIBSON, LOOGOOTEE, IND.

F. M. MOORE, Architect, Cincinnati, Ohio.

N. F. BOLTON, Builder, Loogootee, Indiana.

FIG. 39—60 feet Front, 42 feet Deep.

LIBRARY HALL OF THE GEORGETOWN COLLEGE, KY.

JAMES BAILEY, Architect and Builder, Georgetown, Ky.

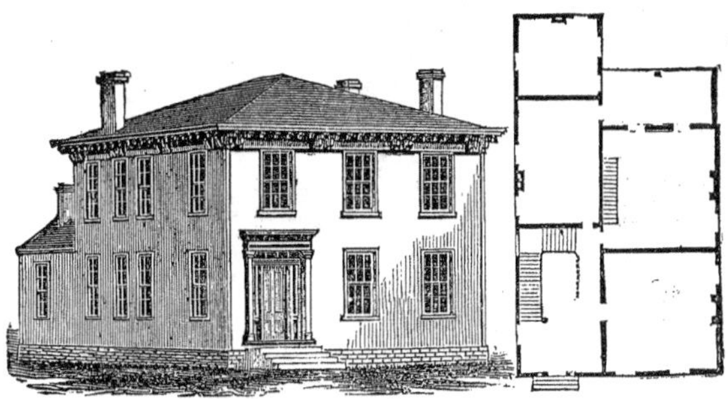

Fig. 40—30 feet Front, 52 feet Deep.

RESIDENCE OF E. G. GARNETT, CAMBRIDGE, MO.

F. M. Moore, Architect, Cincinnati, Ohio.

Fig. 41—46 feet Front, 45 feet Deep.

RESIDENCE OF E. D. GRAVES, CAMBRIDGE, MO.

F. M. Moore, Architect, Cincinnati, Ohio.

Fig. 42—38 feet Front, 47 feet Deep.

RESIDENCE OF CAPT. J. C. CALDWELL, CARTHAGE, O.

F. M. Moore, Architect, Cincinnati, Ohio.
V. Williams, Builder, " "

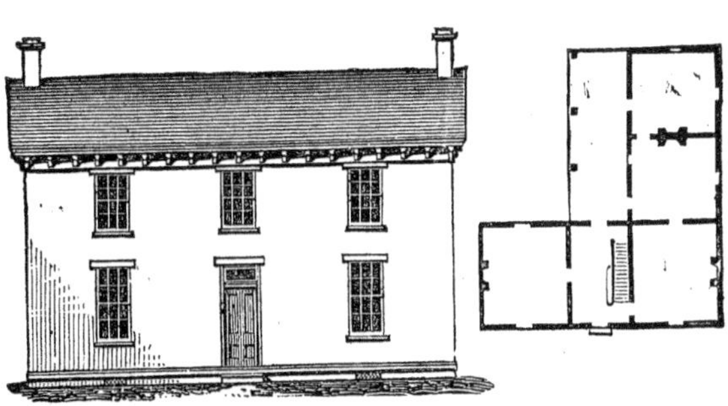

Fig. 43—48 feet Front, 54 feet Deep.

RESIDENCE OF RUSSELL H. TANDY, NEAR GHENT, KY.

W. H. Boudinot, Architect and Builder, Ghent, Ky.

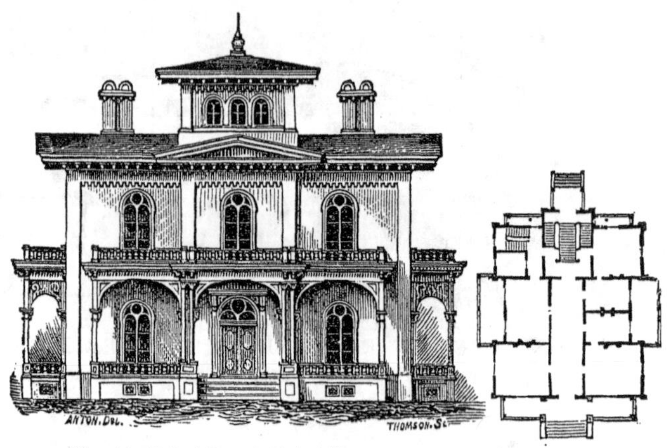

Fig. 44—68 feet Front, 80 feet Deep.
RESIDENCE OF J. W. BODDIE, MADISON COUNTY, MISS.
J. Lamour, Architect and Superintendent, Canton, Miss.

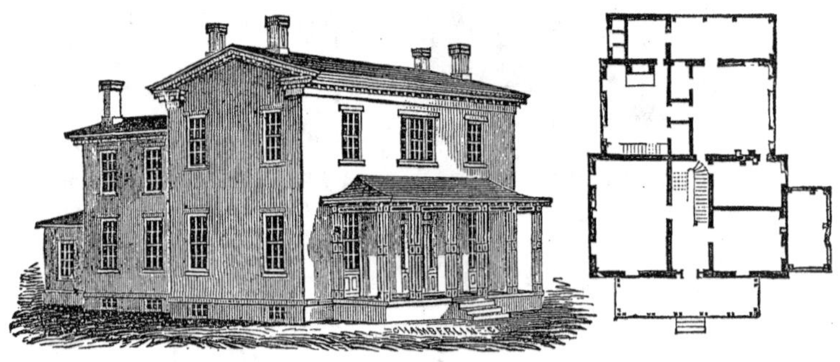

Fig. 45—50 feet Front, 58 Feet Deep.
RESIDENCE OF BENJAMIN T. DALE, OAKLAND, HAMILTON CO., O.
John W. Dale, Architect, Cincinnati.

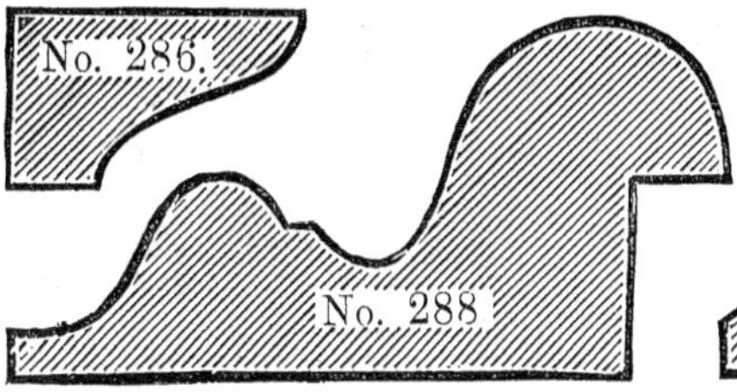

No. 286.

No. 287.

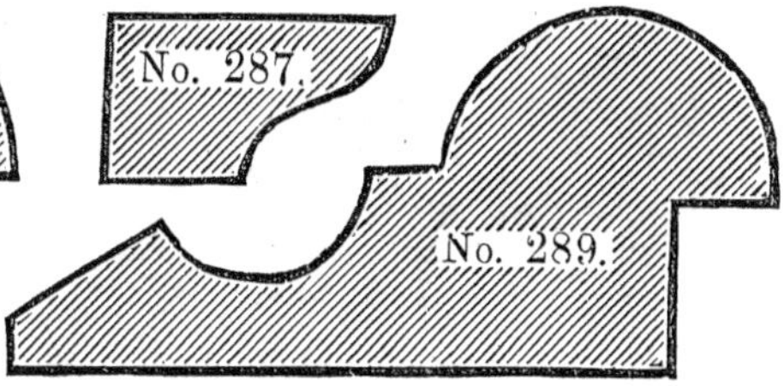

No. 288

No. 289.

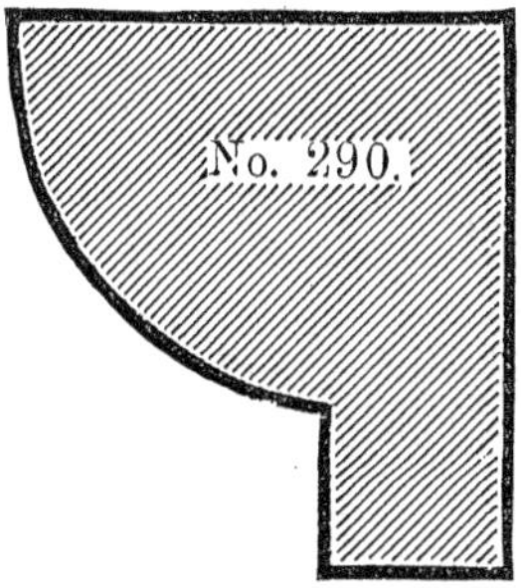

No. 290.

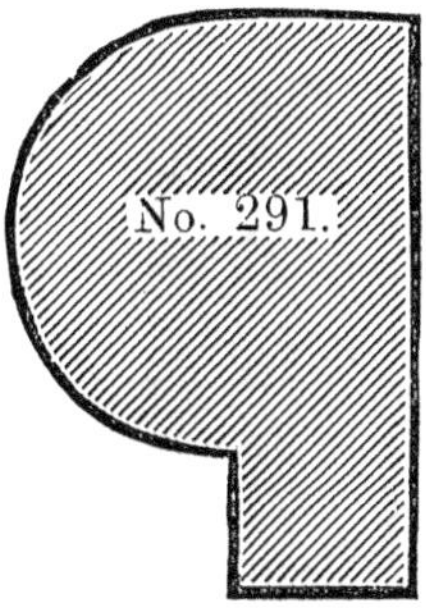

No. 291.

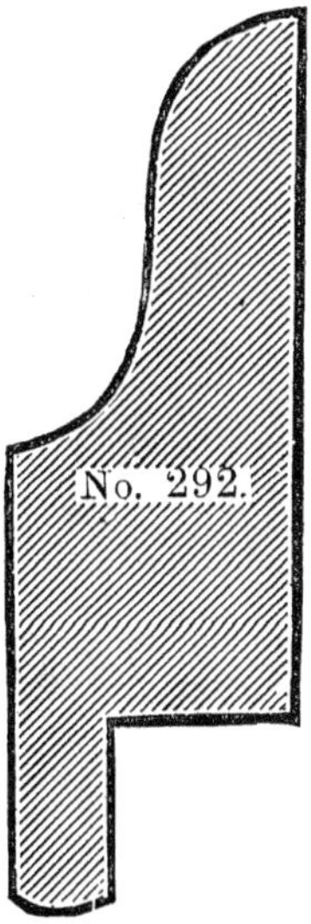

No. 292.

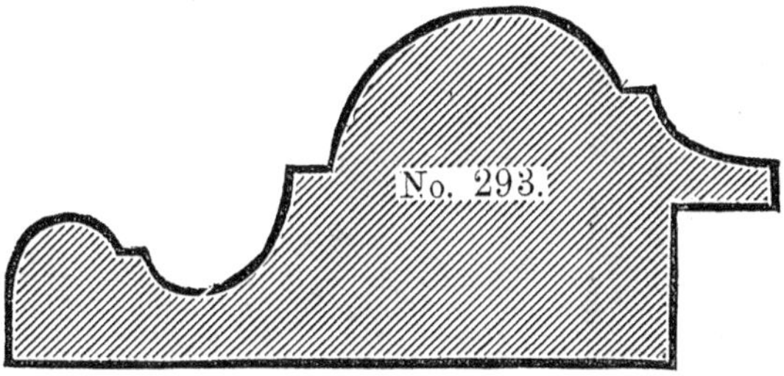

No. 293.

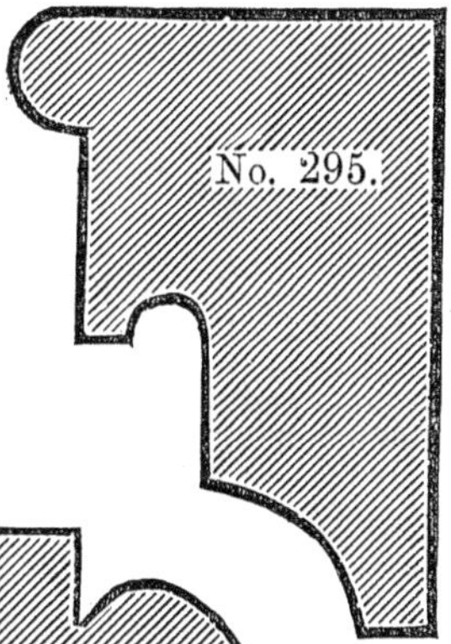

No. 295.

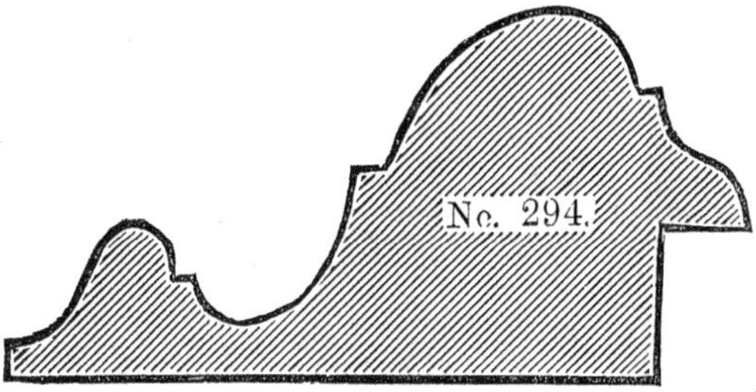

No. 294.

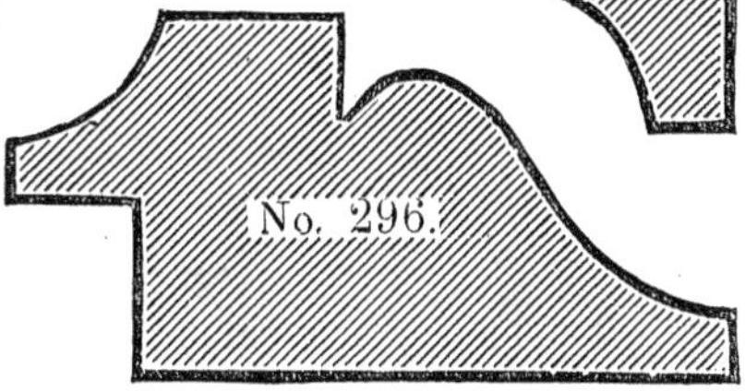

No. 296.

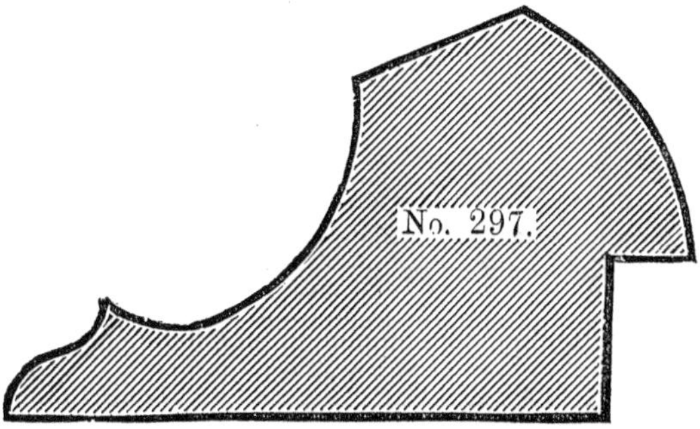

No. 297.

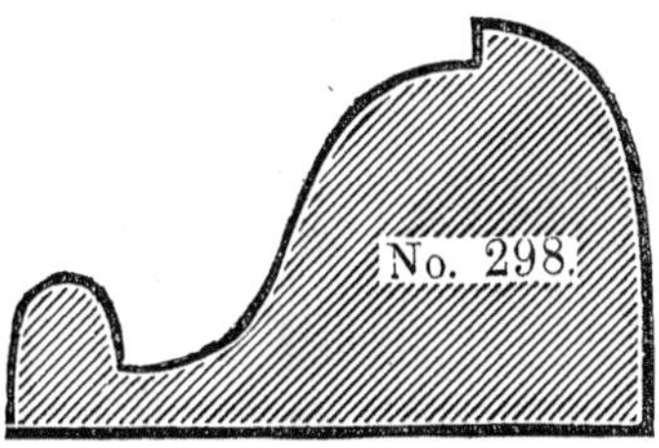

No. 298.

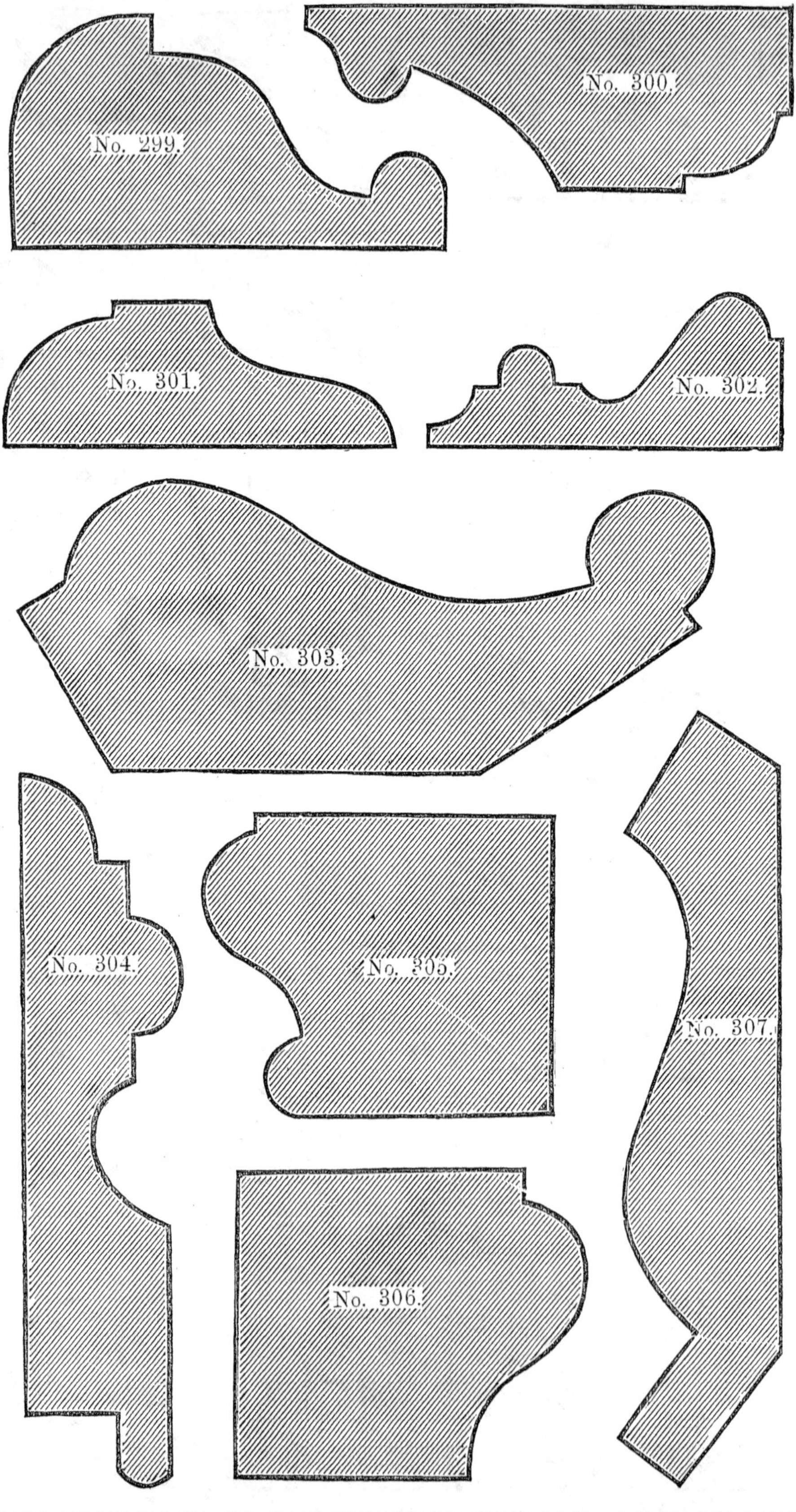

No. 299.

No. 300.

No. 301.

No. 302.

No. 303.

No. 304.

No. 305.

No. 306.

No. 307.

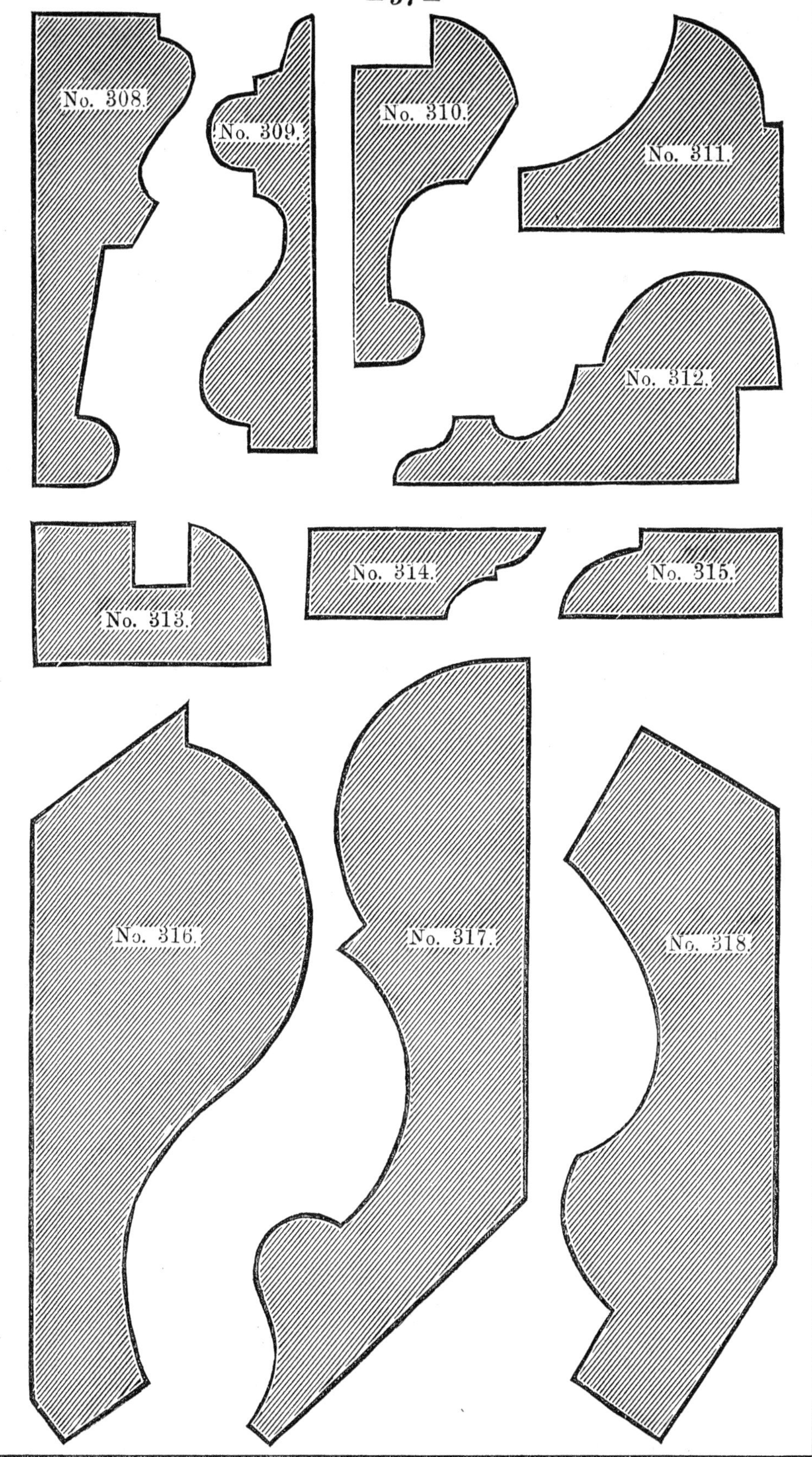
No. 308.
No. 309.
No. 310.
No. 311.
No. 312.
No. 313.
No. 314.
No. 315.
No. 316.
No. 317.
No. 318.

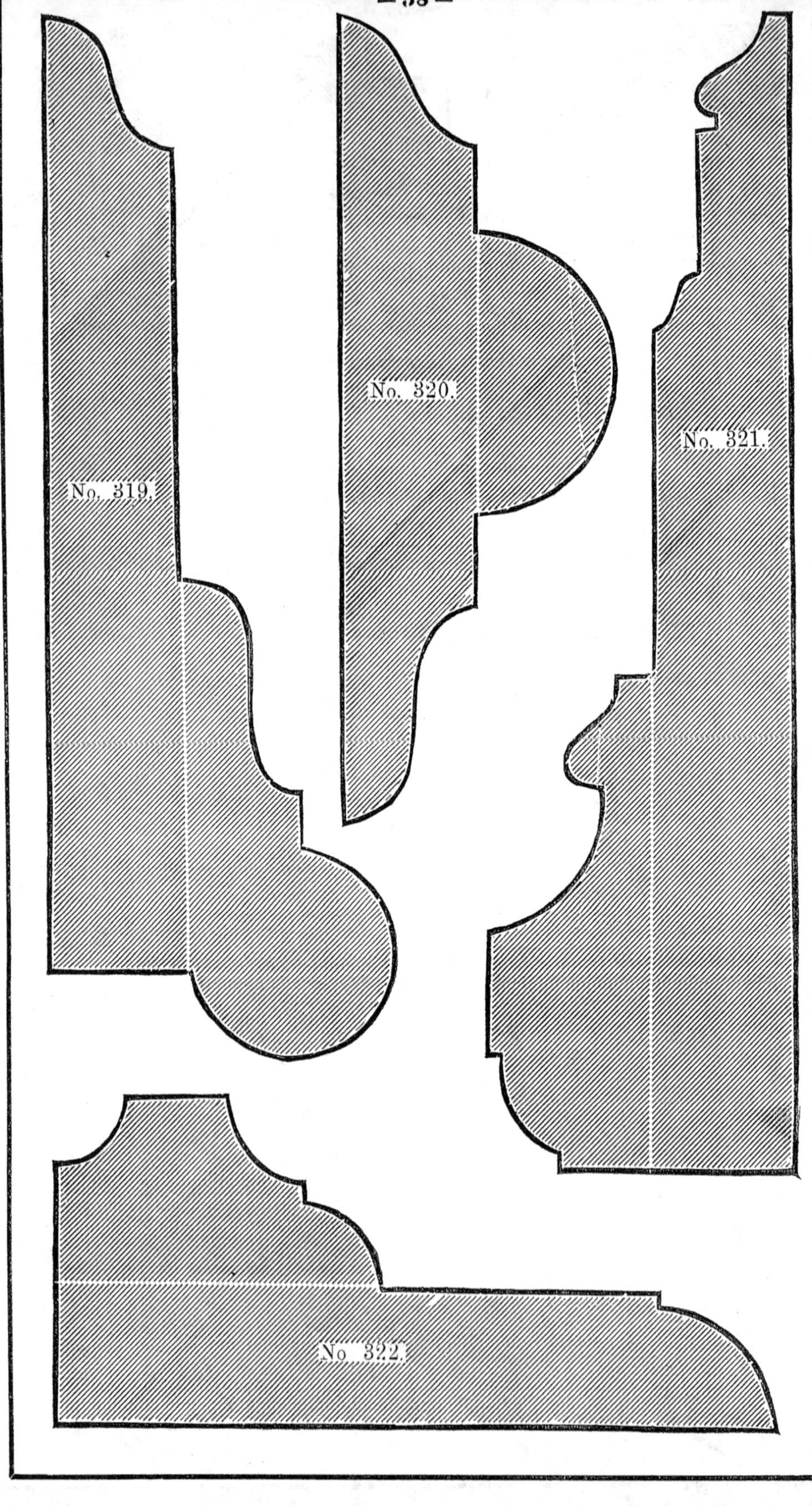
No. 319.
No. 320.
No. 321.
No. 322.

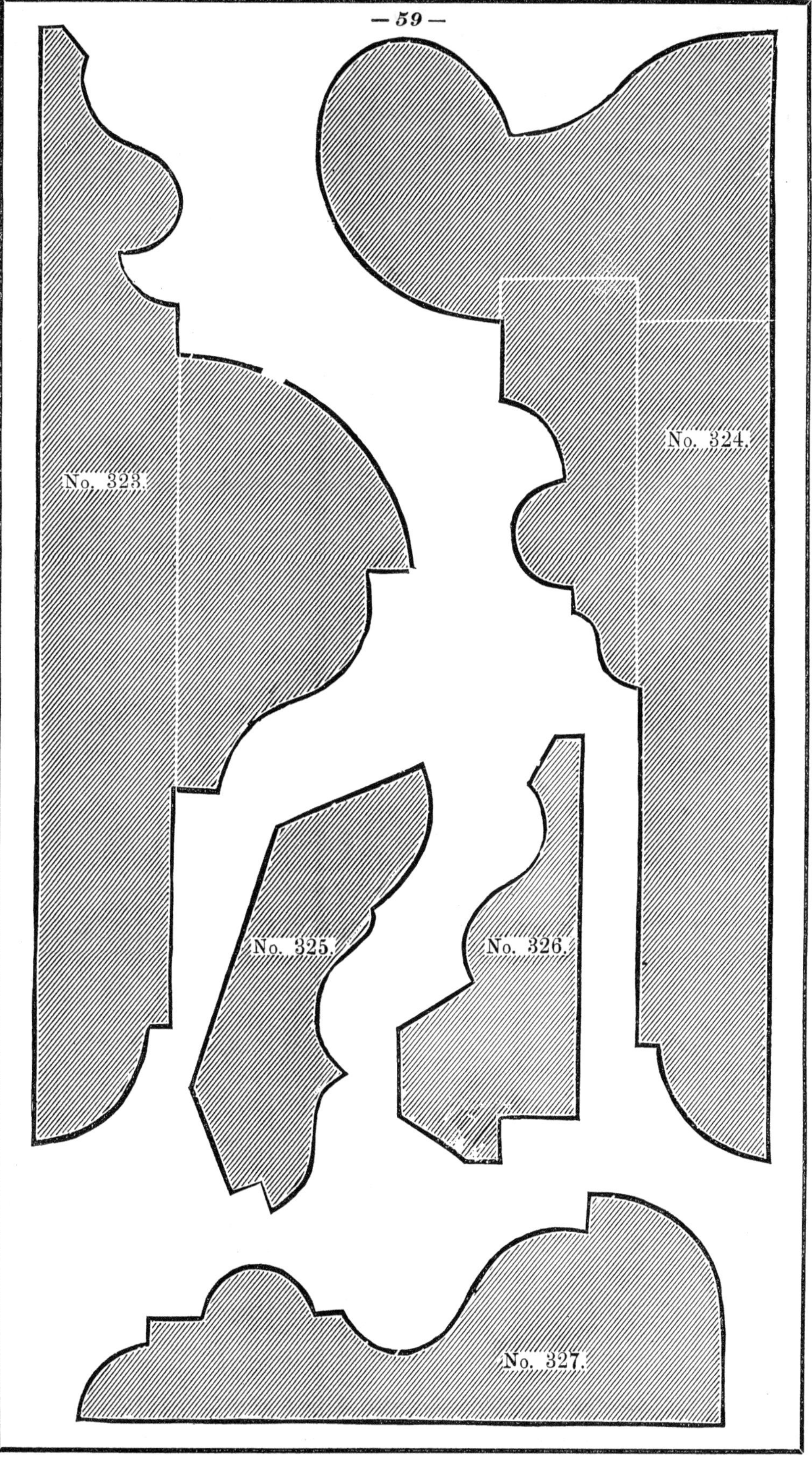
No. 323.
No. 324.
No. 325.
No. 326.
No. 327.

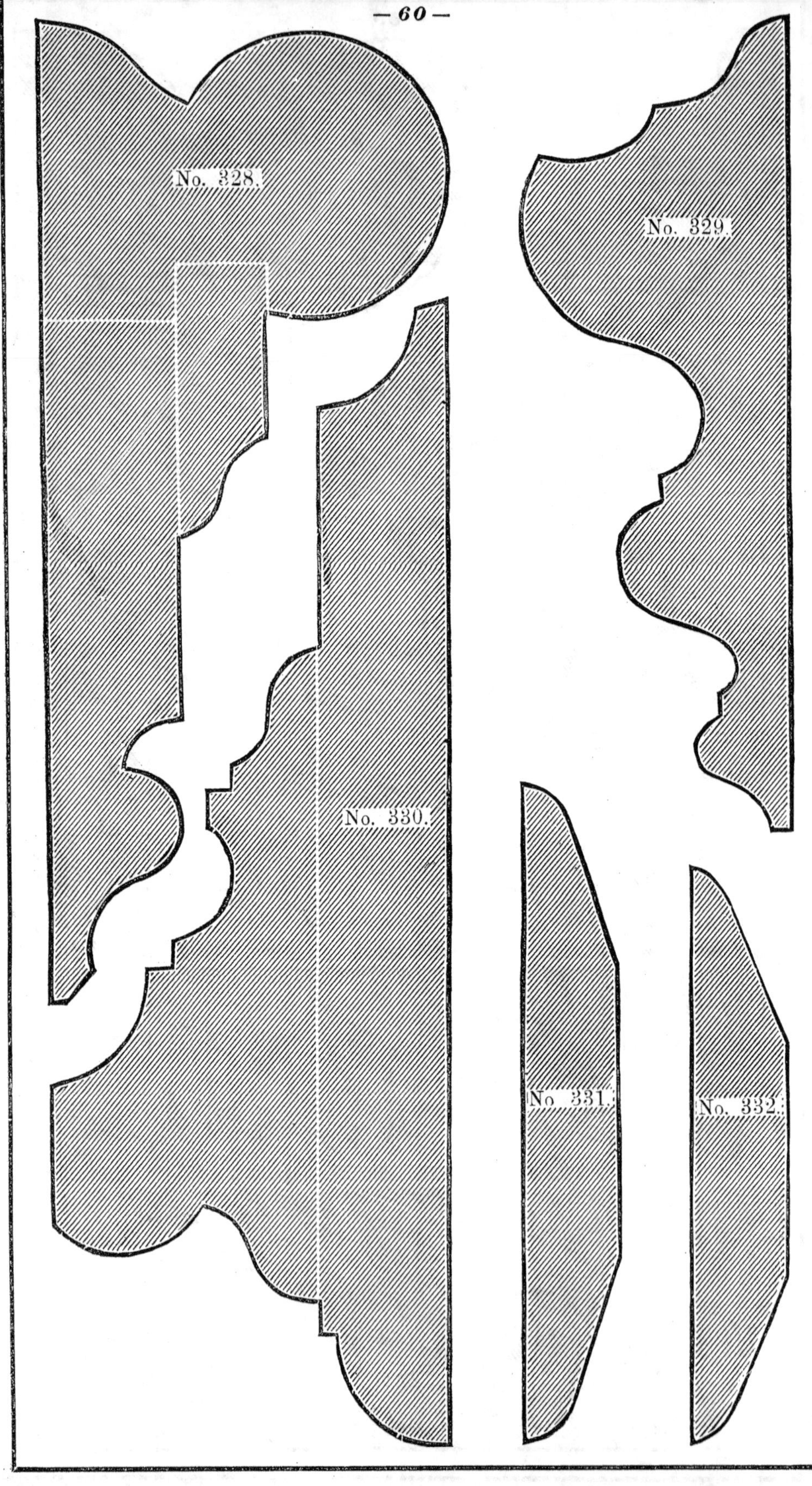
No. 328.
No. 329.
No. 330.
No. 331.
No. 332.

Ornamental Verge Board, Scale 1 inch to the foot.

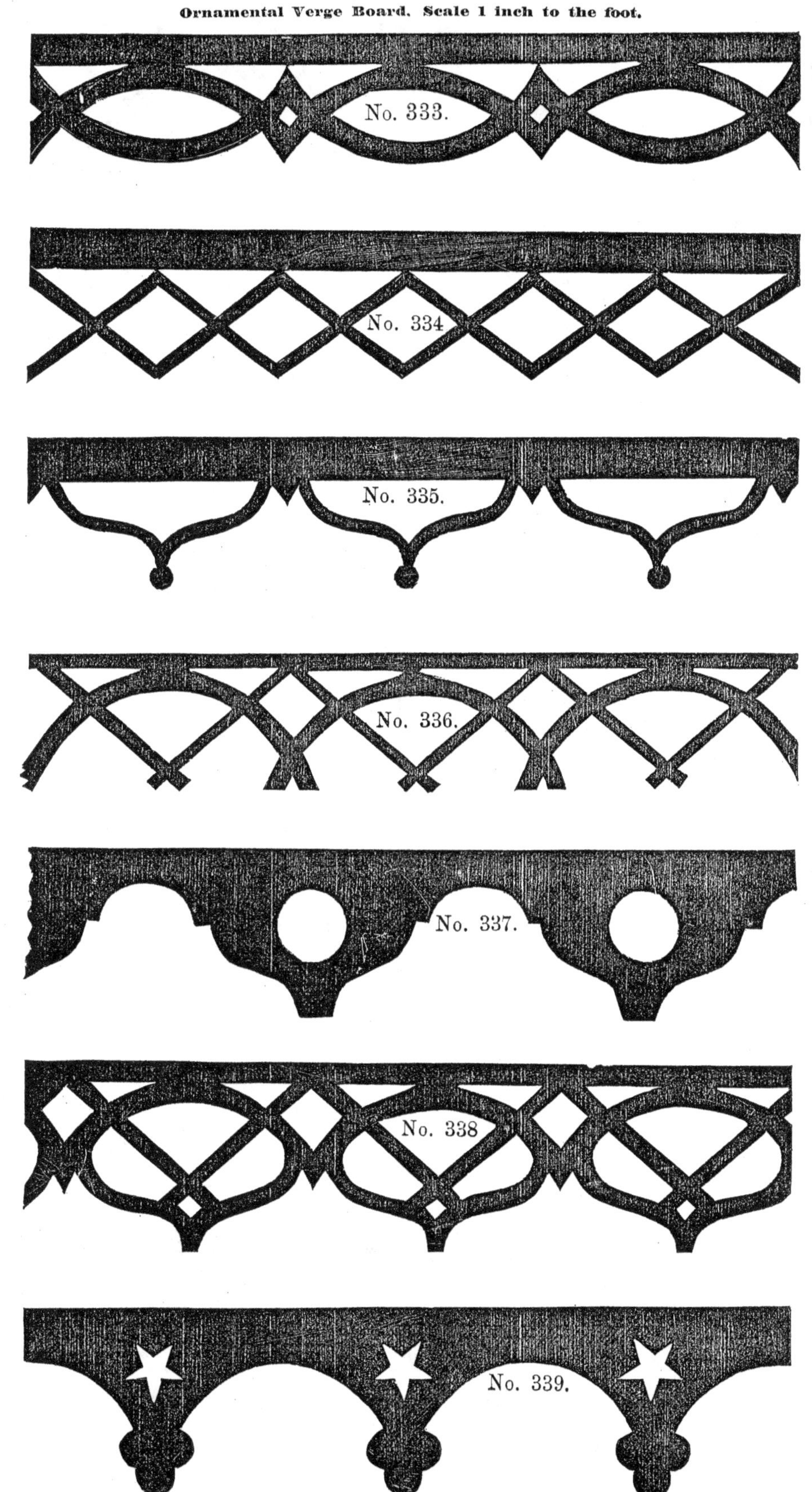

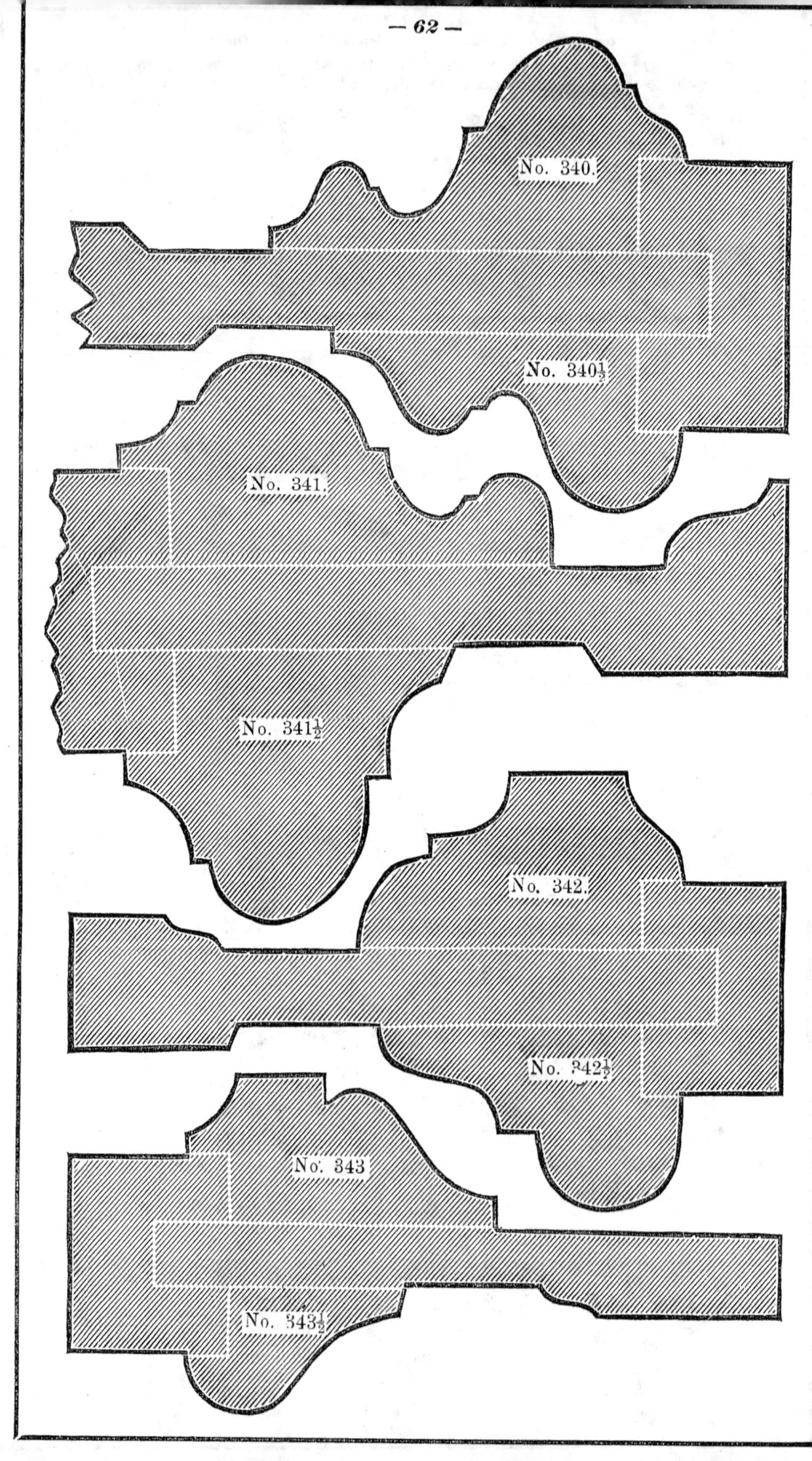
No. 340.
No. 340½
No. 341.
No. 341½
No. 342.
No. 342½
No. 343
No. 343½

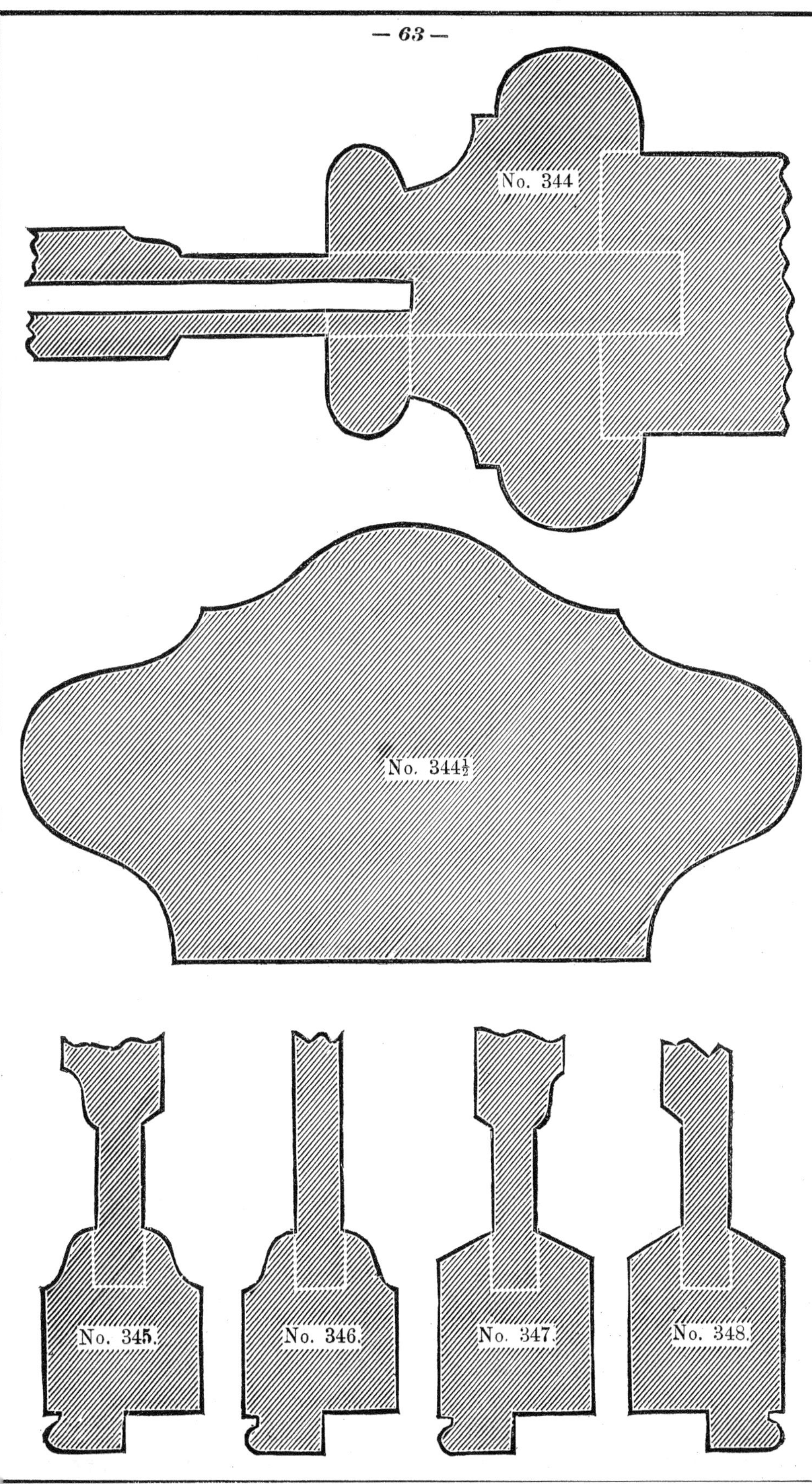
No. 344
No. 344½
No. 345.
No. 346.
No. 347.
No. 348.

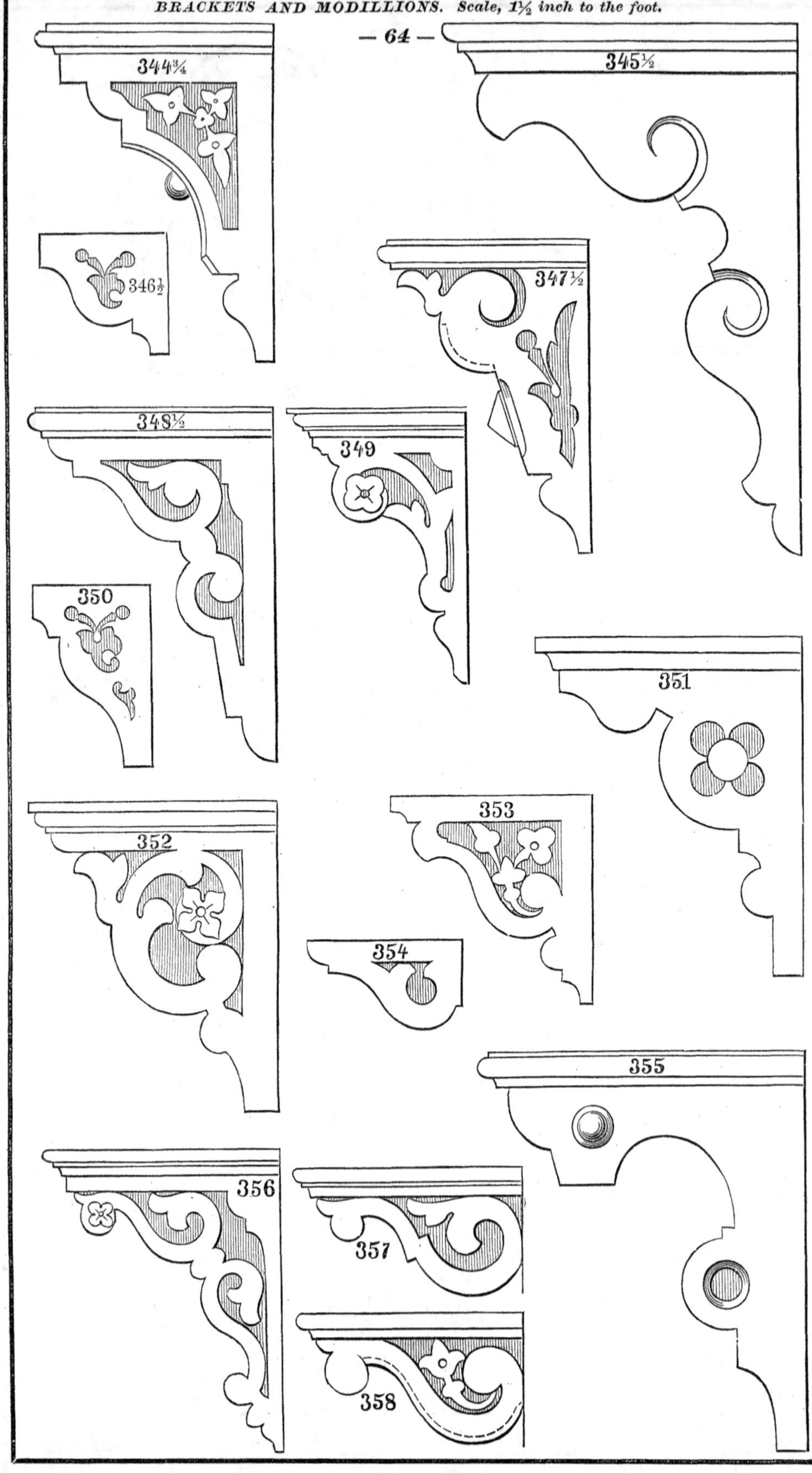
344¾
345½
346½
347½
348½
349
350
351
352
353
354
355
356
357
358

Brackets, Modillions, and Braces. Scale 1 inch to the foot.

359.

360.

361.

362.

363.

364.

365.

366.

367.

368.

369.

370.

371.

374.

373.

375.

372.

377.

376.

378.

379.

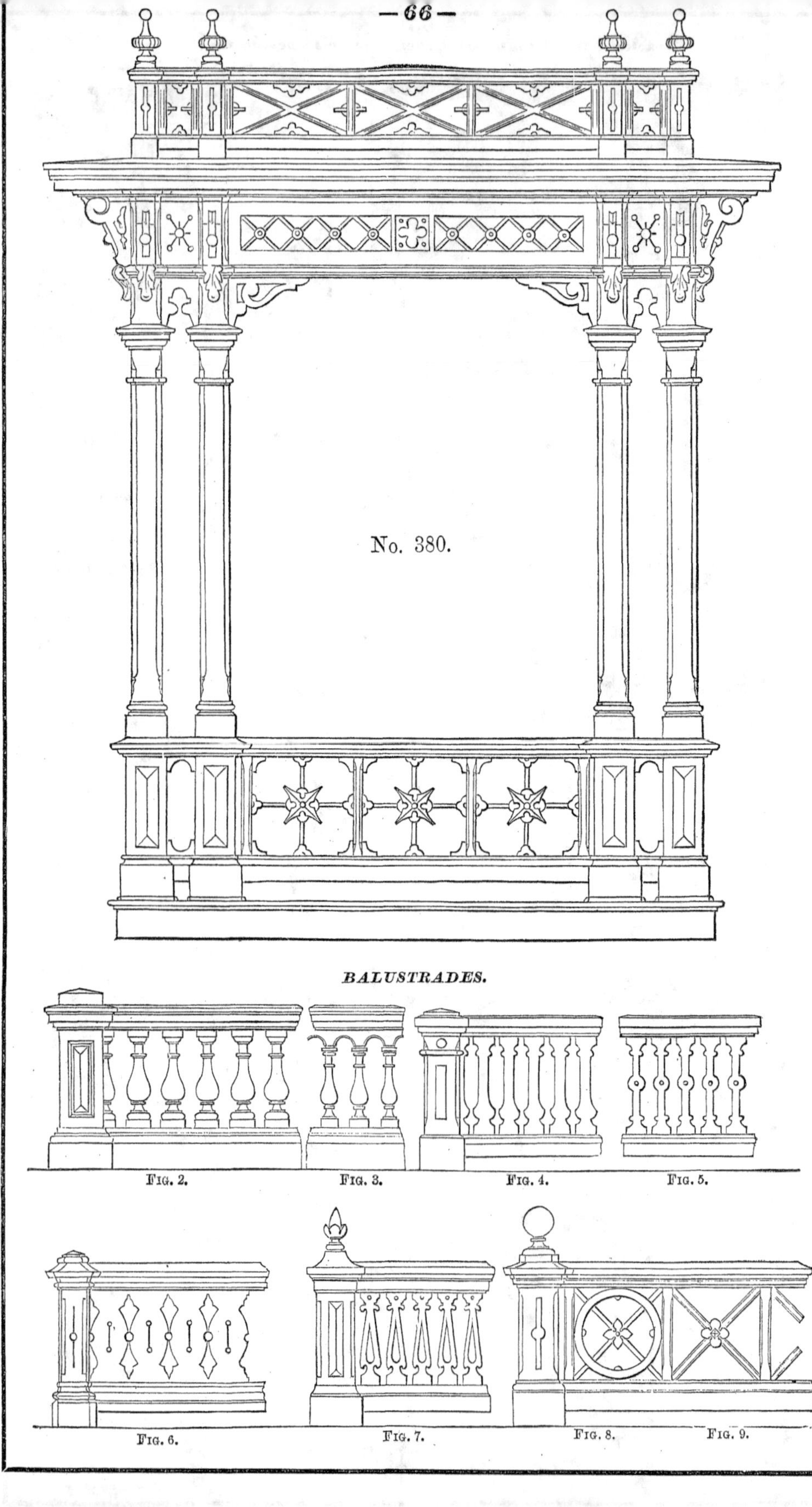
No. 380.
BALUSTRADES.
Fig. 2.
Fig. 3.
Fig. 4.
Fig. 5.
Fig. 6.
Fig. 7.
Fig. 8.
Fig. 9.

No. 381.

No .382.

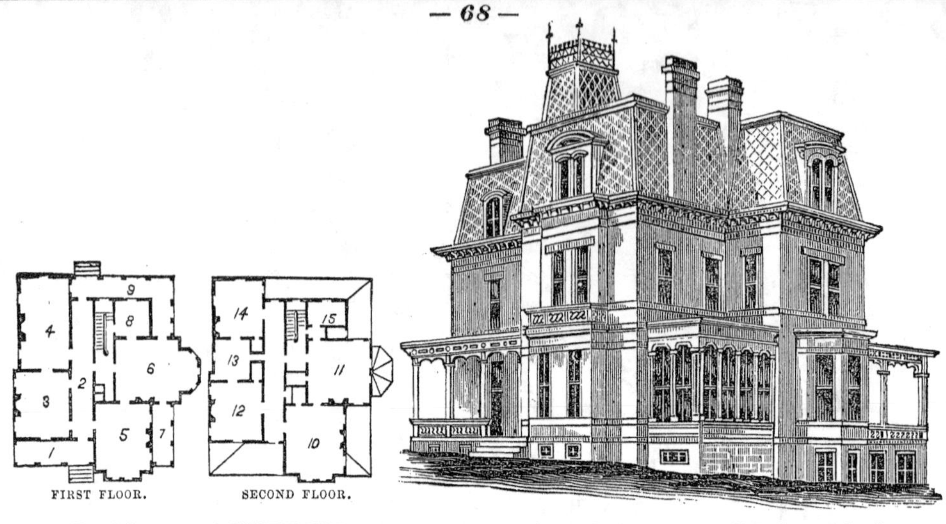

Residence of STEPHEN BURTON, Avondale, near Cincinnati, O.

ARCHITECT, JAS. McLAUGHLIN, CINCINNATI, O.

First Floor.—1, Verandah, 8 by 28 feet; 2, Hall, 9 feet 5½ inches by 38 feet, finished with black walnut, oiled; 3, Library, 18 feet 5 inches by 18 feet 6 inches, white walnut, varnished; 4, Parlor, 18 by 25 feet, white pine, painted; 5, Sitting Room, 16 by 20 feet, white walnut, varnished; 6, Dining Room, 16 feet 3 inches by 22 feet, black walnut, oiled; 7, Conservatory, 8 by 16 feet; 8, China Closet, 12 by 12 feet, black walnut, oiled; 9, Porch, 8 feet wide.

Second Floor.—10, Chamber, 16 by 20 feet, white walnut; 11, Chamber, 16 feet by 21 feet 9 inches, white walnut; 12, Chamber, 17 feet by 18 feet 5 inches, white pine; 13, Bed Room, 11 by 11 feet, white pine; 14, Chamber, 15 feet 9 inches by 16 feet, white pine; 15, Bath Room, 7 feet 6 inches by 12 feet, white walnut.

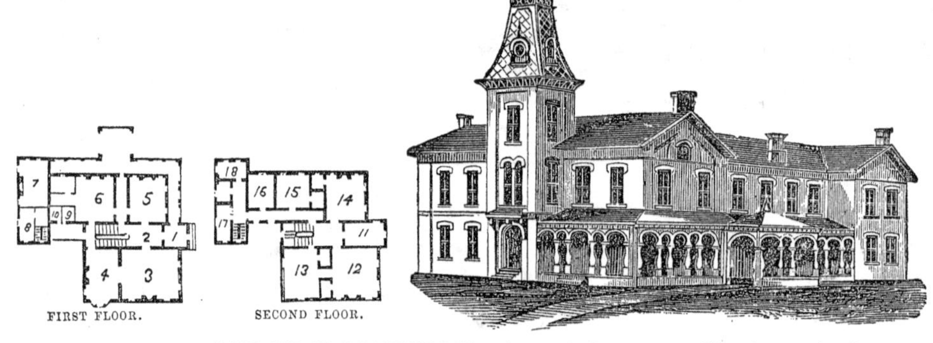

Residence of W. H. DOMINICK, Avondale, near Cincinnati, O.

ARCHITECT, WM. TINSLEY, CINCINNATI, O.

First Floor.—1, Porch, 9 feet 5 inches by 9 feet 6 inches; 2, Hall, 10 feet wide; 3, Parlor, 17 by 24 feet; 4, Library, 14 by 17 feet; 5, Family Room, 16 by 17 feet; 6, Dining Room, 16 by 17 feet; 7, Kitchen, 16 by 18 feet; 8, Servant's Room, 8 feet 6 inches by 12 feet; 9, Pantry, 4 feet 9 inches by 6 feet; 10, Lavatory, 4 feet 9 inches by 6 feet.

Second Floor.—11, Bed Room, 9 feet 5 inches by 17 feet; 12, Bed Room, 17 by 20 feet; 13, Bed Room, 14 feet 6 inches by 17 feet; 14, Bed Room, 16 by 17 feet; 15, Bed Room, 12 feet 6 inches by 15 feet; 16, Bed Room, 10 feet by 12 feet 6 inches; 17, Bath Room, 8 feet 6 inches by 15 feet; 18, Maid's Room, 8 feet 6 inches by 16 feet.

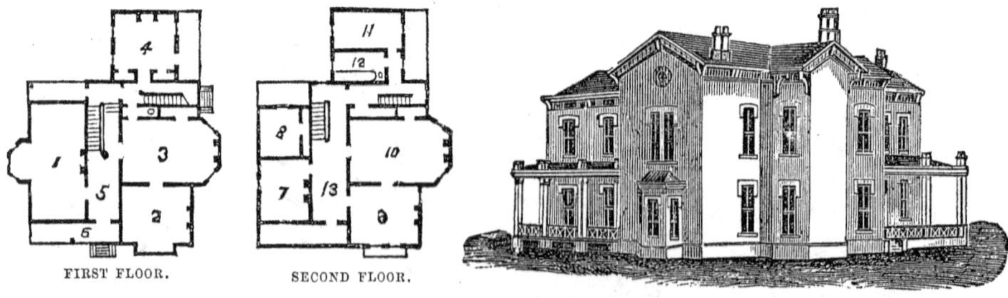

Residence of E. T. KIDD, Clifton, near Cincinnati, O.

ARCHITECTS, WALTERS & STEWART, CINCINNATI, O.

First Floor.—1, Parlor, 15 by 27 feet; 2, Sitting Room, 15 feet by 16 feet 2 inches; 3, Dining Room, 15 feet 2 inches by 18 feet 2 inches; 4, Kitchen, 15 feet 2 inches by 16 feet; 5, Hall, 8 feet; 6, Porch.

Second Floor.—7, Bed Room, 15 feet by 17 feet 6 inches; 8, Dressing Room, 9 by 12 feet; 9, Bed Room, 15 feet by 16 feet 2 inches; 10, Bed Room, 15 feet 2 inches by 18 feet 2 inches; 11, Bed Room, 11 feet 2 inches by 15 feet 2 inches; 12, Bath Room, 7 feet 4 inches by 10 feet 8 inches.

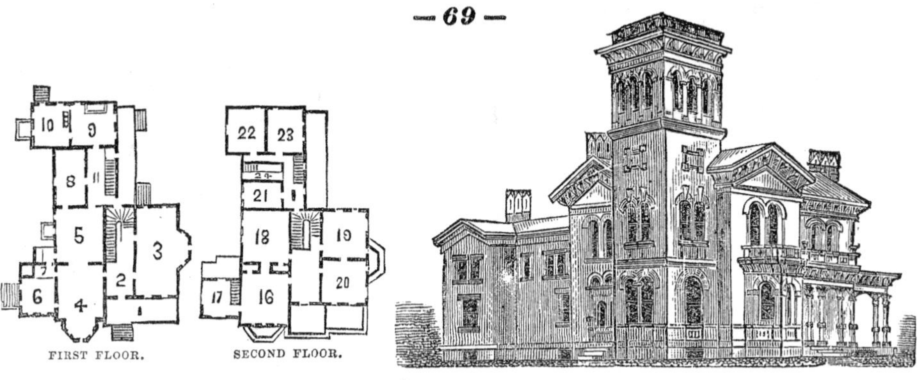

Residence of C. B. ANDERSON, Kentucky, near Cincinnati, O.

ARCHITECTS, ANDERSON & HANNAFORD, CINCINNATI, O.

First Floor.—1, Verandah; 2, Hall; 3, Parlor, 16 by 32 feet; 4, Reception Room, 17 by 20 feet; 5, Dining Room, 18 by 17 feet; 6, Office, 12 by 12 feet; 7, Bath Room, 6 feet 6 inches by 7 feet; 8, Store Room, 12 by 12 feet; 9, Kitchen, 15 feet 6 inches by 15 feet; 10, Laundry, 12 by 15 feet; 11, Rear Hall.

Second Floor.—16, Chamber, 17 feet by 17 feet 7 inches; 17, Dressing Room, 12 by 12 feet; 18, Chamber, 17 feet 7 inches by 17 feet; 19, Chamber, 15 feet 9 inches by 16 feet, 20, Chamber, 15 by 16 feet; 21, Bedding; 22, Chamber, 15 feet by 13 feet 9 inches; 23, Chamber, 15 feet by 13 feet 9 inches; 24, Bath Room, 6 by 14 feet.

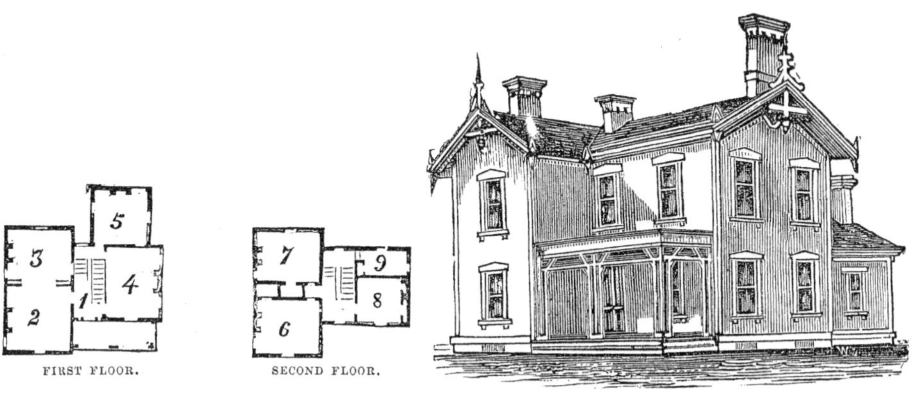

Residence of REV. W. H. BABBITT, Glendale, Ohio.

ARCHITECT, J. B. YOUNG, CINCINNATI, O.

First Floor.—1, Hall, 7 feet 6 inches by 18 feet 1 inch; 2, Parlor, 16 by 17 feet; 3, Study, 16 by 13 feet; 4, Dining Room, 14 by 18 feet; 5, Kitchen, 14 by 14 feet.

Second Floor.—6, Bed Room, 13 feet 6 inches by 16 feet; 7, Bed Room, 16 by 13 feet; 8, Bed Room, 12 feet 4 inches by 11 feet 2 inches; 9, Bed Room, 6 feet 6 inches by 11 feet 8 inches.

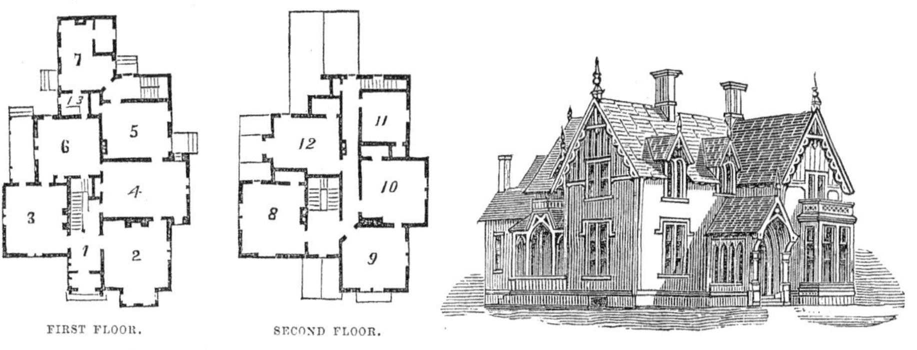

Residence of JOHN S. ESTERBROOK, East Saginaw, Mich.

ARCHITECT, A. BURROWS, EAST SAGINAW, MICH.

First Floor.—1, Hall, 8 feet; 2, Parlor, 17 by 17 feet; 3, Library, 16 by 16 feet; 4, Sitting Room, 15 by 20 feet; 5, Dining Room, 15 by 17 feet; 6, Family Room, 16 by 16 feet; 7, Kitchen, 14 by 17 feet.

Second Floor.—8, Chamber, 16 by 16 feet; 9, Chamber, 15 by 17 feet; 10, Chamber, 17 by 17 feet; 11, Chamber, 12 by 13 feet; 12, Chamber, 16 by 16 feet; 13, Bath Room, 6 by 8 feet.

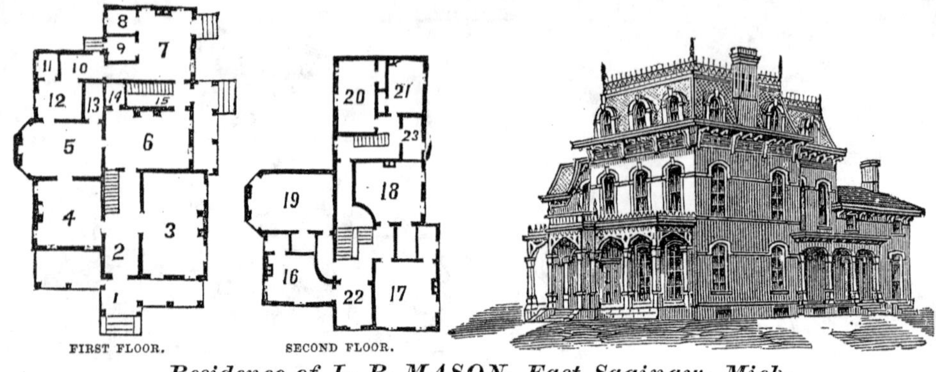

Residence of L. P. MASON, East Saginaw, Mich.

ARCHITECTS, HEARD & BLYTHE, CLEVELAND, O.

First Floor.—1, Porch; 2, Hall, 9 by 25 feet; 3, Parlor, 16 by 25 feet; 4, Sitting Room, 16 by 19 feet; 5, Bed Room, 14 by 22 feet; 6, Dining Room, 15 feet by 21 feet 4 inches; 7, Kitchen, 14 by 17 feet; 8, Pantry, 6 by 7 feet; 9, Store Room, 6 by 7 feet; 10, Bath Room, 6 by 11 feet; 11, Closet, 5 by 6 feet; 12, Child's Bed Room, 9 by 11 feet; 13, Closet, 5 by 9 feet; 14, Fruit Closet, 5 by 6 feet; 15, Rear Hall.

Second Floor.—16, Bed Room, 15 by 16 feet; 17, Chamber, 16 by 17 feet; 18, Bed Room, 15 by 16 feet; 19, Chamber, 14 by 22 feet; 20, Chamber, 9 by 17 feet; 21, Bed Room, 9 by 13 ft.; 22, Bed Room, 9 by 13 ft.; 23, Linen Closet, 5 by 10 ft.

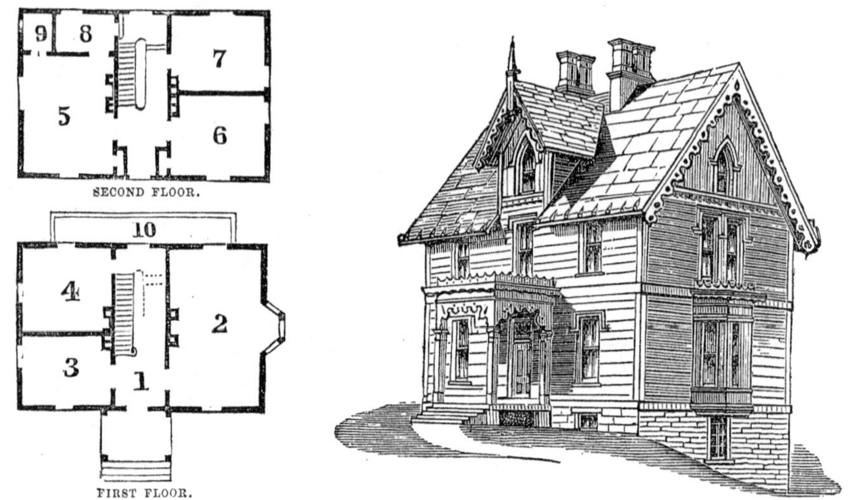

Residence of J. CINNAMON, East Walnut Hills, Cincinnati, O.

ARCHITECTS, WALTER & STEWART, CINCINNATI, O.

First Floor.—1, Hall, 8 feet wide; 2, Parlor, 15 by 25 feet; 3, Library, 11 by 15 feet; 4, Bed Room, 13 feet 6 inches by 15 feet; 10, Balcony, 5 feet wide.

Second Floor.—5, Bed Room, 15 by 18 feet; 6, Bed Room, 12 feet 3 inches by 15 feet; 7, Bed Room, 12 feet 3 inches by 15 feet; 8, Bath Room, 6 feet 6 inches by 9 feet 6 inches; 9, Closet, 6 feet 6 inches by 5 feet.

Dining Room, Kitchen, Store Rooms, etc., located in *Basement Story*. Two Bed Rooms in *Attic*.

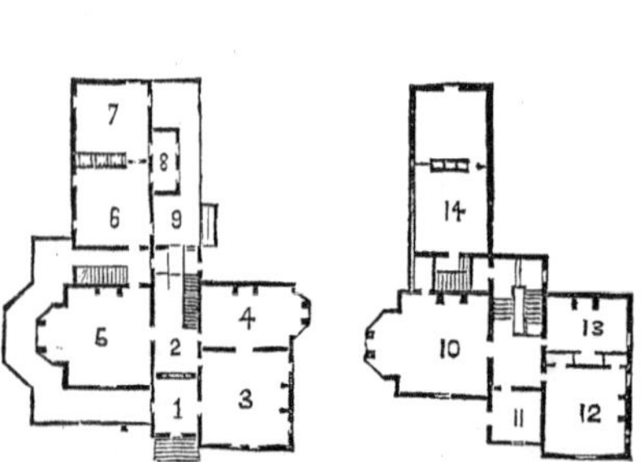

First Floor.—1, Vestibule, 9 by 9 feet; 2, Hall, 9 feet by 26 feet 2 inches; 3, Parlor, 16 by 18 feet; 4, Library, 12 by 16 feet; 5, Family Room, 17 by 21 feet; 6, Dining Room, 16 by 17 feet; 7, Kitchen, 14 by 16 feet; 8, Pantry, 5 feet 4 inches by 11 feet; 9, Back Porch.

Second Floor.—10, Bed Room, 17 by 21 feet; 11, Bed Room, 9 by 9 feet; 12, Bed Room, 16 by 16 feet; 13, Bed Room, 13 by 16 feet; 14, Loft.

Residence of HEZEKIAH WAMPLER, Gosport, Ind.

ARCHITECT, WM. TINSLEY, CINCINNATI, O.

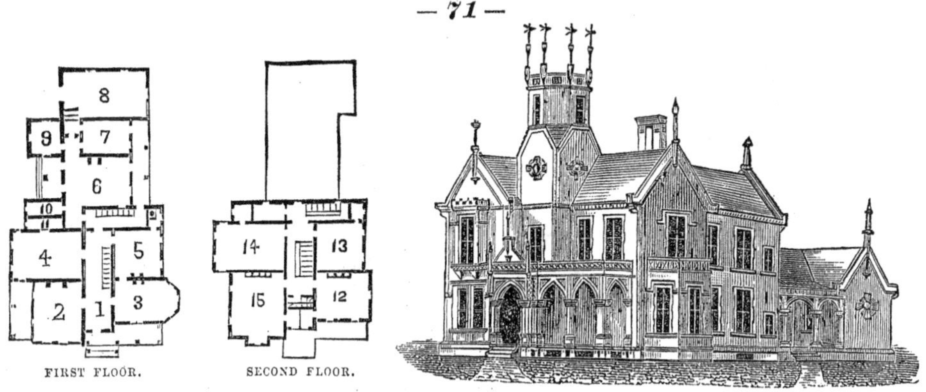

Residence to be built near Cincinnati, Ohio.

ARCHITECTS, WALTER & STEWART, CINCINNATI, O.

First Floor.—1, Hall, 8 feet 6 inches wide; 2, Parlor, 15 by 20 feet; 3, Sitting Room, 15 by 17 feet; 4, Dining Room, 15 feet by 21 feet 6 inches; 5, Bed Room, 15 by 15 feet; 6, Kitchen, 15 feet by 19 feet 2 inches; 7, Wash House, 10 by 14 feet; 8, Wood House, 15 by 24 feet; 9, Store Room, 10 by 10 feet; 10, Pantry, 4 feet 6 inches by 10 feet; 11, China Closet, 3 by 10 feet.

Second Floor.—12, Bed Room, 15 by 17 feet; 13, Bed Room, 15 by 15 feet; 14, Bed Room, 15 feet by 21 feet 6 inches; 15, Bed Room, 15 by 20 feet; 16, Bath Room, 6 by 10 feet.

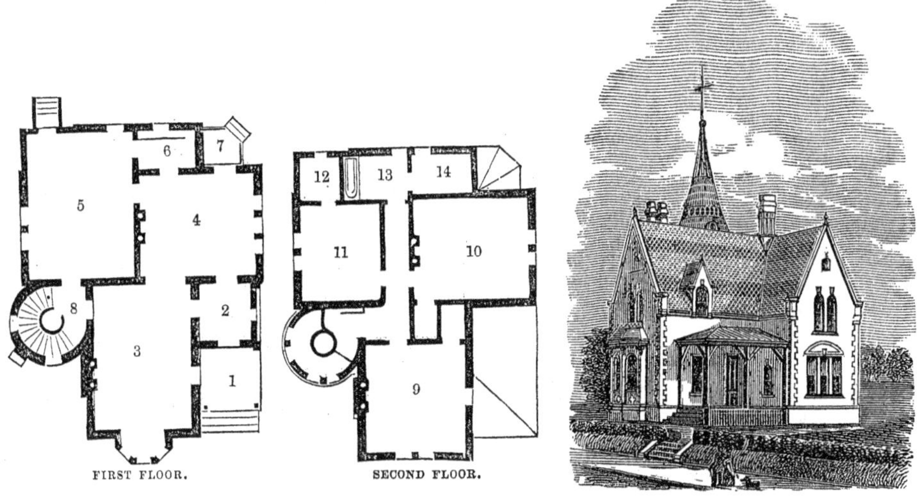

Residence of R. H. COTTLE, Spring Grove Avenue, Cincinnati, O.

ARCHITECTS, A. C. NASH & CO., CINCINNATI, O.

First Floor.—1, Verandah, 8 by 8 feet; 2, Vestibule, 7 by 8 feet; 3, Parlor, 14 by 20 feet; 4, Family Room, 14 by 16 feet; 5, Kitchen, 15 by 20 feet; 6, Pantry, 5 by 8 feet; 7, Lower Staircase, 8 feet diameter; 8, Rear Porch, 5 by 5 feet.

Second Floor.—9, Guest's Chamber, 14 by 15 feet; 10, Chamber, 14 by 16 feet; 11, Bed Room, 11 by 13 feet; 12, Closet, 6 by 6 feet; 13, Bath Room, 6 by 9 feet; 14, Linen Closet, 6 by 8 feet.

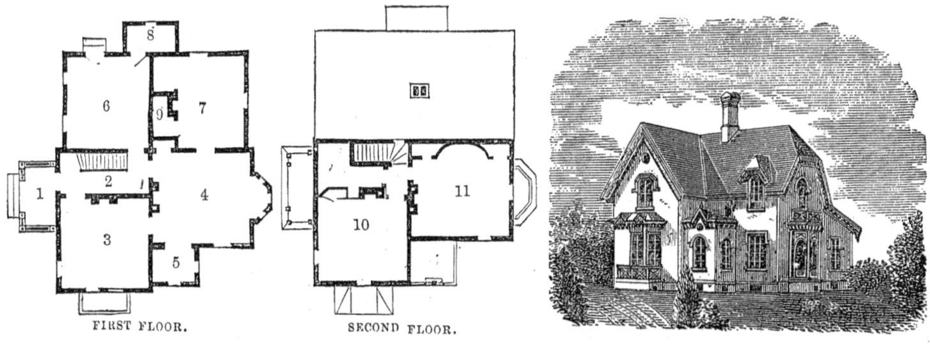

Residence of W. W. NORTHRUP, Belpre, Ohio.

ARCHITECTS, A. C. NASH & CO., CINCINNATI, O.

First Floor.—1, Verandah, 5 by 10 feet; 2, Hall and Stairs, 7 by 15 feet; 3, Parlor, 15 by 15 feet; 4, Family Room, 16 by 15 feet; 5, Library, 6 by 7 feet; 6, Kitchen, 14 by 15 feet; 7, Bed Room, 15 by 15 feet; 8, Pantry, 5 by 8 feet; 9, Closet, 4 by 7 feet.

Second Floor.—10, Chamber, 14 by 15 ft.; 11, Guest's Chamber, 16 by 13 ft.; 12, Linen Closet and Staircase, 7 by 15 ft.

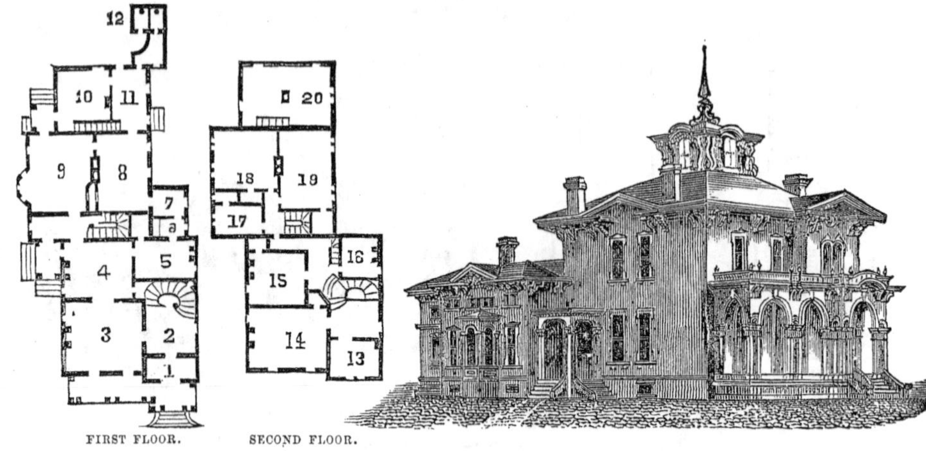

FIRST FLOOR. SECOND FLOOR.

Residence of GEORGE L. BURROWS, Saginaw City, Mich.

ARCHITECT, J. B. DIBBLE, SAGINAW CITY, MICH.

First Floor.—1, Vestibule, 5 by 13 feet; 2, Hall, 13 feet wide; 3, Parlor, 17 by 20 feet; 4, Sitting Room, 14 by 17 feet; 5, Family Bed Room, 10 by 15 feet; 6, Bath Room, 6 by 8 feet; 7, Pantry, 6 feet by 8 feet 6 inches; 8, Kitchen, 13 by 18 feet; 9, Dining Room, 16 by 18 feet; 10, Wash Room, 13 by 16 feet; 11, Laundry, 9 by 16 feet; 12, Privies.

Second Floor.—13, Sewing Room, 9 by 13 feet; 14, Chamber, 16 by 20 feet; 15, Chamber, 14 by 14 feet; 16, Chamber, 9 by 11 feet; 17, Chamber, 8 by 12 feet; 18, Chamber, 15 by 16 feet; 19, Chamber, 13 by 18 feet; 20, Chamber, 15 by 23 feet.

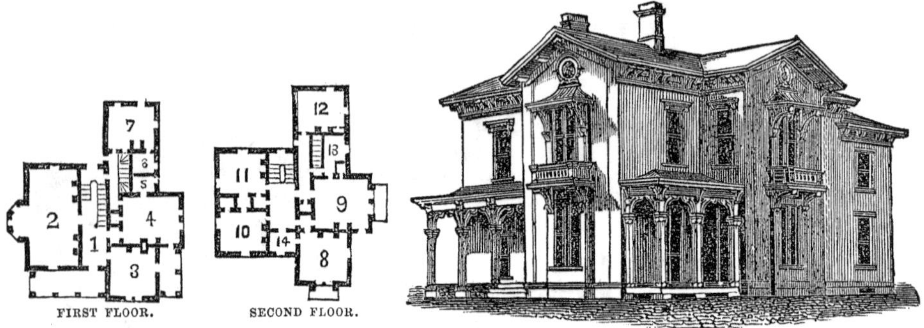

FIRST FLOOR. SECOND FLOOR.

Residence of T. C. ROWLAND, Mt. Auburn, Cincinnati, O.

ARCHITECT AND BUILDER, M. DOUGLASS, MT. AUBURN, CINCINNATI, O.

First Floor.—1, Hall, 8 feet wide; 2, Parlor, 15 feet 6 inches by 30 feet; 3, Sitting Room, 15 by 16 feet; 4, Dining Room, 15 feet 6 inches by 18 feet 6 inches; 5, China Closet, 5 feet by 8 feet 9 inches; 6, Store Room, 5 feet by 8 feet 9 inches; 7, Kitchen, 15 by 16 feet.

Second Floor.—8, Bed Room, 15 by 16 feet; 9, Bed Room, 15 feet by 18 feet 6 inches; 10, Bed Room, 15 feet 6 inches by 13 feet 3 inches; 11, Bed Room, 15 feet 6 inches by 13 feet 3 inches; 12, Bed Room, 15 by 16 feet; 13, Bath Room, 7 feet 9 inches by 8 feet 9 inches; 14, Bed Room, 8 feet by 7 feet 6 inches.

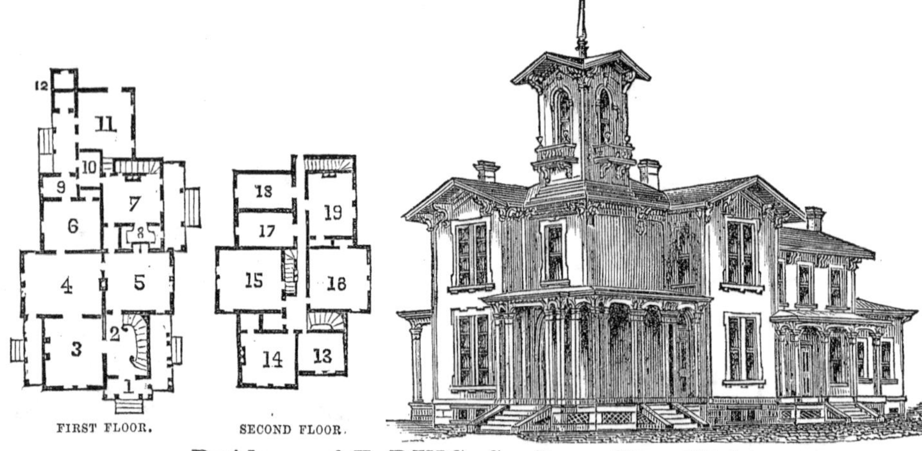

FIRST FLOOR. SECOND FLOOR.

Residence of E. RING, Saginaw City, Mich.

ARCHITECT, J B. DIBBLE; CONTRACTORS, JOHNSON & CROCKER, SAGINAW CITY, MICH.

First Floor.—1, Porch; 2, Hall, 11 by 15 feet; 3, Parlor, 14 by 17 feet; 4, Living Room, 14 by 19 feet; 5, Dining Room, 14 by 17 feet; 6, Family Room, 12 by 15 feet; 7, Kitchen, 12 by 15 feet; 8, Pantry, 6 by 10 feet; 9, Bath Room, 6 by 8 feet; 10, Pantry, 5 by 9 feet; 11, Wood House, 15 by 17 feet; 12, Water Closets.

Second Floor.—13, Chamber, 10 by 11 feet; 14, Chamber, 13 by 14 feet; 15, Chamber, 14 by 18 feet; 16, Chamber, 14 by 17 feet; 17, Chamber, 11 by 13 feet; 18, Chamber, 8 by 13 feet; 19, Chamber, 11 by 15 feet.

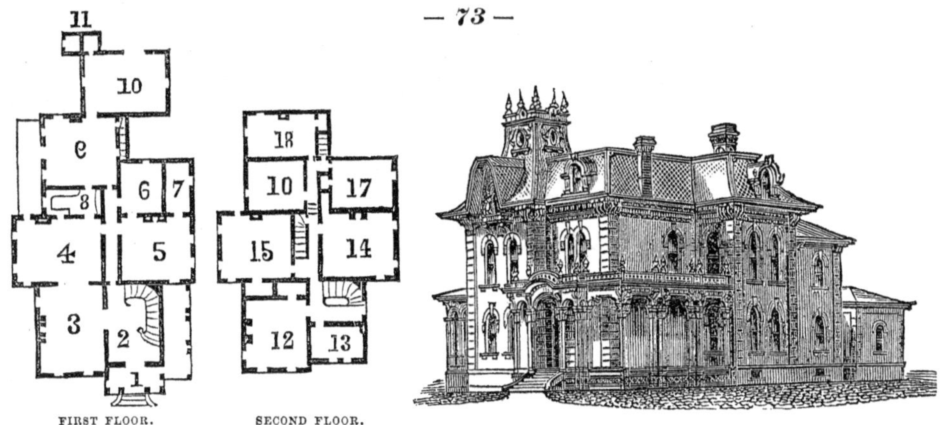

Residence of CHAS. W. GRANT, East Saginaw, Mich.

ARCHITECT, J. B. DIBBLE, SAGINAW CITY, MICH.
CONTRACTORS, PENDALL & McKINNIE, EAST SAGINAW, MICH.

First Floor.—1, Porch; 2, Hall, 14 by 15 feet; 3, Parlor, 15 by 22 feet; 4, Dining Room, 15 by 20 feet; 5, Bed Room, 15 by 18 feet; 6, Bath Room, 11 by 12 feet; 7, Wardrobe, 6 by 12 feet; 8, Pantry, 7 by 12 feet; 9, Kitchen, 16 by 14 feet; 10, Wood House, 14 by 20 feet; 11, Water Closets.
Second Floor.—12, Front Chamber, 15 by 17 feet; 13, Front Chamber, 10 by 14 feet; 14, Chamber, 15 by 18 feet; 15, Chamber, 15 by 16 feet; 16, Bed Room, 12 by 12 feet; 17, Bed Room, 12 by 13 feet; 18, Bed Room, 11 by 16 feet.

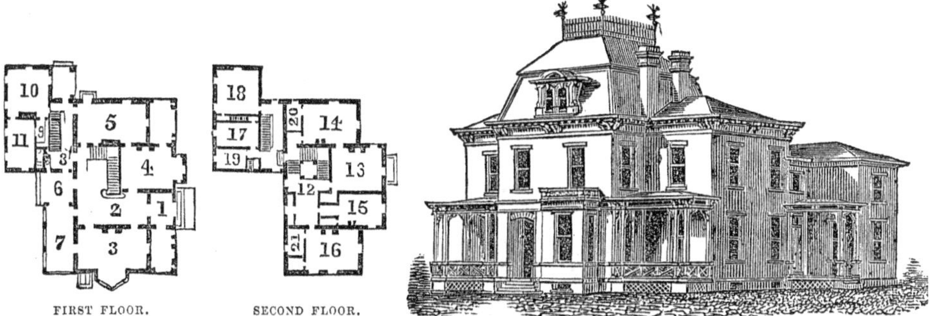

Residence of DR. JAS. TAYLOR, Belmont, Ky., opposite Cincinnati, O.

ARCHITECT, JAS. McLAUGHLIN, CINCINNATI, O.

First Floor.—1, Porch, 7 feet 5 inches by 9 feet 9 inches; 2, Hall, 10 feet wide; 3, Parlor, 15 by 24 feet; 4, Sitting Room, 15 by 18 feet; 5, Dining Room, 15 by 24 feet; 6, Porch, 10 feet 5 inches by 10 feet 5 inches; 7, Conservatory, 10 by 24 feet; 8, Back Stairs; 9, Store Room, 4 feet 6 in. by 10 feet; 10, Kitchen, 15 by 17 ft.; 11, Wash House, 10 by 17 ft.
Second Floor.—12, Hall; 13, Chamber, 15 by 18 feet; 14, Chamber, 15 by 18 feet; 15, Chamber, 10 feet 8 inches by 15 feet; 16, Chamber, 15 by 18 feet; 17, Servant's Bed Room, 10 by 15 feet; 18, Servant's Bed Room, 15 by 15 feet; 19, Bath Room, 6 feet 6 inches by 10 feet; 20 and 21, Dressing Rooms, 5 feet 6 inches by 10 feet.

Residence of EDWARD SARGENT, East Walnut Hills, Cincinnati, O.

ARCHITECT, WM. TINSLEY, CINCINNATI, O.

First Floor.—1, Vestibule; 2, Hall, 12 feet wide; 3, Parlor, 20 by 25 feet; 4, Library, 17 by 20 feet; 5, Family Room, 15 feet by 21 feet 6 inches; 6, Dining Room, 15 feet by 21 feet 6 inches; 7, Kitchen, 15 by 19 feet; 8, Laundry, 15 feet by 18 feet 8 inches; 9, Store Room, 11 feet 8 inches by 8 feet 9 inches.
Second Floor.—10, Bath Rooms, 10 feet 3 inches by 13 feet, and 7 feet by 11 feet 9 inches; 11, Bed Room, 17 by 20 feet; 12, Bed Room, 20 by 20 feet; 13, Bed Room, 12 by 13 feet; 14, Bed Room, 15 feet by 21 feet 6 inches; 15, Bed Room, 15 by 18 feet; 16, Bed Room, 11 by 15 feet; 17, Bed Room, 10 feet 3 inches by 11 feet 3 inches.

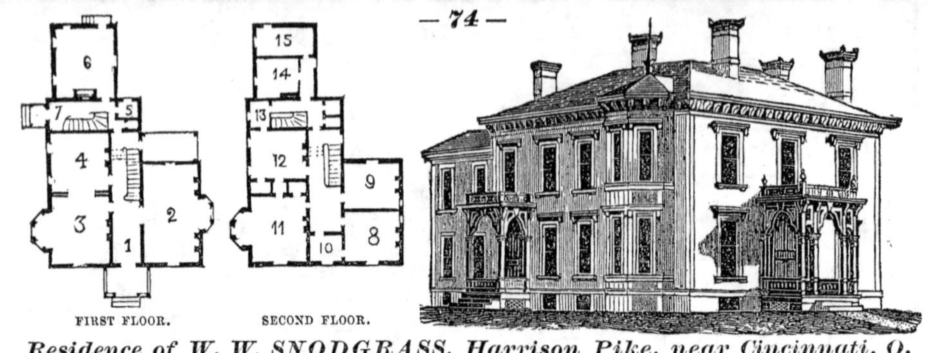

Residence of W. W. SNODGRASS, Harrison Pike, near Cincinnati, O.

ARCHITECT, I. B. YOUNG; BUILDERS, S. L. SNODGRASS & CO., CINCINNATI, O.

First Floor.—1, Hall, 7 feet 8 inches wide; 2, Parlor, 15 feet 2 inches by 25 feet; 3, Sitting Room, 15 feet by 15 feet 4 inches; 4, Dining Room, 15 feet 4 inches by 17 feet; 5, Store Room, 4 by 6 feet; 6, Kitchen, 15 feet 4 inches by 17 feet; 7, Rear Hall, 7 feet 4 inches wide.

Second Floor.—8, Chamber, 12 feet 3 inches by 15 feet 4 inches; 9, Chamber, 12 feet 3 inches by 15 feet 4 inches; 10, Dressing Room, 7 feet 8 inches by 9 feet; 11, Chamber, 15 feet 8 inches by 15 feet 4 inches; 12, Chamber, 14 feet by 15 feet 4 inches; 13, Bath Room, 7 feet 4 inches by 7 feet 6 inches; 14, Bed Room, 9 by 12 feet; 15, Bed Room, 8 by 15 feet.

Residence of JOHN SHILLITO, Mt. Auburn, Cincinnati, O.

ARCHITECT, JAS. McLAUGHLIN; BUILDER, TRUMAN B. HANDY, CINCINNATI, O.

1, Vestibule, 8 feet 6 inches by 11 feet; 2, Hall, 14 feet wide; 3, Grand Staircase, 26 feet 8 inches by 19 feet 6 inches; 4, Reception Room, 18 by 19 feet; 5, Drawing Room, 20 feet by 29 feet 6 inches; 6, Library, 18 by 18 feet; 7, Retiring Room, 8 by 8 feet; 8, Dining Room, 18 by 24 feet; 9, China Pantry, 8 feet 6 inches by 15 feet; 10 Store Room, 10 by 10 feet; 11, Breakfast Room, 16 by 20 feet; 12, Kitchen, 16 by 16 feet; 13, Verandah, 10 feet wide; 14, Verandah, 11 feet 6 inches by 21 feet. Kitchen and Laundry in Basement.

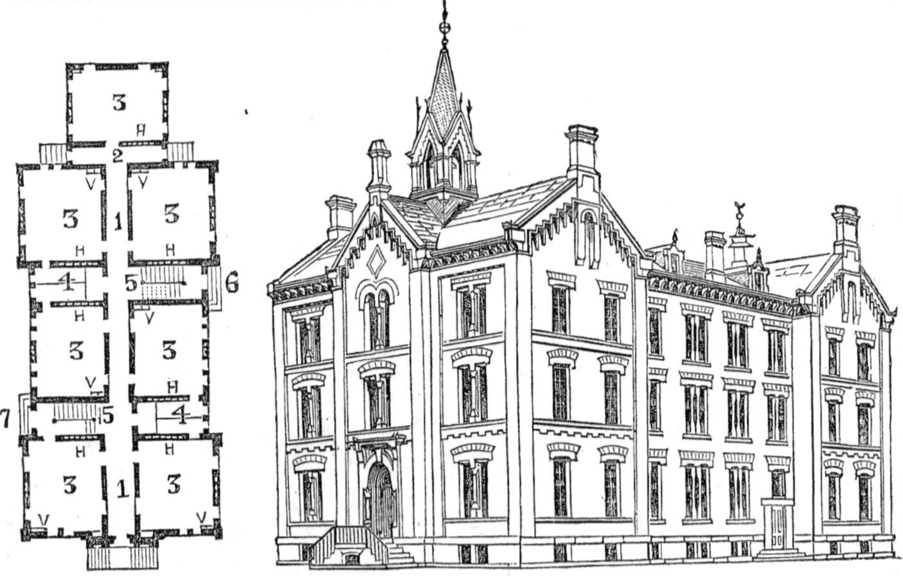

New School House, Findlay Street, Cincinnati, O.

ARCHITECT, I. B. YOUNG, CINCINNATI, O.

First Floor.—1, Main Corridor, 9 feet wide; 2, Rear Corridor to the Yards, 5 feet wide; 3, 3, 3, School Rooms, average 25 by 29 feet; 4, 4, 4, Wardrobes, average 5 by 10 feet; 5, 5, Stairways of Iron construction, 11 feet wide; 6, Boys' Entrance; 7, Girls' Entrance; H, H, H, Hot Air Flues; V, V, V, Ventilating Flues.

Second and Third Stories are similar to the First Story.

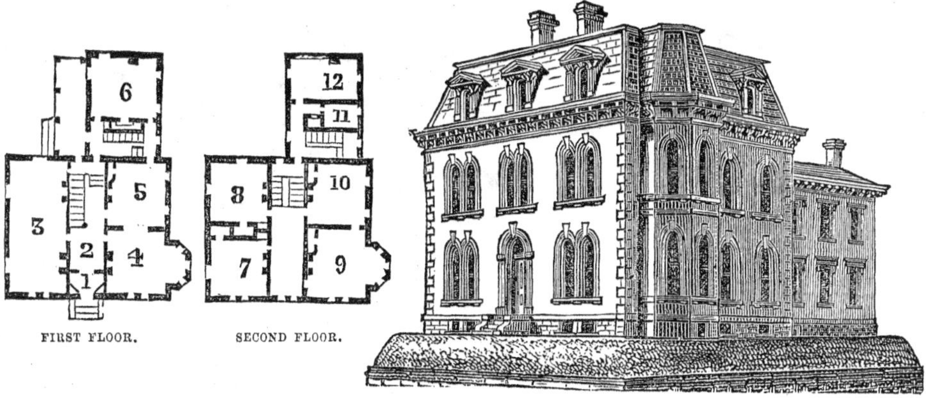

Residence of HENRY MARTIN, Mt. Auburn, Cincinnati, O.

ARCHITECT, F. M. MOORE, CINCINNATI; BUILDER, M. DOUGLASS, MT. AUBURN.

First Floor.—1, Vestibule, 8 feet 2 inches by 4 feet 4 inches; 2, Hall, 8 feet 6 inches wide; 3, Parlor, 15 feet 4 inches by 33 feet 1 inch; 4, Sitting Room, 15 feet 4 inches by 15 feet 4 inches; 5, Dining Room, 15 feet 4 inches by 16 feet 8 inches; 6, Kitchen, 14 feet 11 inches by 18 feet.

Second Floor.—7, Chamber, 15 feet 4 inches by 15 feet; 8, Chamber, 15 feet 4 inches by 14 feet 6 inches; 9, Chamber, 15 feet 4 inches by 16 feet 3½ inches; 10, Chamber, 15 feet 4 inches by 16 feet 3½ inches; 11, Bath Room, 7 feet 6 inches by 10 feet; 12, Servant's Room, 10 by 18 feet.

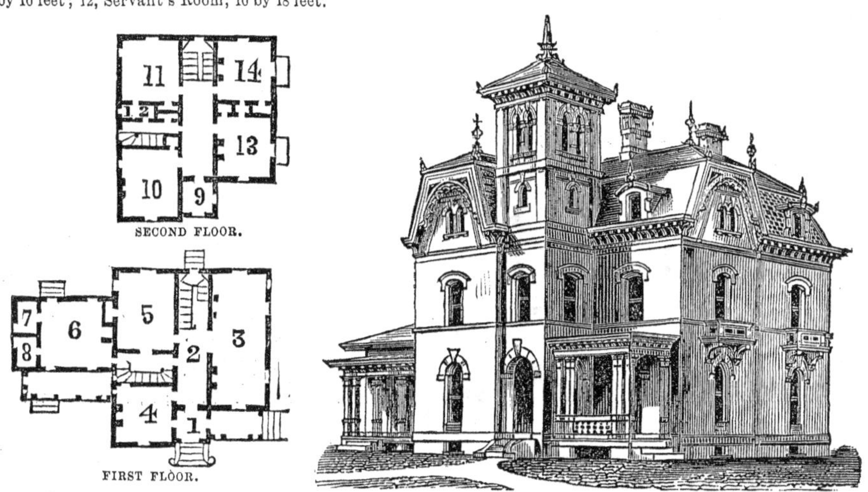

Residence of JOHN R. DAVEY, College Hill, near Cincinnati, O.

ARCHITECTS, ANDERSON & HANNAFORD, CINCINNATI, O.

First Floor.—1, Tower Porch, 7 feet 8 inches by 7 feet 8 inches; 2, Hall, 8 by 34 feet; 3, Parlor, 14 feet 6 inches by 34 feet; 4, Sitting Room, 14 feet 6 inches by 16 feet; 5, Dining Room, 14 feet 6 inches by 20 feet; 6, Kitchen, 17 by 18 feet; 7, Pantry, 5 feet by 8 feet 3 inches; 8, Store Room, 5 feet by 8 feet 3 inches.

Second Floor.—9, Tower Room, 7 feet 8 inches by 7 feet 8 inches; 10, Chamber, 14 feet 6 inches by 16 feet; 11, Chamber, 14 feet 6 inches by 14 feet 6 inches; 12, Bath Room, 5 by 9 feet; 13, Chamber, 14 feet 6 inches by 15 feet; 14, Chamber, 14 feet 6 inches by 15 feet.

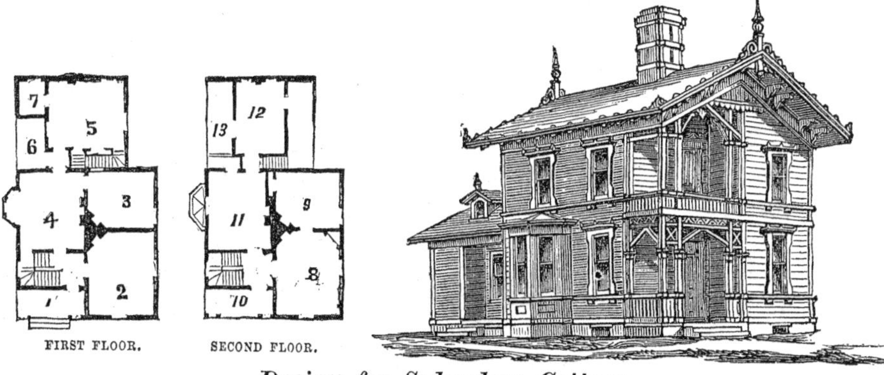

Design for Suburban Cottage.

ARCHITECTS, ANDERSON & HANNAFORD, CINCINNATI, O.

First Floor.—1, Verandah; 2, Parlor, 13 by 16 feet; 3, Bed Room, 11 by 13 feet; 4, Living Room, 13 by 15 feet; 5, Kitchen, 13 by 15 feet; 6, Back Porch, 6 feet 6 inches wide; 7, Pantry, 5 feet by 6 feet 6 inches.

Second Floor.—8, Chamber, 13 by 16 feet; 9, Chamber, 11 by 13 feet; 10, Balcony; 11, Chamber, 13 by 15 feet; 12, Chamber, 10 by 14 feet; 13, Roof.

Residence of FRANK WILSON, Mt. Auburn, Cincinnati, O.

ARCHITECT AND BUILDER, M. DOUGLASS, MT. AUBURN, CINCINNATI, O.

First Floor.—1, Hall, 8 feet wide; 2, Parlor, 15 by 22 feet; 3, Library, 15 by 17 feet; 4, Dining Room, 15 by 18 feet; 5, Kitchen, 14 feet 6 inches by 15 feet; 6, Store Room, 6 by 7 feet.

Second Floor.—7, Chamber, 15 by 17 feet; 8, Chamber, 15 by 17 feet; 9, Linen Closet, 5 by 11 feet; 10, Chamber, 15 by 18 feet; 11, Chamber, 12 by 12 feet; 12, Bath Room, 5 by 12 feet.

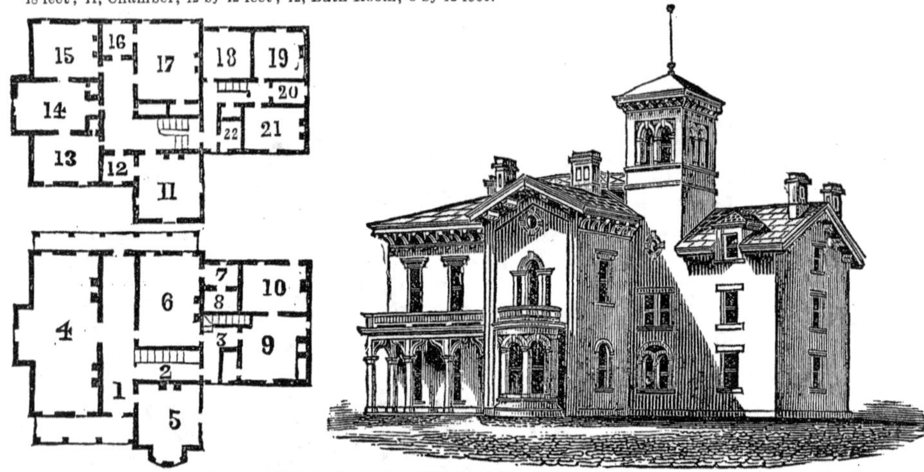

Residence of JETHRO MITCHELL, Mt. Auburn, Cincinnati, O.

First Floor.—1, Hall, 8 by 40 feet; 2, Stairway, 8 by 17 feet; 3, Back Stairs; 4, Parlor, 17 by 40 feet; 5, Sitting Room, 16 by 17 feet; 6, Dining Room, 17 by 22 feet; 7, Pantry, 6 by 9 feet; 8, Store Room, 6 by 9 feet; 9, Kitchen, 17 by 17 feet; 10, Back Kitchen, 12 by 17 feet.

Second Floor.—11, Chamber, 16 by 17 feet; 12, Dressing Room, 8 by 8 feet; 13, Chamber, 13 by 17 feet; 14, Chamber, 13 by 17 feet; 15, Chamber, 13 by 17 feet; 16, Bath Room, 8 by 9 feet; 17, Chamber, 17 feet by 17 feet 6 inches; 18, Chamber, 12 by 13 feet; 19, Chamber, 12 by 13 feet; 20, Bath Room, 5 feet 6 inches by 8 feet 6 inches; 21, Chamber, 11 by 17 feet; 22, Linen Closet, 4 by 6 feet.

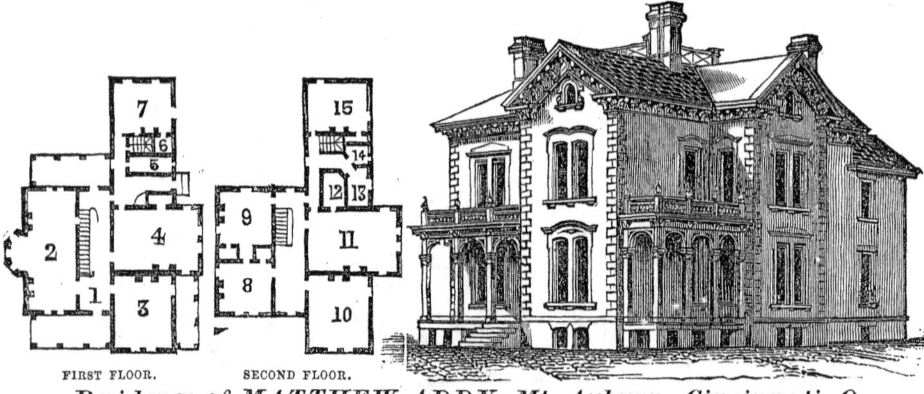

Residence of MATTHEW ADDY, Mt. Auburn, Cincinnati, O.

ARCHITECT AND BUILDER, M. DOUGLASS, MT. AUBURN, CINCINNATI, O.

First Floor.—1, Hall, 8 by 30 feet; 2, Parlor, 15 by 30 feet; 3, Sitting Room, 15 by 18 feet; 4, Dining Room, 15 by 22 feet; 5, Store Room, 5 feet by 11 feet 6 inches; 6, Pantry, 5 feet by 5 feet 6 inches; 7, Kitchen, 14 by 15 feet.

Second Floor.—8, Chamber, 15 feet by 13 feet 6 inches; 9, Chamber, 15 feet by 13 feet 6 inches; 10, Chamber, 15 by 18 feet; 11, Chamber, 15 by 22 feet; 12, Closet, 5 feet 6 inches by 7 feet 6 inches; 13, Bath Room, 9 feet by 5 feet 6 inches; 14, Water Closet, 5 feet by 5 feet 6 inches; 15, Chamber, 14 by 15 feet.

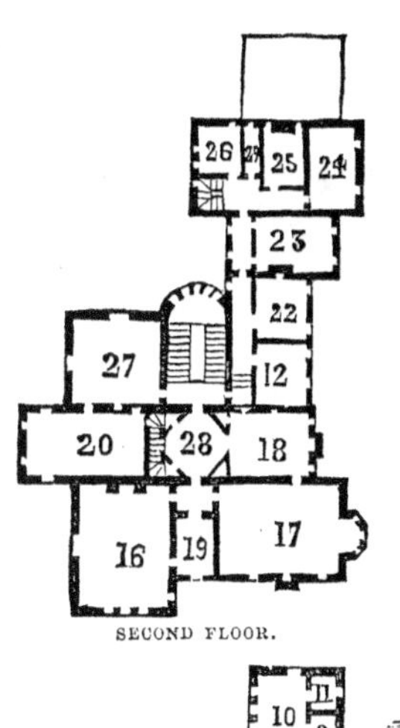
SECOND FLOOR.

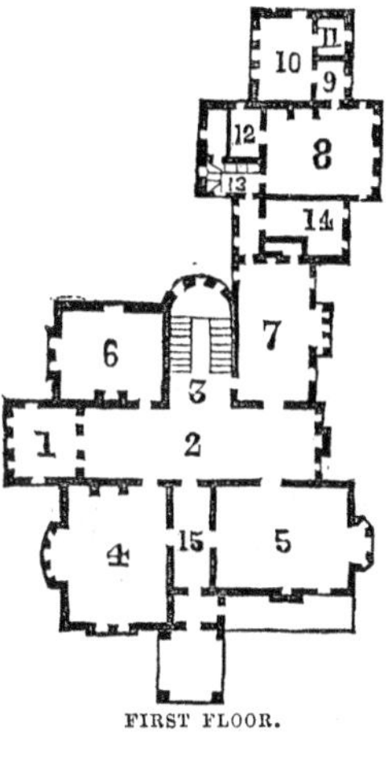
FIRST FLOOR.

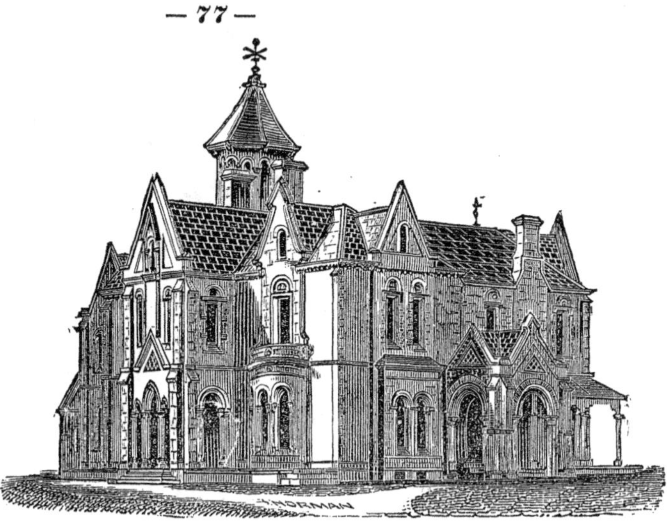

Residence of HENRY PROBASCO, Clifton, near Cincinnati, O.

ARCHITECT, WM. TINSLEY, CINCINNATI, O.

First Floor.—1, Vestibule, 15 by 15 feet; 2, Hall, 15 feet by 47 feet 6 inches; 3, Staircase, 14 feet by 24 feet 6 inches; 4, Parlor, 21 by 28 feet; 5, Library, 21 by 28 feet; 6, Reception Room, 18 by 20 feet; 7, Dining Room, 16 by 27 feet; 8, Kitchen, 18 feet by 21 feet 6 inches; 9, Scullery; 10, Scullery; 11, Store Room; 12, Store Room; 13, Back Stairs; 14, China Closet; 15, Side Hall, 8 feet wide.

Second Floor.—16, Chamber, 21 by 28 feet; 17, Chamber, 21 by 28 feet; 18, Bed Room, 15 feet by 18 feet 6 inches; 19, Dressing Room, 9 feet 4 inches by 14 feet 4 inches; 20, Bed Room, 15 by 24 feet; 21, Bed Room, 11 feet 6 inches by 12 feet 6 inches; 22, Bed Room, 11 feet 6 inches by 14 feet; 23, Bed Room, 14 feet 6 inches by 18 feet 8 inches; 24, Bed Room, 10 feet 6 inches by 18 feet; 25, Bed Room, 11 by 13 feet; 26, Bath Room, 9 feet 4 inches by 10 feet; 27, Chamber, 18 by 20 feet; 28, Rotunda, 14 by 14 feet; 29, Water Closets.

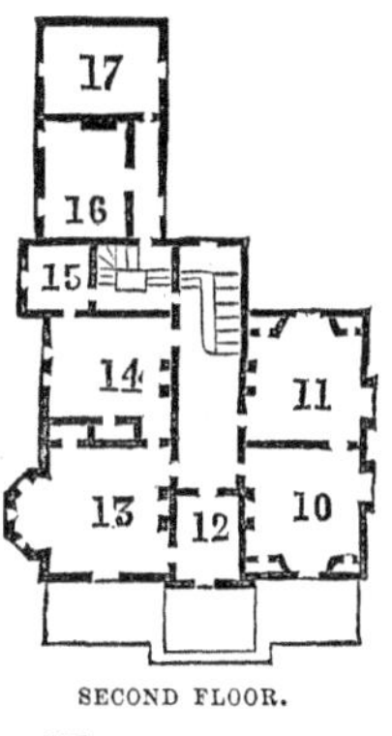
SECOND FLOOR.

FIRST FLOOR.

Residence of RICHARD SMITH, Clifton, near Cincinnati, O.

ARCHITECT, J. K. WILSON, CINCINNATI, O.
CONTRACTORS AND BUILDERS, HOLZINGER & EDWARDS.

First Floor.—1, Verandah, 8 by 40 feet; 2, Hall, 8 feet wide; 3, Parlor, 32 feet 9 inches by 15 feet 6 inches; 4, Library, 15 feet by 15 feet 6 inches; 5, Dining Room, 15 feet 6 inches by 16 feet 9 inches; 6, China Closet, 8 feet 6 inches by 9 feet; 7, Back Stairs, 8 feet 6 inches by 9 feet 11 inches; 8, Kitchen, 15 feet by 15 feet 8 inches; 9, Laundry, 12 feet 3 inches by 15 feet 8 inches.

Second Floor.—10, Chamber, 14 feet 2 inches by 15 feet 6 inches; 11, Chamber, 14 feet 2 inches by 15 feet 6 inches; 12, Sewing Room, 8 feet 6 inches by 11 feet; 13, Chamber, 15 feet 6 inches by 17 feet; 14, Chamber, 13 feet 3 inches by 15 feet 6 inches; 15, Bath Room, 8 feet 6 inches by 9 feet; 16, Servant's Room, 11 feet 8 inches by 15 feet; 17, Servant's Room, 12 feet 3 inches by 15 feet 8 inches.

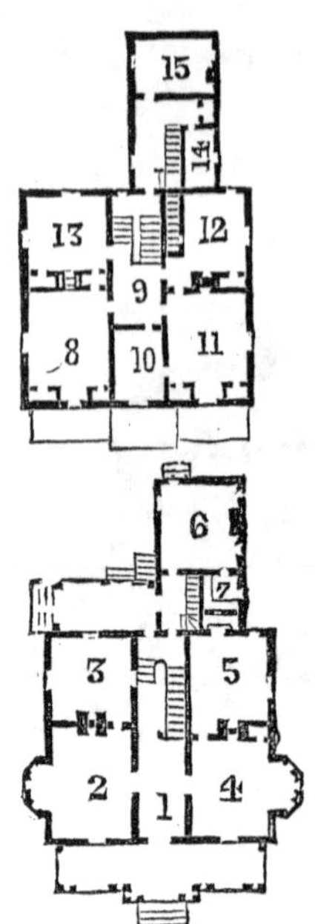

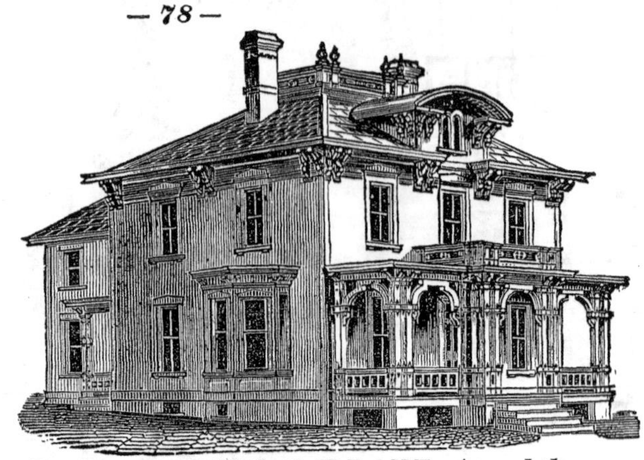

Residence of WM. TALLANT, Avondale, near Cincinnati, O.

ARCHITECT, I. B. YOUNG, CINCINNATI, O.

First Floor.—1, Hall, 8 by 35 feet; 2, Parlor, 15 by 20 feet; 3, Library, 14 feet 4 inches by 15 feet; 4, Sitting Room, 15 by 17 feet; 5, Dining Room, 15 by 20 feet; 6, Kitchen, 14 by 16 feet; 7, Pantry and China Closet, 6 by 9 feet.

Second Floor.—8, Chamber, 15 feet by 16 feet 6 inches; 9, Chamber Hall, 8 by 23 feet; 10, Chamber, 8 by 11 feet; 11, Chamber, 15 by 15 feet; 12, Chamber, 12 by 15 feet; 13, Chamber, 15 feet by 13 feet 6 inches; 14, Bath Room, 6 feet 6 inches by 8 feet; 15, Servant's Room, 12 by 14 feet.

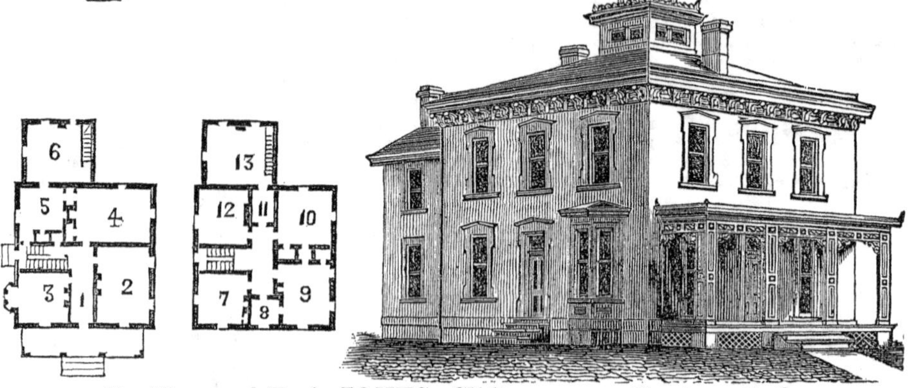

Residence of T. A. JONES, Clifton, near Cincinnati, O.

BUILDERS, THOMPSON & ARTEMUS SMITH, CINCINNATI, O.

First Floor.—1, Hall, 5 feet 6 inches by 20 feet 2 inches; 2, Parlor, 14 feet 2 inches by 20 feet 2 inches; 3, Library, 14 feet 2 inches by 13 feet 8 inches; 4, Dining Room, 14 feet 2 inches by 19 feet 4 inches; 5, Sitting Room, 12 feet 9 inches by 14 feet 2 inches; 6, Kitchen, 15 feet 6 inches by 15 feet 6 inches.

Second Floor.—7, Chamber, 13 feet 8 inches by 14 feet 2 inches; 8, Dressing Room, 6 feet 4 inches by 9 feet; 9, Chamber, 14 feet 8 inches by 17 feet 5 inches; 10, Chamber, 14 feet 8 inches by 14 feet 2 inches; 11, Hall, 5 feet wide; 12, Chamber, 14 feet 2 inches by 14 feet 2 inches; 13, Chamber, 15 feet 6 inches by 15 feet 6 inches.

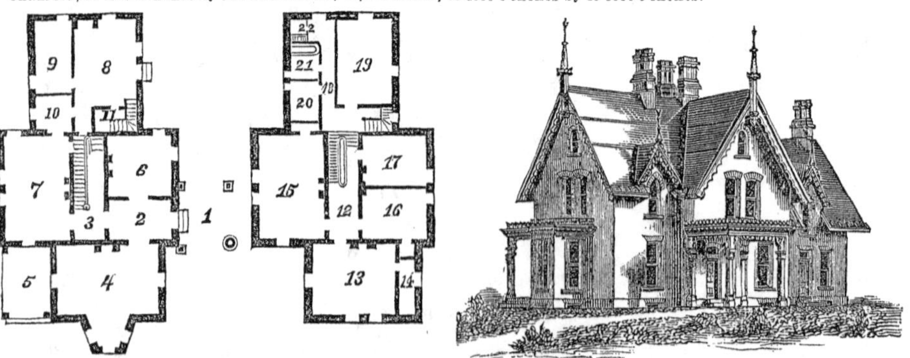

Residence of JOHN CINNAMON, East Walnut Hills, Cincinnati, O.

ARCHITECTS, WALTER & STEWART, CINCINNATI, O.

First Floor.—1, Carriage Porch, 12 feet by 14 feet 6 inches; 2, Hall, 8 feet 6 inches by 14 feet 3 inches; 3, Stair Hall, 6 feet 6 inches by 22 feet; 4, Parlor, 15 by 22 feet; 5, Porch, 11 feet 6 inches by 15 feet; 6, Reception Room, 13 feet by 14 feet 3 inches; 7, Dining Room, 14 feet 3 inches by 22 feet; 8, Kitchen, 13 feet 9 inches by 17 feet 9 inches; 9 Store Room, 7 feet 9 inches by 14 feet 9 inches; 10, Pantry, 7 feet 9 inches by 8 feet; 11, Closet, 5 feet by 9 feet 3 inches.

Second Floor.—12, Hall; 13, Bed Room, 15 by 18 feet; 14, Closet, 3 feet 6 inches by 9 feet 6 inches; 15, Bed Room, 14 feet 3 inches by 22 feet; 16, Bed Room, 10 feet 9 inches by 14 feet 3 inches; 17, Bed Room, 10 feet 9 inches by 14 feet 3 inches; 18, Passage, 3 feet; 19, Bed Room, 11 feet 9 inches by 17 feet 9 inches; 20, Linen Closet, 6 feet 3 inches by 8 feet; 21, Bath Room, 6 feet 3 inches by 6 feet 6 inches; 22, Water Closets, 5 feet 3 inches by 4 feet.

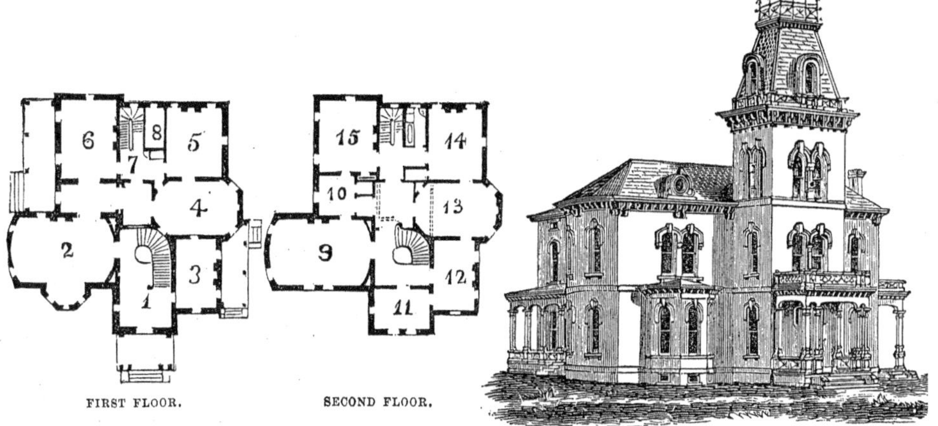

Residence of GEO. M. HORD, East Walnut Hills, Cincinnati, O.

ARCHITECTS, WALTER & STEWART, CINCINNATI, O.

First Floor.—1, Hall, 14 feet 1 inch wide; 2, Parlor, 16 feet 9 inches by 25 feet 6 inches; 3, Library, 11 feet 2 inches by 17 feet 9 inches; 4, Dining Room, 14 feet by 22 feet 9 inches; 5, Breakfast Room, 14 feet 2 inches by 16 feet 2 inches; 6, Winter Parlor, 15 feet by 19 feet 7 inches; 7, Back Hall and Stairs; 8, Store Room, 5 by 9 feet.

Second Floor.—9, Bed Room, 16 feet 7 inches by 25 feet 6 inches; 10, Boudoir, 9 feet 8 inches by 11 feet; 11, Bed Room, 12 feet by 14 feet 1 inch; 12, Bed Room, 11 feet 2 inches by 18 feet 2 inches; 13, Bed Room, 13 feet 5 inches by 18 feet 3 inches; 14, Bed Room, 14 feet 2 inches by 17 feet 3 inches; 15, Bed Room, 15 by 17 feet.

Servants' Rooms, Laundry, and Kitchen in Basement.

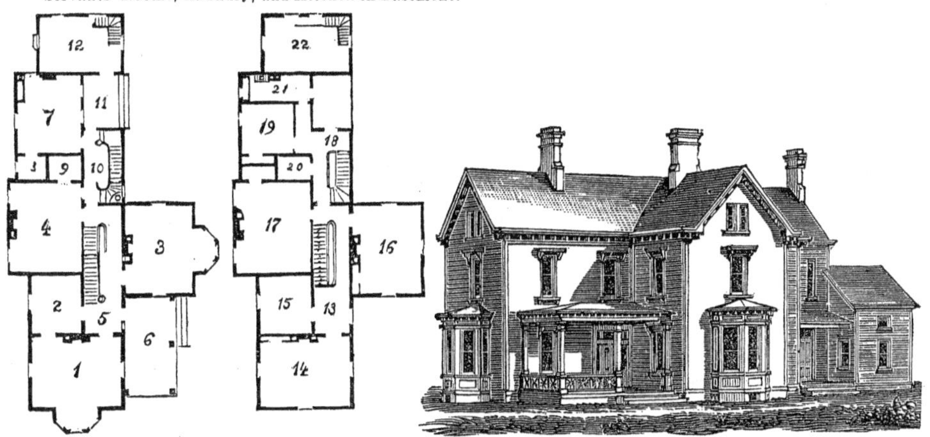

Residence of ISAAC BETTS, College Hill, near Cincinnati, O.

ARCHITECTS, WALTER & STEWART, CINCINNATI, O.

First Floor.—1, Parlor, 15 by 19 feet; 2, Library, 10 feet 6 inches by 12 feet; 3, Sitting Room, 15 by 19 feet; 4, Dining Room, 15 by 19 feet; 5, Hall, 8 by 27 feet; 6, Porch, 11 feet 2 inches by 23 feet 6 inches; 7, Kitchen, 14 by 16 feet; 8, Pantry, 5 feet by 6 feet 9 inches; 9, China Closet, 5 feet by 6 feet 9 inches; 10, Back Stair Hall, 8 by 14 feet; 11, Rear Porch, 8 feet 6 inches by 11 feet 6 inches; 12, Laundry, 12 by 18 feet.

Second Floor.—13, Hall, 8 by 27 feet; 14, Bed Room, 15 by 19 feet; 15, Bed Room, 10 feet 6 inches by 12 feet; 16, Bed Room, 15 feet by 19 feet; 17, Bed Room, 15 by 19 feet; 18, Rear Hall, 8 by 14 feet; 19, Girl's Room, 10 feet 6 inches by 10 feet; 20, Linen Closet, 5 feet by 6 feet 9 inches; 21, Bath Room, 5 feet 6 inches by 14 feet; 22, Man's Room, 12 by 18 ft.

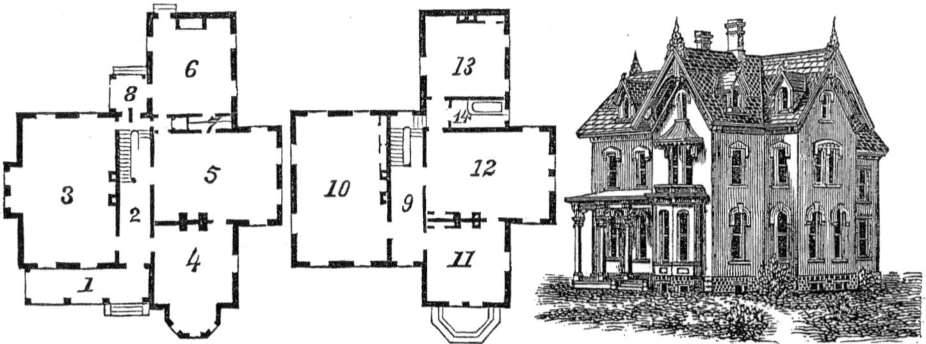

Residence to be built near Cincinnati, O.

First Floor.—1, Porch, 6 by 21 feet; 2, Hall, 6 by 24 feet; 3, Parlor, 16 by 24 feet; 4, Sitting Room, 13 feet 6 inches by 13 feet 6 inches; 5, Dining Room, 16 by 22 feet; 6, Kitchen, 13 feet 6 inches by 15 feet; 7, Closet, 8 feet by 6 feet 6 inches; 8, Porch, 7 by 7 feet.

Second Floor.—9, Hall, 6 by 24 feet; 10, Chamber, 16 by 24 feet; 11, Chamber, 13 feet 6 inches by 13 feet 6 inches; 12, Chamber, 16 by 22 feet; 13, Chamber, 12 feet 6 inches by 13 feet 6 inches; 14, Bath Room, 5 feet 6 inches by 9 feet.

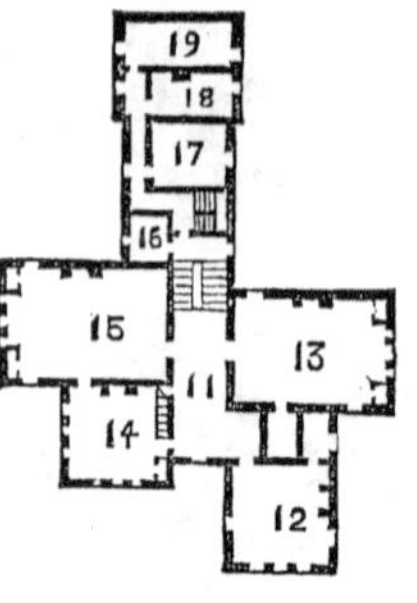
SECOND FLOOR.

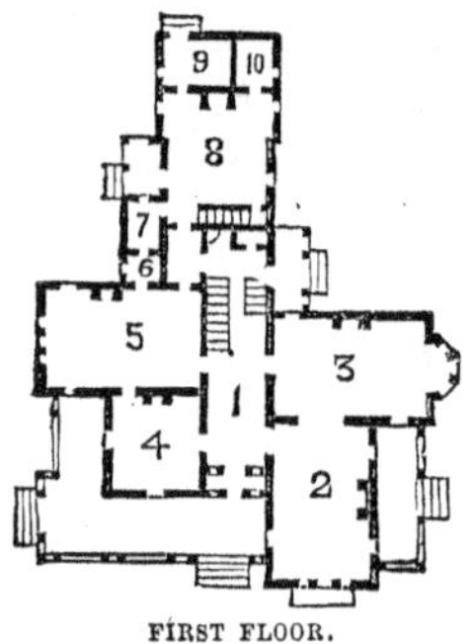
FIRST FLOOR.

Design for an Italian Villa.

ARCHITECT, I. B. YOUNG, CINCINNATI, OHIO.

First Floor.—1, Hall, 11 by 34 feet; 2, Parlor, 16 feet 8 inches by 25 feet; 3, Library, 16 feet 8 inches by 25 feet; 4, Sitting Room, 15 by 15 feet; 5, Dining Room, 16 feet 8 inches by 25 feet; 6, China Closet, 5 by 6 feet; 7, Pantry, 6 by 8 feet; 8, Kitchen, 16 feet by 16 feet 6 inches; 9, Wash Room, 11 by 10 feet; 10, Store Room, 5 by 10 feet.

Second Floor.—11, Chamber Hall, 11 by 34 feet; 12, Chamber, 16 feet 8 inches by 18 feet; 13, Chamber, 16 feet 8 inches by 22 feet; 14, Chamber, 12 by 15 feet; 15, Chamber, 16 feet 8 inches by 22 feet; 16, Bath Room, 6 by 9 feet; 17, Servant's Chamber, 10 by 13 feet; 18, Servant's Chamber, 9 by 13 feet; 19, Servant's Chamber, 9 by 17 feet.

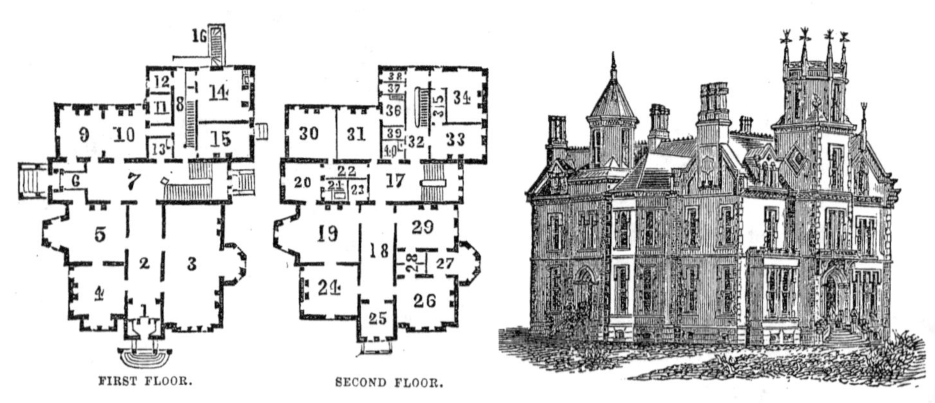
FIRST FLOOR. SECOND FLOOR.

Residence of AMOS SHINKLE, Covington, Ky.

ARCHITECTS, WALTER & STEWART, CINCINNATI, O.

First Floor.—1, Vestibule, 5 feet 8 inches by 11 feet 2 inches; 2, Hall, 12 feet by 31 feet 6 inches; 3, Saloon Parlor, 20 by 40 feet; 4, Library, 18 by 18 feet; 5, Family Room, 18 by 20 feet; 6, Vestibule, 5 feet 6 inches by 8 feet; 7, Hall, 12 by 50 feet; 8, Back Stairs and Hall, 7 feet 6 inches by 29 feet 6 inches; 9, Breakfast Room, 16 by 16 feet; 10, Dining Room, 16 by 16 feet; 11, General Pantry, 9 feet 7 inches by 8 feet; 12, Store Room, 7 feet 6 inches by 8 feet; 13, Safe Room, 6 feet 10 inches by 7 feet 9 inches; 14, Kitchen, 17 by 17 feet; 15, Servant's Room, 12 by 17 feet; 16, Cellar Steps, 3 feet 4 inches wide.

Second Floor.—17, Hall, 12 by 33 feet; 18, Hall, 12 feet by 31 feet 6 inches; 19, Bed Room, 18 by 20 feet; 20, Dressing Room, 11 feet 2 inches by 11 feet 2 inches; 21, Bath Room, 7 feet 4 inches by 9 feet; 22, Hall, 4 feet by 15 feet 6 inches; 23, Closet, 7 feet by 7 feet 4 inches; 24, Bed Room, 18 by 18 feet; 25, Bed Room, 11 feet 2 inches by 11 feet 2 inches; 26, Parlor, 15 by 20 feet; 27, Alcove, 9 feet by 9 feet 9 inches; 28, Closet, 4 feet 8 inches by 9 feet 9 inches; 29, Bed Room, 15 by 20 feet; 30, Bed Room, 16 feet by 16 feet 3 inches; 31, Bed Room, 16 feet by 16 feet 3 inches; 32, Hall, 7 feet 6 inches by 29 feet 6 inches; 33, Bed Room, 12 by 17 feet; 34, Bed Room, 11 feet 4 inches by 17 feet; 35, Closets, 5 feet 4 inches by 5 feet 7 inches; 36, Dressing Room, 8 feet by 8 feet 4 inches; 37, Bath Room, 5 feet 10 inches by 8 feet; 38, Water Closet, 3 feet 6 inches by 8 feet; 39, Closet, 4 by 8 feet; 40, Linen Closet, 6 feet 10 inches by 8 feet; O, Hoister, 2 feet by 3 feet 6 inches.

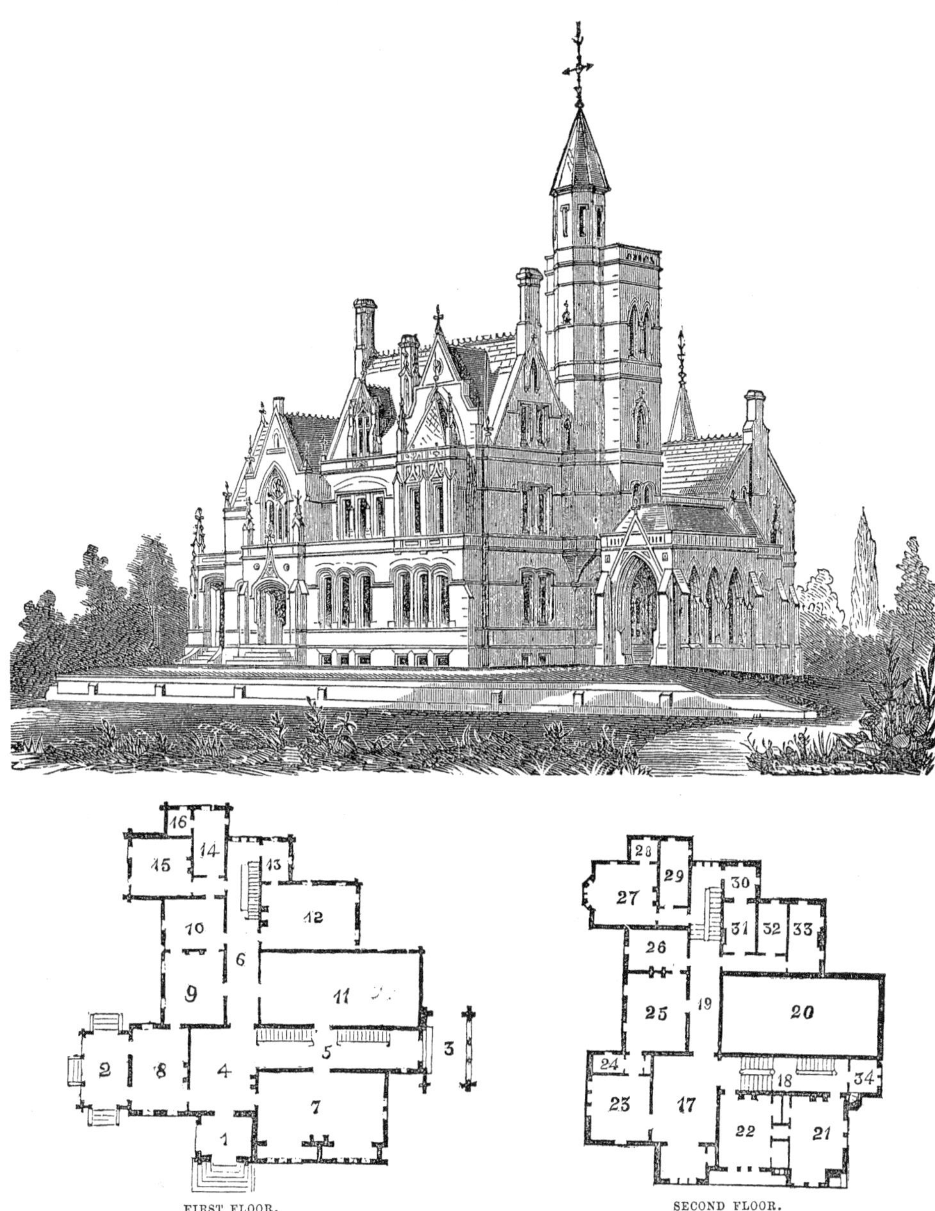

Residence of GEO. K. SHOENBERGER, Clifton, near Cincinnati, O.

ARCHITECT, J. K. WILSON, CINCINNATI, O.

First Floor.—1, Porch, 11 feet 6 by 18 feet; 2, Porch, 15 by 26 feet; 3, Porch, 16 feet by 23 feet 6 inches; 4, Main Hall, 20 by 26 feet; 5, Hall and Stairway, 51 feet 6 inches by 10 feet; 6, Hall and Back Stairs, 56 feet 10 inches by 10 feet; 7, Parlor, 26 feet 11 inches by 40 feet 2 inches; 8, Library, 18 feet 4 inches by 26 feet 6 inches; 9, Dining Room, 17 feet 11 inches by 24 feet; 10, Pantry, 17 feet 11 inches by 13 feet; 11, Picture Gallery, 25 feet 1 inch by 50 feet 5 inches; 12, Billiard Room, 20 feet by 30 feet 5 inches; 13, Bath Room and Water Closet, 9 feet 11 inches by 9 feet; 14, Dressing Room, 9 feet 6 inches by 17 feet 6 inches; 15, Chamber, 18 feet by 18 feet 5 inches; 16, Pantry, 6 by 8 feet.

Second Floor.—17, Hall, 20 by 38 feet; 18, Hall & Stairway, 10 by 40 feet; 19, Hall & Back Stairs, 10 ft. by 56 ft. 10 in.; 20, Picture Gallery continued; 21, Chamber, 18 feet by 26 feet 8 inches; 22, Chamber, 16 by 22 feet; 23, Chamber, 18 feet 4 inches by 21 feet; 24, Bath Room, 5 feet by 10 feet 6 inches; 25, Chamber, 17 feet 11 inches by 24 feet; 26, Chamber, 17 feet 11 inches by 13 feet; 27, Chamber, 18 feet by 18 feet 5 inches; 28, Bath Room, 6 feet 4 inches by 7 feet 10 inches; 29, Dressing Room, 9 feet 6 inches by 17 feet 6 inches; 30, Linen Closet, 8 feet 8 inches by 9 feet 8 inches; 31, Servant's Room, 9 feet 8 inches by 14 feet 6 inches; 32, Servant's Room, 9 feet 8 inches by 14 feet 6 inches; 33, Servant's Room, 10 feet 1 inch by 20 feet; 34, Bath Room, 9 feet 4 inches by 10 feet.

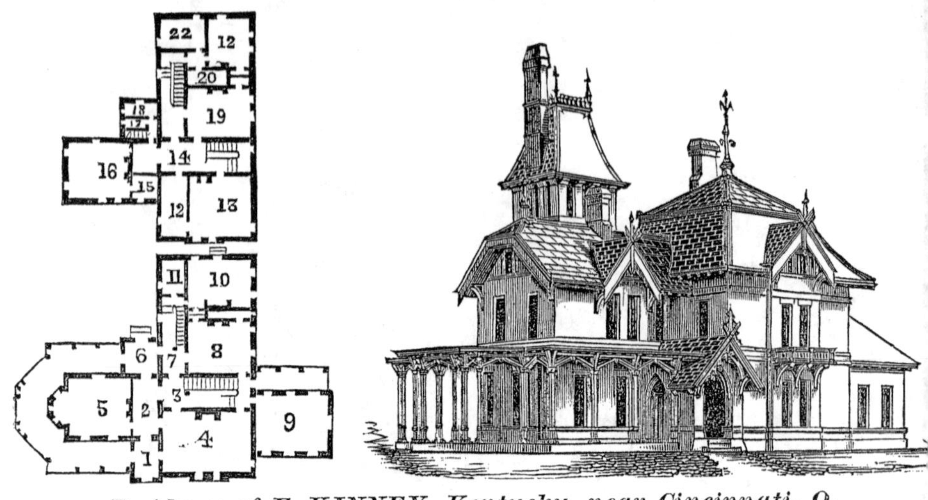

Residence of E. KINNEY, Kentucky, near Cincinnati, O.

ARCHITECT, J. K. WILSON, CINCINNATI, O.

First Floor.—1, Vestibule, 8 feet by 11 feet 6 inches; 2, Hall, 8 by 17 feet; 3, Stairway and Main Hall, 10 by 28 feet; 4, Parlor, 18 feet 28 feet; 5, Library, 17 by 20 feet; 6, Tower, 10 feet 6 inches by 10 feet 6 inches; 7, Rear Hall and Stairway, 7 feet by 25 feet 6 inches; 8, Dining Room, 16 feet 3 inches by 20 feet; 9, Billiard Room, 17 by 22 feet; 10, Kitchen, 15 by 20 feet; 11, Store Room, 7 feet by 10 feet 6 inches.

Second Floor.—12, Bed Room, 8 feet 6 inches by 18 feet; 13, Chamber, 18 by 19 feet; 14, Main Hall and Stairway, 10 by 28 feet; 15, Closet, 8 feet by 6 feet 6 inches; 16, Chamber, 17 by 20 feet; 17, Water Closet, 3 feet 8 inches by 6 feet 4 inches; 18, Bath Room, 4 feet 9 inches by 10 feet 3 inches; 19, Chamber, 16 feet 3 inches by 20 feet; 20, Linen Closet, 4 feet by 12 feet 6 inches; 21, Bed Room, 13 feet 6 inches by 15 feet; 22, Bed Room, 10 feet 6 inches by 13 feet 6 inches.

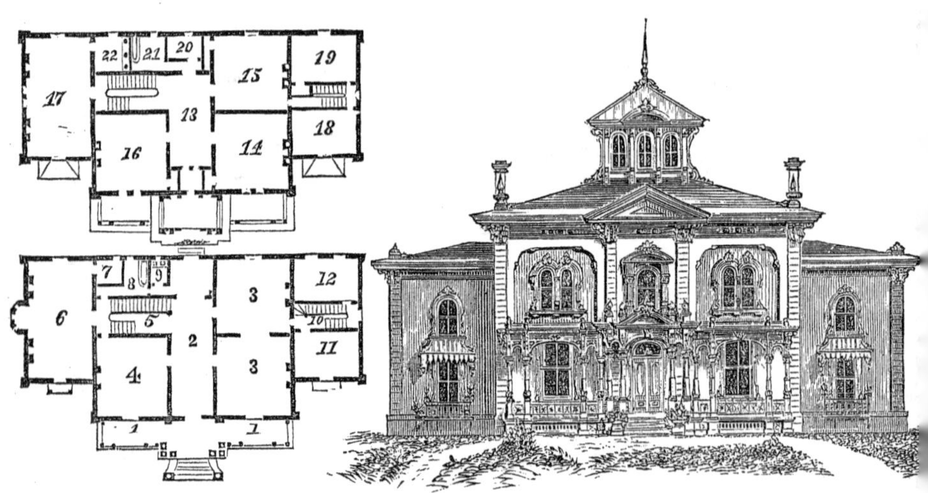

Residence of JASON EVANS, Mt. Auburn, Cincinnati, O.

ARCHITECT AND BUILDER, W. H. STEWART, CINCINNATI, O.

First Floor.—1, Verandah, 7 by 48 feet; 2, Hall, 11 by 39 feet; 3, Parlor, 18 feet 6 inches by 39 feet; 4, Family Room, 18 feet 6 inches by 19 feet 6 inches; 5, Stair Hall, 9 feet by 19 feet 3 inches; 6, Dining Room, 17 feet 6 inches by 29 feet 6 inches; 7, Closet, 7 by 6 feet; 8, Bath Room, 6 feet by 9 feet 6 inches; 9, Water Closet, 4 by 6 feet; 10, Stair Hall, 7 feet by 17 feet 6 inches; 11, Library, 10 feet 6 inches by 17 feet 6 inches; 12, Sitting Room, 10 feet 6 inches by 17 feet 6 inches.

Second Floor.—13, Hall, 11 feet wide; 14, Chamber, 18 feet 3 inches by 18 feet 6 inches; 15, Chamber, 18 feet 3 inches by 18 feet 6 inches; 16, Chamber, 18 feet 6 inches by 19 feet 6 inches; 17, Billiard Room, 17 feet 6 inches by 29 feet 6 inches; 18, Chamber, 10 feet 6 inches by 17 feet 6 inches; 19, Chamber, 10 feet 6 inches by 17 feet 6 inches; 20, Linen Closet, 6 feet by 8 feet 6 inches; 21, Bath Room, 8 feet 6 inches by 9 feet 6 inches; 22, Lavatory, 9 feet 6 inches by 9 feet 6 inches.

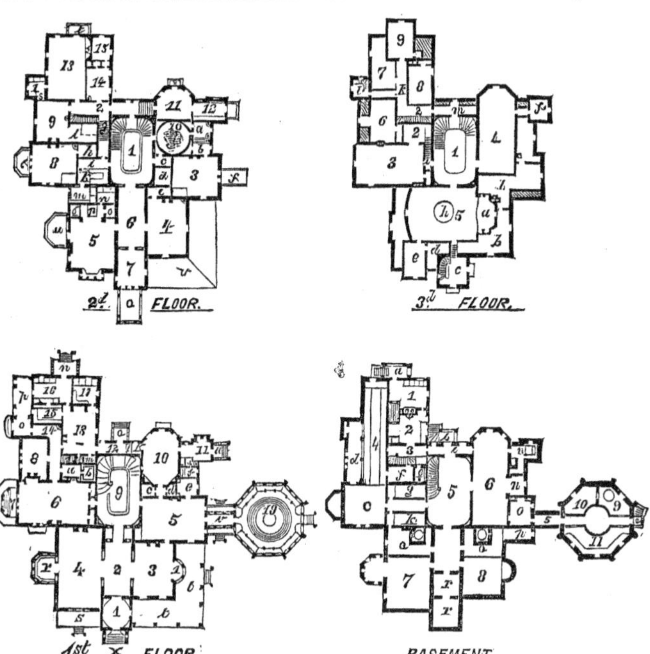

Design for the Residence of ELIAS HOWE, JR., Bridgeport, Ct.

ARCHITECT, A. C. NASH, CINCINNATI, O.

BASEMENT.—1, Wash Room, 11 feet by 15 feet 6 inches; 2, Laundry, 13 feet by 15 feet 6 inches; 3, Back Stairs, 7 feet 6 inches by 16 feet; 4, Bowling Court, 11 by 45 feet; 5, Main Staircase, 20 by 30 feet; 6, Supper Room, 16 feet by 40 feet 6 inches; 7, Light Cellar, 19 feet 6 inches by 23 feet 6 inches; 8, Dark Cellar, 17 feet by 17 feet 6 inches; 9, Heating Room; 10, Coal Room; 11, Potting Room, shelves and benches; a, b, c, Area and Outside Doors; d, Arcade for Seats, 5 feet by 26 feet 6 inches; e, Ante-room, 17 feet by 18 feet 6 inches; f, Coal, 7 by 10 feet; g, Coal for Bowling Court, 5 by 16 feet; i, Water Closet, 3 feet 6 inches by 6 feet 6 inches; k, Coal for Furnaces, 6 by 16 feet; p, Coal for Furnaces, 5 by 14 feet; l, Passage, 4 feet 6 inches by 20 feet; m, Waiters' Room, 6 feet 6 inches by 13 feet 6 inches; n, Side Board, 7 feet 6 inches by 10 feet; o, Wine Room, 10 feet 6 inches by 11 feet; q, Furnace Room, 11 by 18 feet; r, Wine Cellars, 11 by 11 feet.

FIRST FLOOR.—1, Vestibule, 12 by 12 feet; 2, Hall, 12 by 24 feet; 3, Reception Room, 18 by 24 feet; 4, Drawing Room, 20 by 36 feet; 5, Family Parlor, 18 by 28 feet; 6, Dining Hall, 18 by 34 feet; 7, Bay Window, 7 by 11 feet; 8, Smoking Room, 12 by 17 feet; 9, Staircase and Art Gallery, 20 by 30 feet; 10, Library, 16 by 25 feet; 11, Office, 8 by 14 feet; 12, Entry, 5 by 13 feet; 13, Kitchen, 16 by 20 feet; 14, Passage, 5 feet; 15, Pantry, 7 feet 6 inches by 11 feet 6 inches; 16, Wash Room, 12 feet by 17 feet 6 inches; 17, Store Room, 10 by 12 feet; 18, Back Stairs, 3 feet; 19, Conservatory, 29 by 29 feet; a, China Closet, 6 by 10 feet: b, Vault, 3 feet 6 inches by 5 feet 6 inches; c, d, Closets, 5 by 5 feet; e, Dressing Room, 7 by 9 feet; f, Bath Room, 6 by 8 feet; i, Water Closet, 3 feet by 4 feet 6 inches; k, Closet, 4 by 5 feet; l, Closet, 2 by 5 feet; m, Closet, 3 by 5 feet; n, Porch, 7 by 12 feet; o, Porch, 8 by 8 feet; p, Verandah, 8 by 16 feet; r, r, Bay Windows, 9 by 12 feet and 4 by 8 feet; s, Terrace, 6 by 20 feet; t, t, Verandahs, 11 feet 6 inches and 12 feet 6 inches; u, Porch, 6 by 7 feet; v, Glass Passage, 5 by 12 feet.

SECOND FLOOR.—1, Principal Staircase, 20 by 30 feet; 2, Passage and Back Stairs, 3 feet 5 inches by 16 feet; 3, Chamber, 18 by 20 feet; 4, Chamber, 18 by 24 feet; 5, Guest's Chamber, 20 by 22 feet; 6, Hall, 12 by 24 feet; 7, Reading Room, 12 by 18 feet; 8, Chamber, 18 by 22 feet; 9, Chamber, 17 feet by 17 feet 6 inches; 10, Bath Room, 16 feet diameter; 11, Study, 13 by 16 feet; 12, Library, 7 feet 6 inches by 14 feet; 13, Billiard Room, 18 by 27 feet; 14, Serving Room, 10 by 14 feet; 15, Seamstress' Sleeping Room, 8 by 10 feet; a, Dressing Room, 8 by 10 feet; b, Bath Room, 8 by 8 feet; c, Passage, 4 feet 6 inches by 7 feet; d, Closet, 7 by 7 feet; e, Closet, 5 feet 6 inches by 11 feet 6 inches; f, Balcony; g, Back Stairs, 4 by 6 feet; h, Closet, 6 by 8 feet; i, Passage, 4 feet 6 inches by 13 feet: k, Linen Room, 6 by 13 feet; l, Alcove, 8 by 11 feet; m, Linen Room, 6 feet 6 inches by 11 feet; n, Bath Room, 7 by 8 feet; o, Closets, 4 by 6 feet; p, Alcove, 6 by 11 feet; q, Verandah, 10 by 15 feet; r, Wash Room, 6 by 8 feet; s, Closet, 3 feet 6 inches by 5 feet; t, Gallery, 7 by 12 feet; u, Balcony, 9 by 14 feet; v, Roof; w, Seats, 2 feet 4 inches by 9 feet; x, Balcony, 3 by 6 feet; y, Balcony, 7 feet 6 inches by 13 feet.

THIRD FLOOR.—1, Hall, 20 by 30 feet; 2, Back Staircase, 7 by 15 feet; 3, Children's Play Room, 18 feet by 32 feet 6 inches; 4, Gymnasium, 16 by 38 feet; 5, Private Theatre, 24 feet by 31 feet 6 inches; 6, Servant's Bed Room, 14 by 18 feet; 7, Lumber Room, 11 by 13 feet; 8, Bed Room, 10 by 16 feet; 9, Servant's Bed Room, 11 feet 6 inches by 17 feet; a, Stage, 9 feet by 17 feet 6 inches; b, b, Dressing Rooms; c, Tower, 12 by 12 feet; d, Wardrobe, 9 by 10 feet; e, Common Room, 10 by 15 feet; f, Dressing Room, 8 by 8 feet; g, Recess, 8 by 11 feet; h, Sky Light, 9 feet 6 inches diameter; i, Stairs to Roof, 3 feet wide; k, Passage, 4 feet 6 inches wide; l, Tower, 8 by 8 feet; m, Passage, 3 feet 6 inches by 20 feet.

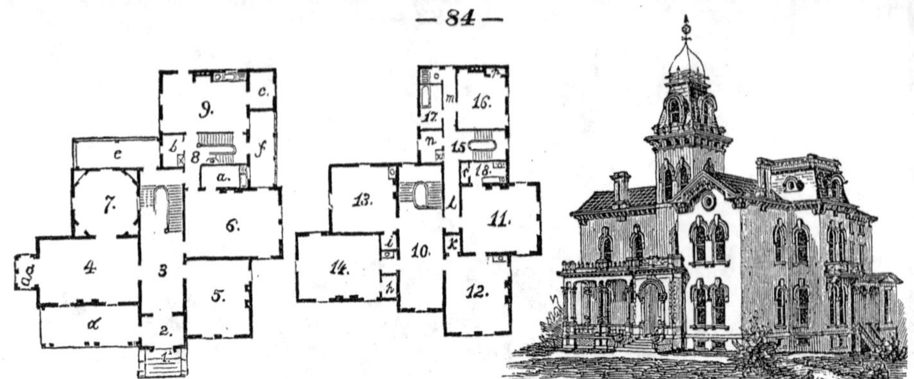

Residence of WM. SUMNER, Walnut Hills, Cincinnati, O.

ARCHITECTS, WALTER & STEWART, CINCINNATI, O.

First Floor.—1, Front Door Steps, 7 feeet 2 inches by 12 feet 6 inches; 2, Vestibule, 7 feet 6 inches by 10 feet 6 inches; 3, Hall, 10 by 35 feet; 4, Parlor, 16 by 25 feet; 5, Sitting Room, 16 by 19 feet; 6, Dining Room, 16 by 24 feet; 7, Library, 16 by 16 feet; 8, Back Stairs, 8 by 16 feet; 9, Kitchen, 15 feet by 21 feet 6 inches; *a*, Pantry, 5 feet 6 inches by 11 feet 6 inches; *b*, Store Room, 5 feet by 8 feet 8 inches; *c*, Pantry, 6 by 9 feet; *d*, Porch, 9 feet 6 inches by 25 feet; *e*, Porch, 8 by 17 feet; *f*, Porch, 6 feet 9 in. by 20 feet; *g*, Bay Window, 5 feet by 8 feet 9 in.; *x*, Dumb Waiter, 2 ft. by 2 ft. 6 in.

Second Floor.—10, Hall, 10 by 35 feet; 11, Bed Room, 16 by 19 feet; 12, Bed Room, 16 by 19 feet; 13, Bed Room, 16 feet 8 inches by 16 feet; 14, Bed Room, 16 feet by 20 feet 6 inches; 15, Back Stairs, 8 by 16 feet; 16, Bed Room, 12 by 15 feet; 17, Bath Room, 5 by 11 feet; 18, Dressing Room, 5 feet 6 inches by 9 feet; *h*, Closet, 4 feet by 5 feet 6 inches; *i*, Closet, 4 feet by 3 feet 6 inches; *k*, Closet, 4 feet by 4 feet 3 inches; *l*, Passage, 4 by 18 feet; *m*, Passage, 3 feet 6 inches by 15 feet 6 inches; *n*, Linen Room, 5 feet by 8 feet 8 inches; *o*, Water Closet, 3 feet 6 inches by 5 feet; *p*, Closet, 1 foot 8 inches by 5 feet; *r*, Closet, 2 feet by 5 feet 6 inches; *x*, Dumb Waiter, 2 feet by 2 feet 6 inches.

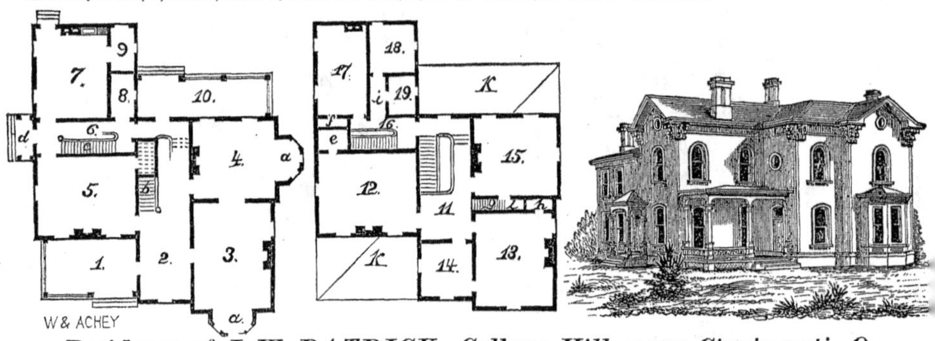

Residence of J. W. PATRICK, College Hill, near Cincinnati, O.

ARCHITECTS, WALTER & STEWART, CINCINNATI, O.

First Floor.—1, Porch, 10 by 18 feet; 2, Hall, 10 feet by 33 feet 6 inches; 3, Parlor, 15 by 20 feet; 4, Sitting Room, 15 by 16 feet; 5, Dining Room, 15 by 19 feet; 6, Rear Stair Hall, 6 by 19 feet; 7, Kitchen, 14 by 17 feet; 8, Store Room, 4 feet 6 inches by 8 feet 3 inches; 9, Pantry, 4 feet 6 inches by 8 feet 3 inches; 10, Porch, 8 by 26 feet; *a*, *a*, Bay Windows, 4 feet 8 in. by 9 feet; *b*, Main Stairs, 3 feet 6 in. wide; *c*, Rear Stairs, 2 feet 8 in. wide; *d*, Portico, 4 feet 6 in. by 8 feet.

Second Floor.—11, Hall, 10 feet by 33 feet 6 inches; 12, Bed Room, 15 by 19 feet; 13, Bed Room, 15 by 17 feet; 14, Bed Room, 10 by 10 feet; 15, Bed Room, 15 by 16 feet; 16, Rear Staircase, 6 feet by 12 feet 6 inches; 17, Girl's Room, 9 feet 6 inches by 17 feet; 18, Bath Room, 9 by 9 feet; 19, Linen Room, 5 feet 6 inches by 7 feet 6 inches; *e*, Closet, 4 by 6 feet; *f*, Closet, 1 foot 6 inches by 6 feet; *g*, Garret Stairs, 2 feet 6 inches wide; *h*, Closet, 2 feet 6 inches by 5 feet; *i*, Passage, 3 feet by 7 feet 6 inches; *k*, *k*, Porch Roofs; *l*, Closet, 2 feet 6 inches by 9 feet.

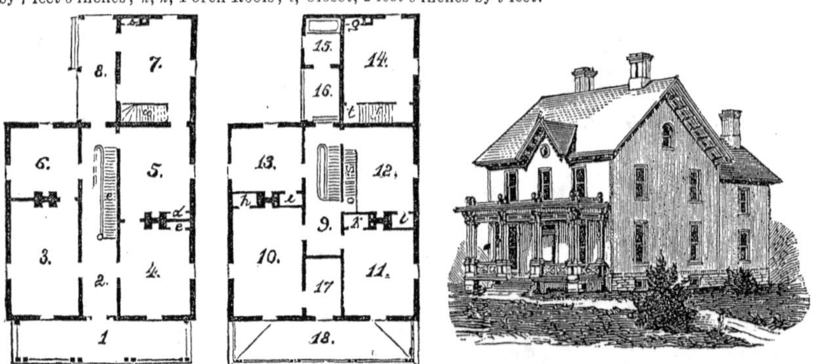

Residence of R. H. GIVEN, Mt. Auburn, Cincinnati, O.

ARCHITECT, J. C. ANTON, CINCINNATI, O.

First Floor.—1, Verandah, 7 by 31 feet; 2, Hall, 6 feet by 30 feet 6 inches; 3, Parlor, 12 by 18 feet; 4, Sitting Room, 12 by 15 feet; 5, Dining Room, 12 by 15 feet; 6, Library, 12 by 12 feet; 7, Kitchen, 12 by 14 feet; 8, Porch, 6 feet by 17 feet 8 inches; *a*, Back Stairs, 2 feet 6 inches wide; *b*, Closet, 1 foot 2 inches by 3 feet 6 inches; *c*, Principal Stairs, 2 feet 9 inches wide; *d*, Closet, 1 foot by 3 feet 9 inches; *e*, Closet, 1 foot by 3 feet 9 inches.

Second Floor.—10, Bed Room, 12 by 16 feet; 11, Bed Room, 12 by 13 feet 10 inches; 12, Bed Room, 12 feet by 13 feet 10 inches; 13, Bed Room, 12 feet by 10 feet 10 inches; 14, Servant's Room, 12 by 14 feet; 15, Bath Room, 6 by 8 feet; 16, Porch, 6 feet 6 inches by 10 feet 6 inches; 17, Dressing Room, 6 by 10 feet; 18, Porch Roof, flat; *f*, Back Stairs, 2 feet 6 inches wide; *g*, Closet, 1 foot 2 inches by 3 feet 6 inches; *h*, Closet, 2 feet 4 inches by 3 feet 9 inches; *i*, Closet, 2 feet 4 inches by 3 feet 9 inches; *k*, Closet, 2 feet 4 inches by 3 feet 9 inches; *l*, Closet, 2 feet 4 inches by 3 feet 9 inches; *o*, Closet, 2 by 5 feet; *s*, Garret Stairs, 2 feet wide; *t*, Closet, 2 feet 6 inches by 2 feet 6 inches.

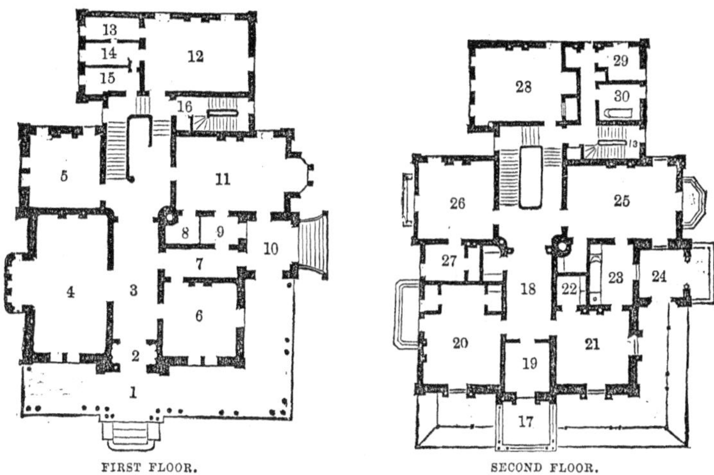

Residence of A. H. HINKLE, Mt. Auburn, Cincinnati, O.

ARCHITECTS, A. C. NASH & CO., CINCINNATI, O.

First Floor.—1, Verandah, 11 feet wide; 2, Vestibule, 5 by 10 feet; 3, Main Hall, 10 feet wide; 4, Drawing Room, 16 by 30 feet; 5, Library, 16 by 16 feet; 6, Reception Room, 16 by 16 feet; 7, Passage, feet wide; 8, Closet, 5 by 6 feet; 9, Wash Room, 6 by 8 feet; 10, Tower Vestibule, 10 by 10 feet; 11, Family Room, 16 by 24 feet; 12, Dining Room, 16 by 24 feet; 13, Butler's Pantry, 5 by 12 feet; 14, Dish Pantry, 5 by 12 feet; 15, Store Room, 5½ by 12 feet; 16, Hall and Servants' Stairs.

Second Floor. —17, Balcony, 9 by 11 feet; 18, Hall, 10 feet wide; 19, Siesta, 10 by 11 feet; 20, Guest's Chamber, 17 by 22 feet; 21, Front Chamber, 16 by 16 feet; 22, Closet, 7 by 8 feet; 23, Bath Room, 10 by 13 feet; 24, Arcade, 10 by 11 feet; 25, Chamber, 16 by 24 feet; 26, Chamber, 16 by 16 feet; 27, Dressing Room, 8 by 9 feet; 28, Sewing Room, 16 by 19 feet; 29, Linen Closet, 8 by 10 feet; 30, Bath Room, by 10 feet.

Servants' Rooms, Kitchens, and Laundry in Basement. Several Bed Rooms in Attic.

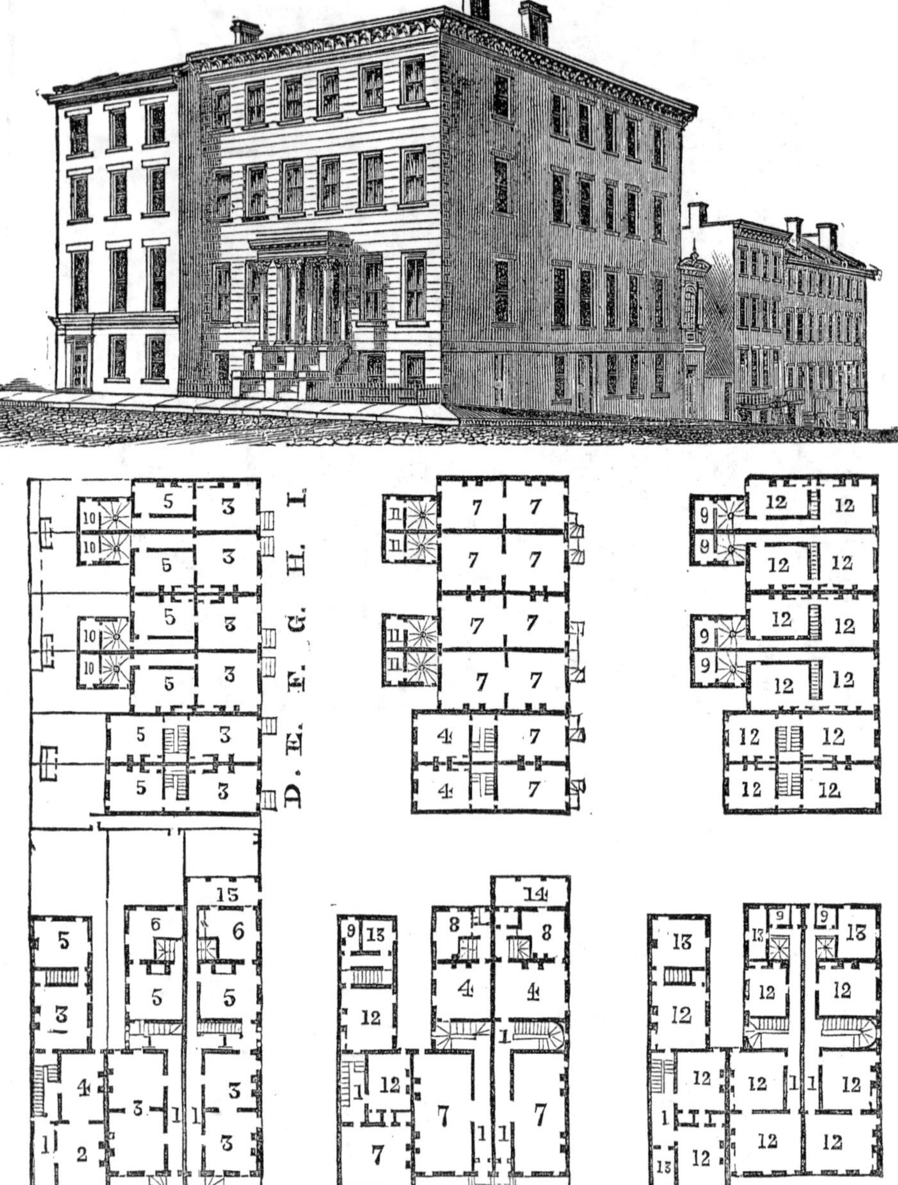

BASEMENT. FIRST FLOOR. SECOND FLOOR.

HINKLE'S BUILDINGS,

Corner Fourth and Smith Streets, Cincinnati, Ohio.

NINE DWELLING HOUSES,

BUILT ON A LOT 60 BY 180 FEET, ON FIVE DIFFERENT PLANS.

Plans marked A, B, C, are each 20 feet front.
Plans marked D, E, are each 12½ feet front.
Plans marked F, G, H, I, are each 15 feet front.

With a scale to this, the size of all the rooms can be ascertained.

1, Hall; 2, Office; 3, Dining Room; 4, Sitting Room; 5, Kitchen; 6, Laundry; 7, Parlor; 8, Library; 9, Bath Room; 10, Store Room; 11, Closet; 12, Chamber; 13, Bed Room; 14, Conservatory; 15, Porch.

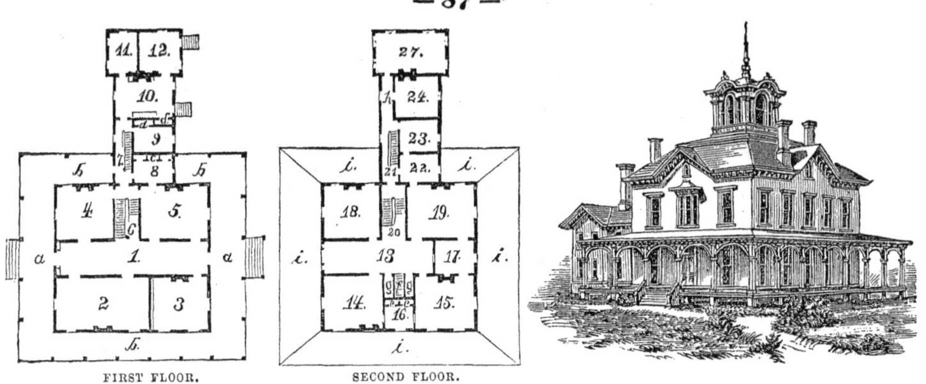

FIRST FLOOR. SECOND FLOOR.

Design for a Southern Residence.

ARCHITECT, J. C. ANTON, CINCINNATI, O.

First Floor.—1, Hall, 12 by 53 feet; 2, Parlor, 18 by 32 feet; 3, Bed Room, 18 by 20 feet; 4, Library, 18 by 20 feet; 5, Dining Room, 18 by 24 feet; 6, Staircase, 8 by 18 feet; 7, Rear Hall and Stairs, 6 feet 6 inches by 21 feet 6 inches; 8, Butler's Room, 8 by 13 feet; 9, Store Room, 9 by 13 feet; 10, Kitchen, 14 by 20 feet; 11, Servants' Hall, 11 feet 6 inches by 15 feet; 12, Laundry, 13 by 15 feet; *a, a,* Verandah, 12 feet wide; *b, b, b,* Verandah, 10 feet wide; *c, c, c,* Closets, 1 foot 10 inches by 4 feet; *d, d,* Closets, 1 foot 6 inches by 6 feet.

Second Floor.—13, Hall, 12 by 38 feet; 14, Bed Room, 18 feet by 21 feet 6 inches; 15, Bed Room, 18 feet by 21 feet 6 inches; 16, Dressing Room, 8 by 10 feet; 17, Dressing Room, 12 feet by 14 feet 6 inches; 18, Bed Room, 18 by 20 feet; 19, Bed Room, 18 by 24 feet; 20, Staircase, 8 by 18 feet; 21, Rear Hall and Stairs, 6 feet 6 inches by 21 feet 6 inches; 22, Bath Room, 10 by 13 feet; 23, Bed Room, 11 by 13 feet; 24, Bed Room, 14 by 15 feet; 27, Bed Room, 15 by 25 feet; *e, e,* Closet, 2 feet by 4 feet 10 inches; *f,* Garret Stairs, 3 feet wide; *g, g,* Closets, 3 by 7 feet; *h,* Passage, 4 feet 6 inches by 14 feet 6 inches; *i, i, i, i,* Porch Roofs.

First Floor.—1, Family Room, 15 feet 4 inches by 15 feet 6 inches; 2, Kitchen, 12 feet 9 inches by 15 feet 6 inches; 3, Stairs, 2 feet 6 inches wide; 4, Closet under Stairs; 5, Closet, 1 foot 7 inches by 5 feet 2 inches.

Second Floor.—6, Landing, 3 feet by 7 feet 8 inches; 7, Bed Room, 7 feet 8 inches by 15 feet 6 inches; 8, Bed Room, 7 feet 8 inches by 12 feet 4 inches; 9, Closet, 1 foot by 3 feet 2 inches; 10, Closet, 1 foot by 3 feet 2 inches; 11, Passage, 2 feet 6 inches wide; 12, Bed Room, 8 feet by 14 feet 3 inches; 13, Bed Room, 7 feet by 7 feet 6 inches; *a,* Closet, 2 by 4 feet; *b,* Closet, 1 foot 3 inches by 2 feet 6 inches; *c,* Closet, 1 foot 3 inches by 2 feet.

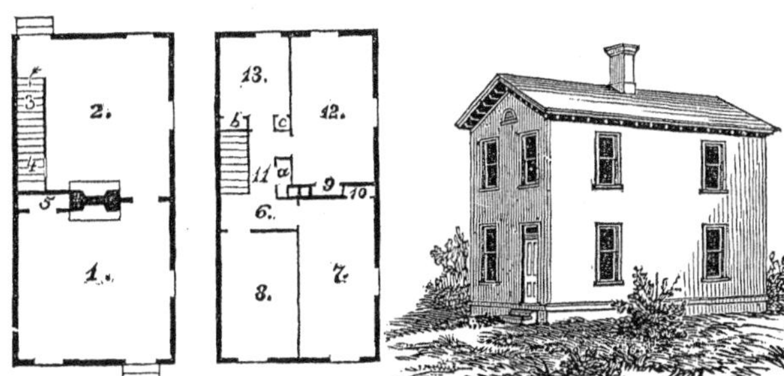

No. 10.

HINKLE & CO., Cottage Building.

ARCHITECT, J. C. ANTON, CINCINNATI, O.

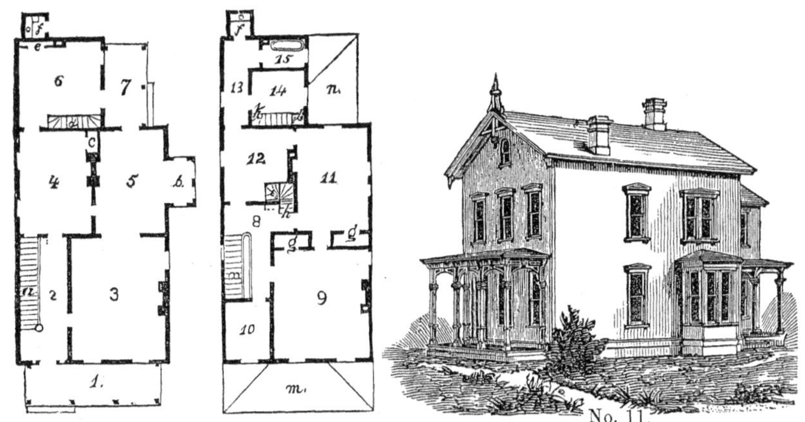

No. 11.

HINKLE & CO., Cottage Building to be erected on Mt. Auburn.

ARCHITECT, J. C. ANTON, CINCINNATI, O.

First Floor.—1, Porch, 6 feet by 22 feet 6 inches; 2, Hall, 7 feet 2 inches by 18 feet 9 inches; 3, Parlor, 15 feet by 18 feet 8 inches; 4, Dining Room, 11 feet 1 inch by 15 feet 9 inches; 5, Sitting Room, 11 feet 1 inch by 15 feet 9 inches; 6, Kitchen, 13 feet by 13 feet 6 inches; 7, Porch, 6 feet 6 inches by 12 feet 6 inches; *a,* Stairs, 3 feet wide; *b,* Bay Window, 4 feet 2 inches by 6 feet 6 inches; *c,* Closet, 1 foot 3 inches by 3 feet 6 inches; *d,* Back Stairs, 2 feet wide; *e,* Closet, 1 foot by 5 feet 9 inches; *f, f,* Water Closets, 3 feet by 3 feet 6 inches.

Second Floor.—8, Hall, 7 feet 2 inches by 11 feet; 9, Bed Room, 15 feet by 16 feet 3 inches; 10, Bed Room, 7 feet 2 inches by 9 feet; 11, Bed Room, 11 feet 1 inch by 15 feet 9 inches; 12, Bed Room, 11 feet 1 inch by 11 feet 3 inches; 13, Passage, 4 feet by 13 feet 6 inches; 14, Servant's Room, 8 feet 6 inches by 8 feet 6 inches; 15, Bath Room, 4 feet 6 inches by 7 feet 3 inches; *g, g,* Closets, 2 feet by 5 feet 6 inches; *h,* Garret Stairs, 2 feet 4 inches wide; *i,* Closet, 2 feet 4 inches by 3 feet 6 inches; *k,* Stairs to Kitchen, 2 feet wide; *l,* Closet, 2 by 2 feet; *m,* Porch Roof; *n,* Porch Roof.

Hinkle & Co.'s Cottage Buildings, Cincinnati, O.

We call the attention of the public to the following plans of buildings. They are framed with Sills, Posts, Studs, Joists, and Rafters; the weather-boards are narrow, to be put on horizontal; roofed with shingles, or, if preferred, saturated paper painted with Fire Proof Composition, and sanded; the flooring and partition of white pine boards, narrow, planed, tongued and grooved, beveled base; Doors and Windows furnished with plain casing. We furnish these buildings, all framed, the lumber, shingles, or paper and composition for roof, carpenter work, hardware and sash glazed, all packed and delivered at railroad depot, or Wharf at Cincinnati, at the following prices:

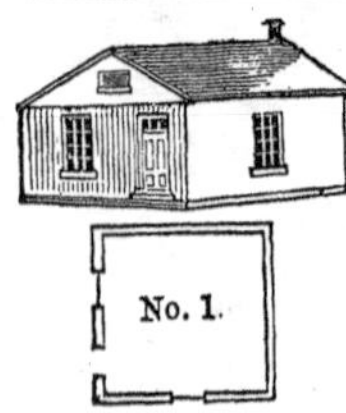

Price $115, subject to change.

CUT No. 1 represents a house of one room, 15 feet square, one story, 7 feet 10 inches high. It has two windows, glazed, and one door.

CALCULATIONS FOR SHIPPING.—It contains 1,349 feet of lumber, and 413 pounds hardware, etc. Total weight 3,011 pounds. For shingle roof add 3,000 shingles.

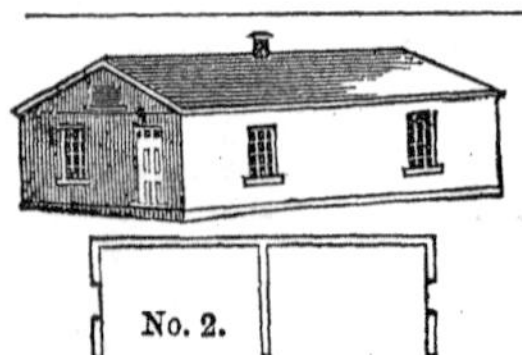

Price $210, subject to change.

CUT No. 2 represents a house 15 by 30 feet, divided into two rooms, one story, 7 feet 10 inches high. It has four windows, glazed, and three doors.

CALCULATIONS FOR SHIPPING.—It contains 2,420 feet of lumber and 807 pounds hardware, etc. Total weight 5,647 pounds. For shingle roof add 5,500 shingles.

Price $250, subject to change.

WE also furnish a No. 2, 15 by 30 feet, 10 feet story, with same number of doors and windows as above, of a larger size.

CALCULATIONS FOR SHIPPING.—It contains 2,730 feet of lumber, and 1,118 pounds of hardware, etc. Total weight 6,578 pounds. For shingle roof add 5,500 shingles.

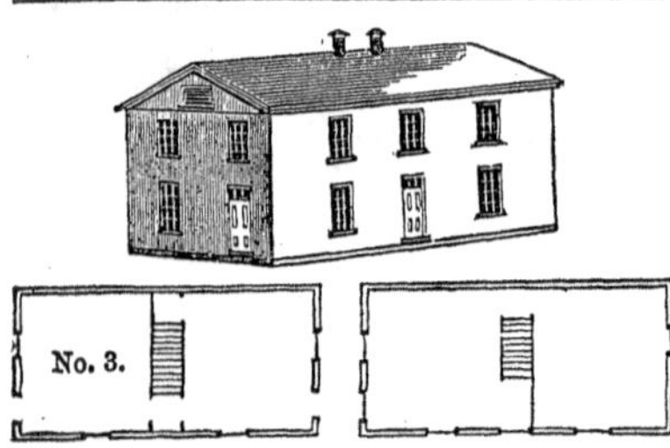

Price $350, subject to change.

CUT No. 3 represents a house 15 by 30 feet, two stories; first story 8 feet high, divided into two rooms; second story 7 feet high, divided into two rooms. It has ten windows, glazed, and eight doors.

CALCULATIONS FOR SHIPPING.—It contains 4,435 feet of lumber and 1,240 pounds hardware, etc. Total weight 10,110 pounds. For shingle roof add 5,500 shingles.

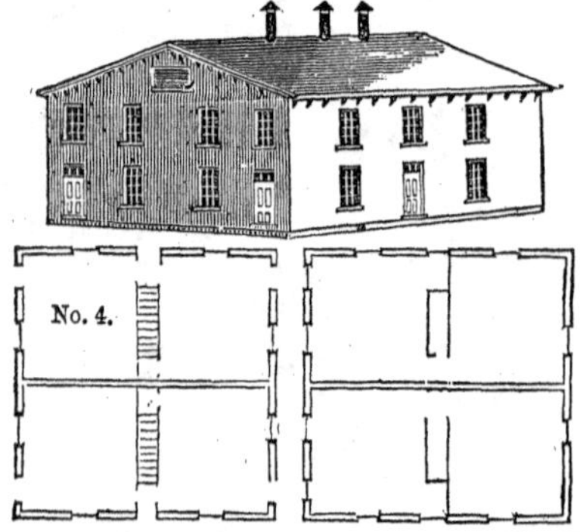

Price $715, subject to change.

CUT No. 4 represents a house 30 by 30 feet, two stories; first story 8 feet high, divided into four rooms; second story 7 feet high, divided into four rooms. It has twenty windows, glazed, and sixteen doors.

CALCULATIONS FOR SHIPPING.—It contains 8,682 feet of lumber, and 2,392 pounds of hardware, etc. Total weight 19,757 pounds. For shingle roof add 11,500 shingles.

The materials in these buildings are light, yet sufficiently strong, and the small space which they occupy, when in parts, renders them easy of transportation. It will require but a few days carpenter work to set up the buildings and finish them. They are designed to be plastered inside or can be ceiled with thin boards, and papered, which is cheaper than plastering.

☞ We furnish written directions for putting up and finishing these buildings, which can be done by any carpenter.

HINKLE & CO., Cincinnati, Ohio,

PORTABLE DWELLINGS, STORES, CHAPELS, ETC.,

WITH IRON ROOF.

We have invented a Portable Building to meet the present demand for houses. We call the attention of the public to the following plans:

They are framed with sills and plates; grooved to receive perpendicular siding, which is of inch boards, planed on one side, tongued and grooved, with the necessary Flooring, dressed, tongued and grooved. Ceiling over head, of thin, common boards, dressed, jointed for papering to make the building complete. The roof is of iron. The Doors, Windows and Partition are made so their location can be changed, if desired. The buildings are so constructed that they can be put together or taken apart in a few hours. The materials are all light, but of sufficient strength, and are easy of transportation by Wagon, Railroad, or Steamboat. We furnish these buildings, all made and fitted together, Doors and Windows hung and trimmed, packed and delivered to Railroad Depot or Wharf, at Cincinnati, at the price attached. Also, the number of feet of Lumber, and the weight of Hardware, etc., to ascertain the cost of shipping.

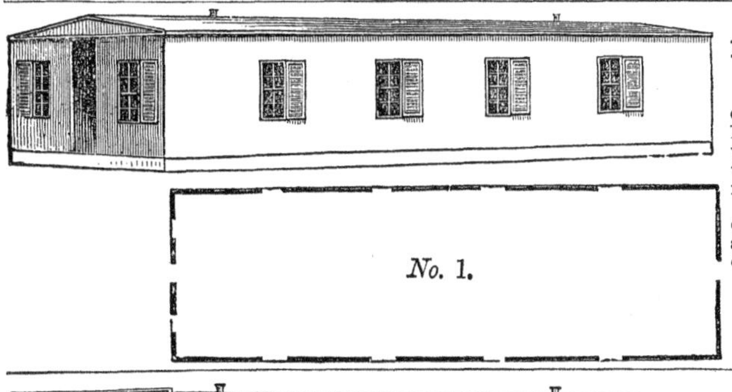

Price $590, subject to change.

Cut No. 1 represents a building of one room, 19x60 feet, one story 10 feet high. It has ten windows with glass in, and shutters, and two doors, all hung and trimmed.

Calculations for Shipping.—It contains 4,830 feet of Lumber, and 2,557 pounds of hardware, etc.

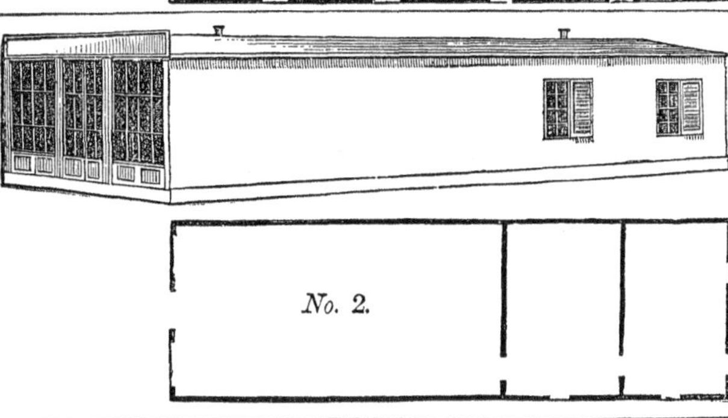

Price $675, subject to change.

Cut No. 2 represents a store and dwelling, 19x60 feet, one story, 10 feet high, divided into three rooms; it has one pair of sash store doors, two windows and glass, but not glazed in front, with shutters, and three windows with glass in and shutters, and three doors in rear, all hung and trimmed.

Calculations for Shipping.—It contains 5,220 feet of Lumber, and 2,400 pounds Hardware, etc.

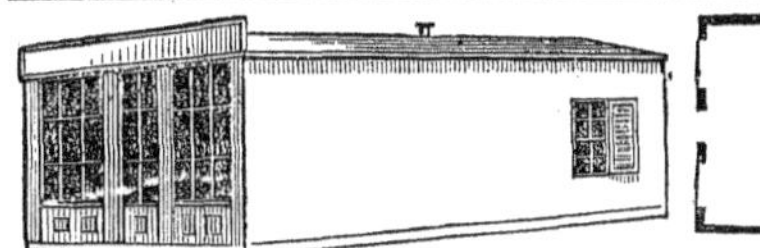

No. 3.

Price $350, subject to change.

Cut No. 3 represents a store and dwelling, 15x30 feet, one story, 10 feet high, divided into two rooms; it has one sash store door, two windows and glass, but not glazed in front, with shutters; and two windows with glass in, and shutters, and two doors in rear all hung and trimmed.

Calculations for Shipping.—It contains 1,922 feet of Lumber, and 1,158 pounds of Hardware, etc.

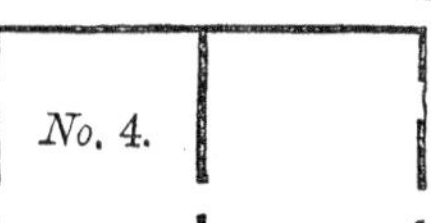

Price $250, subject to change.

Cut No. 4 represents a dwelling, 15x30 feet, one story, 7 feet 10 inches high, divided into two rooms; it has four windows with glass in and shutters, and three doors, all hung and trimmed.

Calculations for Shipping.—It contains 2,232 feet of Lumber, and 784 pounds of Hardware, etc.

Price $140, subject to change.

Cut No. 5 represents a house of one room, 15 feet square, one story, 7 feet 10 inches high. It has two windows with glass in and one door.

Calculations for Shipping.—It contains 1,116 ft. of Lumber, and 392 lbs. of Hardware, etc.

These buildings are made 15 feet or 19 feet wide, to suit iron for roof; Story 7 feet 10 inches, or 10 feet high, and can be made any depth required, with store or dwelling front, with any number of Rooms, Doors, and windows desired.

We have furnished a number of these Buildings to persons, who have taken them with goods to the Southern and Western country, landed, put up the store and shelving the same day, and opened to sell goods the next morning Owners of unimproved real estate, in city or country, will find, in many places, that the rent of these Buildings will pay the cost of them in one year. They could be removed at pleasure when larger buildings would be required.

The great demand for these Portable Houses has compelled us to increase our facilities for manufacturing. We are now prepared to furnish fifty per week.

☞ We furnish written directions for putting up these buildings, which can be done by any carpenter.

JAMES HUNTER & CO.

169 CENTRAL AVENUE,

CINCINNATI, OHIO,

MANUFACTURERS OF

Ornamental Galvanized Iron Cornice,

DORMER WINDOWS, FINEALS, WINDOW CAPS, &C.

TIN AND SLATE ROOFERS,

Gutters, Spouting, &c.

ALL ORDERS PROMPTLY ATTENDED TO.

M. CLEMENTS,

MANUFACTURER OF

PLAIN AND ORNAMENTAL

IRON RAILINGS,

Balconies and Verandas, Iron Stairs, Sashes, Sky-Lights and Roofs,

Jail Cells, Doors, Bank Vaults, &c.

And all kinds of Iron Work for Private and Public Buildings.

Nos. 447 and 452 West Sixth St.

Near Cincinnati, Hamilton and Dayton Railroad Depot,

CINCINNATI.

HINKLE & CO., 365 West Front Street, Cincinnati.

LUMBER CIRCULAR.

Our Yard is situated very advantageously on the river bank, upper part of the City, which gives us every facility for taking in lumber. We yard annually several million feet, also a large quantity of Shaved and Sawed Shingles and Lath, and have arrangements for a constant supply of the same, from the head waters of the Alleghany and the Lakes, which, with the advantage of our large Yard, containing several acres and 375 feet of wharf, enables us to purchase, yard, and sell wholesale, retail, or manufacture into building materials, cheaper than any other establishment in the West.

Orders filled for Boards, Plank, Shaved and Sawed Shingles, Joist, Lath, Framing and Cornice Timber of every description.

Below we give the manner in which we sort and name our lumber. Prices omitted as they are subject to change. Prices furnished on application,

CLEAR WHITE PINE.		
1 inch thick, per 100 feet, face measure, seasoned		
1½ " " " "		
2 " " " "		
FIRST COMMON WHITE PINE.		
1 inch thick, per 100 feet, face measure, seasoned		
1½ " " " "		
2 " " " "		
SECOND COMMON WHITE PINE.		
⅝ inch thick, per 100 feet, face measure, seasoned		
1 " " " "		
1½ " " " "		
2 " " " "		
THIRD COMMON WHITE PINE.		
½ inch thick, per 100 feet, face measure, seasoned		
1 " " " "		
GRUB PLANK.		
1½ inch thick, per 100 feet, face measure, seasoned		
2 " " " "		
LATH.		
Pine, sawed, 4 feet long, per thousand		
Poplar, " " "		
" Cut " "		
SHINGLES.		
Pine, sawed, No. 1, 16 inches long, per thousand		
" " 2, 16 " "		
" " 1, 18 " "		
" " 2, 18 " "		
" shaved, 1, 16 " "		
" " 2, 16 " "		
" " 1, 18 " "		
" " 2, 18 " "		
GREEN TIMBER FROM SAW MILL.		
Poplar Joist and Scantling, 20 feet long and under, and Framing Timber, 30 feet long and under, per 100 feet, board measure		
Pine Joist and Scantling, 20 feet long and under, and Framing Timber, 30 feet long and under, per 100 feet, board measure		
Pine Cornice Timber, 30 feet long and under, per 100 feet, board measure		
Hemlock Joist and Scantling, 20 feet long and under, per 100 feet, board measure		
Additional lengths, extra price		
SEASONED JOIST.		
Poplar, per 100 feet, board measure		
Pine " " "		
Hemlock " " "		
FLOORING, CEILING AND PARTITION.		
Dressed, tongued and grooved, face measure. Tongue of board not included in measurement.		
Flooring or Sheeting, 3d Com. white Pine, ⅞ or 1 inch thick, per 100 feet		
Flooring and Ceiling, 2d " " ⅞ or 1 inch thick, "		
" " 1st " " ⅞ or 1 inch thick, "		
" " 2d Clear. " ⅞ or 1 inch thick, "		
" Yellow Pine, 1 inch thick, per 100 feet		
" " " 1⅛ " "		
Partition, White Pine, 1st Common, 1 inch, "		
Weatherboards, 1st Common White Pine, undressed		
" 2d " " " "		
" 2d Clear, " " "		
Planing Weatherboards, one side, per 100 feet, Face measure		
Planing 1 inch Boards, two sides, " "		
Planing 1½ and 2 inch Plank, two sides, per 100 feet, Face measure		
Boards or Plank selected to a width or extra wide, additional price		

Bundling and Drayage extra.

HINKLE & CO.'S
(365 WEST FRONT STREET, CINCINNATI, O.)
NEW BOOK ON BUILDING

SENT FREE OF POSTAGE ON RECEIPT OF ONE DOLLAR

It contains One Hundred and Eleven Plans and Elevations of Buildings,

Taken from Houses Already Built, or in Course of Erection.

Fifty-six of them give the plans of the first and second stories, and description of rooms attached, *as sample below.* They vary in cost from $115 to $350,000.

Also, six hundred and fifteen plans of Moldings, Architraves, Bases, Brackets, Stairs, Newels, Balusters, Rails, Cornice, Mantels, Window Frames, Sash, Doors, Columns, Church Pews, Store Counters, Porticos, Etc. Adapted to the style of building in the United States; containing valuable information on building.

RESIDENCE ON MOUNT AUBURN, CIN., O. A. C. NASH & CO., Architects, Cin, O.

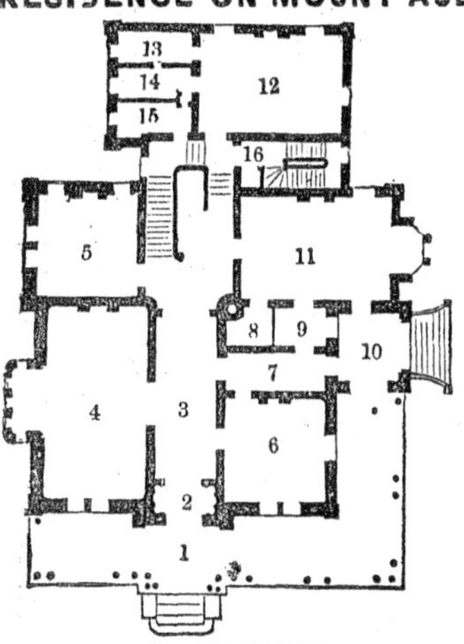

FIRST FLOOR.

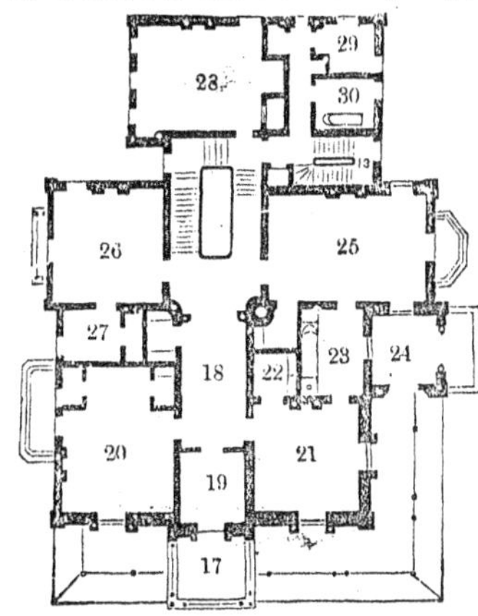

SECOND FLOOR.

FIRST FLOOR.—1. Veranda 11 ft. wide; 2 Vestibule, 5x10 ft.; 3. Main Hall, 10 ft. wide; 4. Drawing Room, 16x30 ft.; 5. Library, 16x16 ft.; 6 Reception Room 16x 6 ft.; 7 Passage, 6 ft. wide; 8. Closet, 5x6 ft.; 9. Wash Room 6x8 ft.; 10. Tower Vestibule, 10x10 ft.; 11. Family Room, 16x24 ft.; 12. Dining Room, 16x24; 13 Butler's Pantry, 5x12 ft; 14. Dish Pantry, 5x12 ft.; 15. Store Room, 5¼x12 ft.; 16. Hall and Servants' Stairs.

SECOND FLOOR.—17. Balcony, 9x11 ft.; 18. Hall, 10 ft. wide; 19 Siesta, 10x11 ft.; 20. Guest's Chamber, 17x22 ft.; 21. Front Chamber, 16x16 ft; 22. Closet, 7x8 ft; 23 Bath Room 10x13 ft; 24 Arcade, 0x11 ft.; 25. Chamber, 16x24 ft.; 26. Chamber, 16x16 ft; 27. Dressing Room, 8x9 ft.; 28. Sewing Room, 16x19 ft.; 29 Linen Closet. 8x10 ft.; 30. Bath Room 8x10 ft.

Servants' Rooms, Kitchens and Laundry in basement.

www.ingramcontent.com/pod-product-compliance
Lightning Source LLC
LaVergne TN
LVHW021425110826
845150LV00007B/2090

* 9 7 8 1 4 2 5 5 0 7 9 7 8 *